GETTING STARTED

WELCOME

Thanks for purchasing these training notes for the **AWS Certified Solutions Architect Associate** exam from Digital Cloud Training. While we can't update the title of this book, the information in this document has been fully updated to cover the latest SAA-C02 version of the exam.

The SAA-C02 exam covers a broad set of AWS services and the aim of putting this information together is to provide a centralized, detailed list of the facts you need to know before you sit the exam. This will shortcut your study time and maximize your chance of passing the exam first time.

I hope you get great value from this popular resource that has been well received by our pool of over 40,000 students. Wishing you all the best with your AWS Certified Solutions Architect Associate exam.

Neal Davis

AWS Solutions Architect & Founder of Digital Cloud Training

ABOUT THESE TRAINING NOTES

This document does not read like a book or instructional text. We provide a raw, point-to-point list of facts backed by tables and diagrams to help with understanding.

For easy navigation, the information on each AWS service in this document is organized into the same categories as they are in the AWS Management Console.

The scope of coverage of services, and what information is included for each service, is based on feedback from our pool of over 40,000 students who have taken the exam, as well as our own experience - and may differ between AWS services.

To test your understanding, we have added **80 quiz questions** that you will find at the end of each major chapter. Please note that quiz questions that are **numbered**, are primarily designed as a tool to review your knowledge of the content that was presented within the section. Quiz questions that are **lettered** represent the AWS exam style or difficulty. You will also find examples of exam style practice questions within the next chapter "How to best prepare for your exam".

YOUR PATHWAY TO SUCCESS

If you're new to AWS, we'd suggest first enrolling in the online instructor-led AWS Certified Solutions Architect Associate Hands-on Labs Video Course from Digital Cloud Training to familiarize yourself with the AWS platform before returning to the Training Notes to get a more detailed understanding of the AWS services.

To assess where you are at on your AWS journey, we recommend taking the AWS Certified Solutions Architect Associate Practice Exams on the Digital Cloud Training website. The **online exam simulator** with over **500 unique questions** will help you identify your strengths and weaknesses. These practice tests are designed to reflect the difficulty of the AWS exam and are the closest to the real exam experience available.

As a final step, use these training notes to focus your study on the knowledge areas where you need to most.

BONUS OFFER

To assess your AWS exam readiness, we have included one full-length practice exam from Digital Cloud Training. These 65 exam-difficulty practice questions are timed and scored and simulate the real

AWS exam experience. To gain access to your free practice test on our interactive exam simulator online, simply navigate to the CONCLUSION at the back of this book where you'll find detailed instructions.

CONTACT, SUPPORT & FEEDBACK

We hope you get great value from these training resources. If for any reason you are not 100% satisfied, please message us at feedback@digitalcloud.training.

For technical support, contact us at:

support@digitalcloud.training.

If you enjoy reading reviews, please consider paying it forward. It's the best way you can help us improve our books and help your fellow AWS students make the right choices. We celebrate every honest review and truly appreciate it. You can leave a review at any time at amazon.com/ryp.

The AWS platform is evolving quickly, and the exam tracks these changes with a typical lag of around 6 months. We are therefore reliant on student feedback to keep track of what is appearing in the exam. Our private Facebook group is a great place to ask questions and share knowledge and exam tips with the AWS community. Please join the discussion and share your exam feedback to our Facebook group:

https://www.facebook.com/groups/awscertificationqa

HOW TO BEST PREPARE FOR YOUR EXAM

THE AWS EXAM BLUEPRINT

The AWS Certified Solutions Architect Associate exam is recommended for individuals with at least one year of hands-on experience. The exam is intended for Solutions Architects and requires you to demonstrate knowledge of how to define a solution using architectural design principles based on customer requirements and provide implementation guidance based on best practices to the organization throughout the lifecycle of the project.

In the official Exam Guide for the AWS Certified Solutions Architect, the following **AWS knowledge is recommended:**

- One year of hands-on experience designing available, cost-efficient, fault-tolerant, and scalable distributed systems on AWS.
- Hands-on experience using compute, networking, storage and database AWS services.
- Hands-on experience with AWS deployment and management services.
- Ability to identify and define technical requirements for an AWS-based application.
- Ability to identify which AWS services meet a given technical requirement.
- Knowledge of recommended best practices for building secure and reliable applications on the AWS platform.
- An understanding of the basic architectural principles of building on the AWS cloud.
- An understanding of the AWS global infrastructure.
- An understanding of network technologies as they relate to AWS.
- An understanding of security features and tools that AWS provides and how they relate to traditional services.

The exam includes 65 questions and has a time limit of 130 minutes. You need to score a minimum of 720 out of 1000 points to pass the exam.

The question format of the exam is multiple-choice (one correct response from four options) and multiple response (two or more correct responses from five or more options). The questions are 100% scenario based with most scenarios being just a couple to a few lines long.

You will find there are often multiple correct answers and you must select the answer that best fits the scenario. For instance, you may be asked to select the MOST secure, MOST cost-effective, BEST architecture or LEAST complex option.

Important: Be very careful reading the wording of the question to ensure you select correctly. Sometimes small details can be easily missed that change the answer so take your time when sitting the exam.

DOMAINS, OBJECTIVES AND EXAMPLES

The knowledge required is organized into four test "domains". Within each test domain, there are several objectives that broadly describe the knowledge and experience required to pass the exam.

Test Domain 1: Design Resilient Architectures

This domain makes up 30% of the exam and includes the following four objectives:

1.1 Design a multi-tier architecture solution.

1.2 Design highly available and/or fault-tolerant architectures.

1.3 Design decoupling mechanisms using AWS services.

1.4 Choose appropriate resilient storage.

What you need to know

You need to understand the various block, file and object storage technologies such as Amazon EBS, Instance Store, Amazon EFS, Amazon S3, and Amazon FSx and know their use cases.

You must be able to design multi-tier application architectures and know-how to decouple application components using technologies such as Amazon SQS and Amazon SWF.

The architectures also need to be highly available in the case of component failure, and able to recover in the case of major outages, so you need to know the various ways of implementing high availability and fault tolerance.

Technologies you need to understand include Amazon Elastic Load Balancing, Amazon Route 53 and Amazon RDS Read Replicas and Multi-AZ.

You also need to understand the AWS Global Infrastructure in order to determine how to design application stacks to best use the underlying infrastructure architecture.

Example Questions

Question: You are a Solutions Architect at a media company, and you need to build an application stack that can receive customer comments from sporting events. The application is expected to receive significant load that could scale to millions of messages within a short space of time following high-profile matches.

As you are unsure of the load required for the database layer what is the most cost-effective way to ensure that the messages are not dropped?

1. Use RDS Auto Scaling for the database layer which will automatically scale as required
2. Create an SQS queue and modify the application to write to the SQS queue. Launch another application instance that polls the queue and writes messages to the database
3. Write the data to an S3 bucket, configure RDS to poll the bucket for new messages
4. Use DynamoDB and provision enough write capacity to handle the highest expected load

Answer: 2, Amazon Simple Queue Service (Amazon SQS) offers a reliable, highly scalable, hosted queue for storing messages in transit between computers and is used for distributed/decoupled applications. This is a great use case for SQS as you don't have to over-provision the database layer or worry about messages being dropped.

Question: A new Big Data application you are developing will use hundreds of EC2 instances to write data to a shared file system. The file system must be stored redundantly across multiple AZs within a region and allow the EC2 instances to concurrently access the file system. The required throughput is multiple GB per second.

From the options presented which storage solution can deliver these requirements?

1. Amazon EBS using multiple volumes in a RAID 0 configuration
2. Amazon S3
3. Amazon EFS
4. Amazon Storage Gateway

Answer: 3, Amazon EFS is the best solution as it is the only solution that is a file-level storage solution (not block/object-based), stores data redundantly across multiple AZs within a region and you can concurrently connect up to thousands of EC2 instances to a single filesystem.

Test Domain 2: Design High-Performing Architectures

This domain makes up 28% of the exam and includes the following **objectives**:

2.1 Identify elastic and scalable compute solutions for a workload.

2.2 Select high-performing and scalable storage solutions for a workload.

2.3 Select high-performing networking solutions for a workload.

2.4 Choose high-performing database solutions for a workload.

What you need to know

You need to be able to select the best storage and database services to use for a given scenario, taking into account requirements for performance.

Technologies to increase performance may include a caching layer such as Amazon ElastiCache, Amazon DynamoDB DAX, or Amazon CloudFront and you must be able to select the best service to use in the situation presented.

You must know how to effectively implement elasticity and scalability to your application architectures. This means understanding at an architectural and implementation level what to use and how to build it.

Elasticity and scalability services you need to understand include AWS Auto Scaling, EC2 Auto Scaling, and how to implement these features at the application, storage, and database layers of your application using AWS technology.

Example Questions

Question: A developer is creating a solution for a real-time bidding application for a large retail company that allows users to bid on items of end-of-season clothing. The application is expected to be extremely popular and the back-end DynamoDB database may not perform as required.

How can the Solutions Architect enable in-memory read performance with microsecond response times for the DynamoDB database?

1. Configure DynamoDB Auto Scaling
2. Enable read replicas
3. Increase the provisioned throughput
4. Configure Amazon DAX

Answer: 4, Amazon DynamoDB Accelerator (DAX) is a fully managed, highly available, in-memory cache for DynamoDB that delivers up to a 10x performance improvement – from milliseconds to microseconds – even at millions of requests per second. You can enable DAX for a DynamoDB database with a few clicks.

Question: A Solutions Architect is designing a workload that requires a high-performance object-based storage system that must be shared with multiple Amazon EC2 instances.

Which AWS service delivers these requirements?

1. Amazon S3
2. Amazon EFS
3. Amazon EBS
4. Amazon ElastiCache

Answer: 1, Amazon S3 is an object-based storage system. Though object storage systems aren't mounted and shared like filesystems or block-based storage systems, they can be shared by multiple instances as they allow concurrent access.

Test Domain 3: Design Secure Applications and Architectures

This domain makes up 24% of the exam and includes the following three objectives:

3.1 Design secure access to AWS resources.

3.2 Design secure application tiers.

3.3 Select appropriate data security options.

What you need to know

You need to understand how to use native AWS technologies and solution architecture to create secure applications. This includes configuring security controls for authentication, authorization, and access and applying encryption to data.

You need to know how to design isolation and separation through AWS service architecture, Amazon EC2 instance deployment options and Amazon VPC configuration.

It is also recommended to understand the best practices for implementing services in the most secure manner and best practices for creating users, groups, and roles using AWS IAM. Which services can use multi-factor authentication is also required knowledge and you should understand the available AWS Directory Services at a high-level and when to use them.

Questions often come up asking you to identify which technologies include DDoS mitigation and these include AWS Auto Scaling, Amazon CloudFront, and Amazon Route 53.

You should also know how to implement monitoring and logging using Amazon CloudWatch and AWS CloudTrail, when and what penetration testing you are allowed to perform within the AWS cloud and what compliance programs AWS comply with.

Technologies you need to know for domain 3 include Amazon VPC, AWS KMS, AWS CloudHSM, AWS IAM, Amazon Cognito, and AWS Directory Services.

Example Questions

Question: The development team at your company have created a new mobile application that will be used by users to access confidential data. The developers have used Amazon Cognito for authentication, authorization, and user management. Due to the sensitivity of the data, there is a requirement to add another method of authentication in addition to a username and password.

You have been asked to recommend the best solution. What is your recommendation?

1. Integrate IAM with a user pool in Cognito
2. Enable multi-factor authentication (MFA) in IAM
3. Integrate a third-party identity provider (IdP)
4. Use multi-factor authentication (MFA) with a Cognito user pool

Answer: 4, You can use MFA with a Cognito user pool (not in IAM) and this satisfies the requirement. A user pool is a user directory in Amazon Cognito. With a user pool, your users can sign-in to your web or mobile app through Amazon Cognito. Your users can also sign-in through social identity providers like Facebook or Amazon, and through SAML identity providers.

Question: You have been asked to come up with a solution for providing single sign-on to existing staff in your company who manage on-premise web applications and now need access to the AWS management console to manage resources in the AWS cloud.

Which product combinations provide the best solution to achieve this requirement?

1. Use your on-premise LDAP directory with IAM

2. Use IAM and MFA
3. Use the AWS Secure Token Service (STS) and SAML
4. Use IAM and Amazon Cognito

Answer: 3, Single sign-on using federation allows users to log-in to the AWS console without assigning IAM credentials. The AWS Security Token Service (STS) is a web service that enables you to request temporary, limited-privilege credentials for IAM users or for users that you authenticate (such as federated users from an on-premise directory). Federation (typically Active Directory) uses SAML 2.0 for authentication and grants temporary access based on the users' AD credentials. The user does not need to be a user in IAM.

Test Domain 4: Design Cost-Optimized Architectures

This domain makes up 18% of the exam and includes the following objectives:

4.1 Identify cost-effective storage solutions.

4.2 Identify cost-effective compute and database service.

4.3 Design cost-optimized network architectures.

What you need to know

A relatively small but still important area of the exam requires architects to consider cost-effectiveness when deploying application on AWS. You need to understand the various cost models of compute and storage services, what you pay for and what the best choices would be given a specific scenario.

Example Questions

Question: You need to run a production batch process quickly that will use several EC2 instances. The process cannot be interrupted and must be completed within a short time period.

What is likely to be the MOST cost-effective choice of EC2 instance type to use for this requirement?

1. Reserved instances
2. Spot instances
3. On-demand instances
4. Flexible instances

Answer: 3, the key requirements here are that you need to deploy several EC2 instances quickly to run the batch process and you must ensure that the job completes. The on-demand pricing model is the best for this ad-hoc requirement. Though spot pricing may be cheaper, you cannot afford to risk that the instances are terminated by AWS when the market price increases.

Question: An Architect is designing a serverless application that will accept images uploaded by users from around the world. The application will make API calls to back-end services and save the session state data of the user to a database.

Which combination of services would provide a solution that is cost-effective while delivering the least latency?

1. Amazon CloudFront, API Gateway, Amazon S3, AWS Lambda, DynamoDB
2. API Gateway, Amazon S3, AWS Lambda, DynamoDB
3. Amazon CloudFront, API Gateway, Amazon S3, AWS Lambda, Amazon RDS
4. Amazon S3, API Gateway, AWS Lambda, Amazon RDS

Answer: 1, Amazon CloudFront caches content closer to users at Edge locations around the world. This is the lowest latency option for uploading content. API Gateway and AWS Lambda are present in all options. DynamoDB can be used for storing session state data.

TABLE OF CONTENTS

COMPUTE

AMAZON EC2

GENERAL

Amazon Elastic Compute Cloud (Amazon EC2) is a web service that provides resizable compute capacity in the cloud. It is designed to make web-scale computing easier for developers.

With Amazon EC2 you launch virtual server instances on the AWS cloud.

Each virtual server is known as an "instance".

You are limited to running up to a total of 20 On-Demand instances across the instance family, purchasing 20 Reserved Instances, and requesting Spot Instances per your dynamic spot limit per region (by default).

AWS are transitioning to a vCPU based, rather than instance based, limit. This is currently being rolled out and may not feature on the exam yet.

Amazon EC2 currently supports a variety of operating systems including: Amazon Linux, Ubuntu, Windows Server, Red Hat Enterprise Linux, SUSE Linux Enterprise Server, Fedora, Debian, CentOS, Gentoo Linux, Oracle Linux, and FreeBSD.

EC2 compute units (ECU) provide the relative measure of the integer processing power of an Amazon EC2 instance.

With EC2 you have full control at the operating system layer.

Key pairs are used to securely connect to EC2 instances:

- A key pair consists of a **public key** that AWS stores, and a **private key file** that you store.
- For Windows AMIs, the private key file is required to obtain the password used to log into your instance.
- For Linux AMIs, the private key file allows you to securely SSH (secure shell) into your instance.

Metadata and User Data:

- User data is data that is supplied by the user at instance launch in the form of a script.
- Instance metadata is data about your instance that you can use to configure or manage the running instance.
- User data is limited to 16KB.
- User data and metadata are not encrypted.
- Instance metadata is available at http://169.254.169.254/latest/meta-data/ (the trailing "/" is required).
- Instance user data is available at: http://169.254.169.254/latest/user-data.
- The IP address 169.254.169.254 is a link-local address and is valid only from the instance.
- On Linux you can use the curl command to view metadata and userdata, e.g. "curl http://169.254.169.254/latest/meta-data/".
- The Instance Metadata Query tool allows you to query the instance metadata without having to type out the full URI or category names.

BILLING AND PROVISIONING

On demand:

- Pay for hours used with no commitment.
- Low cost and flexibility with no upfront cost.
- Ideal for auto scaling groups and unpredictable workloads.
- Good for dev/test.

Spot:

- Amazon EC2 Spot Instances let you take advantage of unused EC2 capacity in the AWS cloud.
- Spot Instances are available at up to a 90% discount compared to On-Demand prices.
- You can use Spot Instances for various stateless, fault-tolerant, or flexible applications such as big data, containerized workloads, CI/CD, web servers, high-performance computing (HPC), and other test & development workloads.
- You can request Spot Instances by using the Spot management console, CLI, API or the same interface that is used for launching On-Demand instances by indicating the option to use Spot.
- You can also select a Launch Template or a pre-configured or custom Amazon Machine Image (AMI), configure security and network access to your Spot instance, choose from multiple instance types and locations, use static IP endpoints, and attach persistent block storage to your Spot instances.
- **New pricing model:** The Spot price is determined by long term trends in supply and demand for EC2 spare capacity.
- You don't have to bid for Spot Instances in the new pricing model, and you just pay the Spot price that's in effect for the current hour for the instances that you launch.
- Spot Instances receive a two-minute interruption notice when these instances are about to be reclaimed by EC2, because EC2 needs the capacity back.
- Instances are not interrupted because of higher competing bids.
- To reduce the impact of interruptions and optimize Spot Instances, diversify and run your application across multiple capacity pools.
- Each instance family, each instance size, in each Availability Zone, in every Region is a separate Spot pool.
- You can use the RequestSpotFleet API operation to launch thousands of Spot Instances and diversify resources automatically.
- To further reduce the impact of interruptions, you can also set up Spot Instances and Spot Fleets to respond to an interruption notice by stopping or hibernating rather than terminating instances when capacity is no longer available.

Reserved:

- Purchase (or agree to purchase) usage of EC2 instances in advance for significant discounts over On-Demand pricing.
- Provides a capacity reservation when used in a specific AZ.
- AWS Billing automatically applies discounted rates when you launch an instance that matches your purchased RI.

- Capacity is reserved for a term of 1 or 3 years.
- EC2 has three RI types: Standard, Convertible, and Scheduled.
- Standard = commitment of 1 or 3 years, charged whether it's on or off.
- Scheduled = reserved for specific periods of time, accrue charges hourly, billed in monthly increments over the term (1 year).
- Scheduled RIs match your capacity reservation to a predictable recurring schedule.
- For the differences between standard and convertible RIs, see the table below.
- RIs are used for steady state workloads and predictable usage.
- Ideal for applications that need reserved capacity.
- Upfront payments can reduce the hourly rate.
- Can switch AZ within the same region.
- Can change the instance size within the same instance type.
- Instance type modifications are supported for Linux only.
- Cannot change the instance size of Windows RIs.
- Billed whether running or not.
- Can sell reservations on the AWS marketplace.
- Can be used in Auto Scaling Groups.
- Can be used in Placement Groups.
- Can be shared across multiple accounts within Consolidated Billing.
- If you don't need your RI's, you can try to sell them on the Reserved Instance Marketplace.

	Standard	Convertible
Terms	1 year, 3 year	1 year, 3 year
Average discount off On-Demand price	40% - 60%	31% - 54%
Change AZ, instance size, networking type	Yes via ModifyReservedInstance API or console	Yes via ExchangeReservedInstance API or console
Change instance family, OS, tenancy, payment options	No	Yes
Benefit from price reductions	No	Yes

RI Attributes:

- Instance type – designates CPU, memory, networking capability.
- Platform – Linux, SUSE Linux, RHEL, Microsoft Windows, Microsoft SQL Server.
- Tenancy – Default (shared) tenancy, or Dedicated tenancy.

- Availability Zone (optional) – if AZ is selected, RI is reserved, and discount applies to that AZ (Zonal RI). If no AZ is specified, no reservation is created but the discount is applied to any instance in the family in any AZ in the region (Regional RI).

Comparing Amazon EC2 Pricing Models

The following table provides a brief comparison of On-demand, Reserved and Spot pricing models:

On-Demand	Reserved	Spot
No upfront fee	Options: No upfront, partial upfront or all upfront	No upfront fee
Charged by hour or second	Charged by hour or second	Charged by hour or second
No commitment	1-year or 3-year commitment	No commitment
Ideal for short term needs or unpredictable workloads	Ideal for steady-state workloads and predictable usage	Ideal for cost-sensitive, compute intensive use cases that can withstand interruption

Dedicated hosts:

- Physical servers dedicated just for your use.
- You then have control over which instances are deployed on that host.
- Available as On-Demand or with Dedicated Host Reservation.
- Useful if you have server-bound software licences that use metrics like per-core, per-socket, or per-VM.
- Each dedicated host can only run one EC2 instance size and type.
- Good for regulatory compliance or licensing requirements.
- Predictable performance.
- Complete isolation.
- Most expensive option.
- Billing is per host.

Dedicated instances:

- Virtualized instances on hardware just for you.
- Also uses physically dedicated EC2 servers.
- Does not provide the additional visibility and controls of dedicated hosts (e.g. how instance are placed on a server).
- Billing is per instance.
- May share hardware with other non-dedicated instances in the same account.
- Available as On-Demand, Reserved Instances, and Spot Instances.
- Cost additional $2 per hour per region.

The following table describes some of the differences between dedicates instances and dedicated hosts:

Characteristic	Dedicated Instances	Dedicated Hosts
Enables the use of dedicated physical servers	X	X
Per instance billing (subject to a $2 per region fee)	X	
Per host billing		X
Visibility of sockets, cores, host ID		X
Affinity between a host and instance		X
Targeted instance placement		X
Automatic instance placement	X	X
Add capacity using an allocation request		X

Partial instance-hours consumed are billed based on instance usage.

Instances are billed when they're in a running state – need to stop or terminate to avoid paying.

Charging by the hour or second (by the second with Linux instances only).

Data between instances in different regions is charged (in and out).

Regional Data Transfer rates apply if at least one of the following is true, but are only charged once for a given instance even if both are true:

- The other instance is in a different Availability Zone, regardless of which type of address is used.
- Public or Elastic IP addresses are used, regardless of which Availability Zone the other instance is in.

INSTANCE TYPES

Amazon EC2 provides a wide selection of instance types optimized to fit different use cases.

Instance types comprise varying combinations of CPU, memory, storage, and networking capacity and give you the flexibility to choose the appropriate mix of resources for your applications.

Each instance type includes one or more instance sizes, allowing you to scale your resources to the requirements of your target workload.

Category	Families	Purpose/Design
General Purpose	A1, T3, T3a, T2, M5, M5a, M4	General purpose instances provide a balance of compute, memory and networking resources, and can be used for a variety of diverse workloads
Compute Optimized	C5, C5n, C4	Compute Optimized instances are ideal for compute bound applications that benefit from high performance processors
Memory Optimized	R5, R5a, R4, X1e, X1, High Memory, z1d	Memory optimized instances are designed to deliver fast performance for workloads that process large data sets in memory
Accelerated Computing	P3, P2, G4, G3, F1	Accelerated computing instances use hardware accelerators, or co-processors, to perform functions, such as floating-point number calculations, graphics processing, or data pattern matching
Storage Optimized	I3, I3en, D2, H1	This instance family provides Non-Volatile Memory Express (NVMe) SSD-backed instance storage optimized for low latency, very high random I/O performance, high sequential read throughput and provide high IOPS at a low cost

Options when launching Instances

Choose whether to auto-assign a public IP – default is to use the subnet setting.

Can add an instance to a placement group.

Instances can be assigned to IAM roles which configures them with credentials to access AWS resources.

Termination protection can be enabled and prevents you from terminating an instance.

Basic monitoring is enabled by default (5-minute periods), detailed monitoring can be enabled (1 minute periods, chargeable).

Can define shared or dedicated tenancy.

T2 unlimited allows applications to burst past CPU performance baselines as required (chargeable).

Can add a script to run on startup (user data).

Can join to a directory (Windows instances only).

There is an option to enable an Elastic GPU (Windows instances only).

Storage options include adding additional volumes and choosing the volume type.

Non-root volumes can be encrypted.

Root volumes can be encrypted if the instance is launched from an encrypted AMI.

There is an option to create tags (or can be done later).

You can select an existing security group or create a new one.

You must create or use an existing key pair – this is required.

AMAZON MACHINE IMAGES

An Amazon Machine Image (AMI) provides the information required to launch an instance.

An AMI includes the following:

- A template for the root volume for the instance (for example, an operating system, an application server, and applications).
- Launch permissions that control which AWS accounts can use the AMI to launch instances.
- A block device mapping that specifies the volumes to attach to the instance when it's launched.

AMIs are regional. You can only launch an AMI from the region in which it is stored. However, you can copy AMI's to other regions using the console, command line, or the API.

Volumes attached to the instance are either EBS or Instance store:

- Amazon Elastic Block Store (EBS) provides persistent storage. EBS snapshots, which reside on Amazon S3, are used to create the volume.
- Instance store volumes are ephemeral (non-persistent). That means data is lost if the instance is shut down. A template stored on Amazon S3 is used to create the volume.

NETWORKING

Networking Limits (per Region or as Specified):

Name	Default Limit
EC2-Classic Elastic IPs	5
EC2-VPC Elastic IPs	5
VPCs	5
Subnets per VPC	200
Security groups per VPC	500
Rules per VPC security group	50
VPC security groups per elastic network interface	5
Network interfaces	350
Network ACLs per VPC	200
Rules per network ACL	20
Route tables per VPC	200
Entries per route table	50
Active VPC peering connections	50
Outstanding VPC peering connection requests	25
Expiry time for an unaccepted VPC peering connection	168

IP Addresses

There are three types of IP address that can be assigned to an Amazon EC2 instance:

- Public – public address that is assigned automatically to instances in public subnets and reassigned if instance is stopped/started.
- Private – private address assigned automatically to all instances.
- Elastic IP – public address that is static.

Public IPv4 addresses are lost when the instance is stopped but private addresses (IPv4 and IPv6) are retained.

Public IPv4 addresses are retained if you restart the instance.

Elastic IPs are retained when the instance is stopped.

Elastic IP addresses are static public IP addresses that can be remapped (moved) between instances.

All accounts are limited to 5 elastic IP's per region by default.

AWS charge for elastic IP's when they're not being used.

An Elastic IP address is for use in a specific region only.

You can assign custom tags to your Elastic IP addresses to categorize them.

By default, EC2 instances come with a private IP assigned to the primary network interface (eth0).

Public IP addresses are assigned for instances in public subnets (VPC).

Public IP addresses are always assigned for instances in EC2-Classic.

DNS records for elastic IP's can be configured by filling out a form.

Secondary IP addresses can be useful for hosting multiple websites on a server or redirecting traffic to a standby EC2 instance for HA.

You can choose whether secondary IP addresses can be reassigned.

You can associate a single private IPv4 address with a single Elastic IP address and vice versa.

When reassigned the IPv4 to Elastic IP association is maintained.

When a secondary private address is unassigned from an interface, the associated Elastic IP address is disassociated.

You can assign or remove IP addresses from EC2 instances while they are running or stopped.

All IP addresses (IPv4 and IPv6) remain attached to the network interface when detached or reassigned to another instance.

You can attach a network interface to an instance in a different subnet as long as it's within the same AZ.

The following table compares the different types of IP address available in Amazon EC2:

Name	Description
Public IP address	Lost when the instance is stopped Used in Public Subnets No charge Associated with a private IP address on the instance Cannot be moved between instances
Private IP address	Retained when the instance is stopped Used in Public and Private Subnets
Elastic IP address	Static Public IP address You are charged if not used Associated with a private IP address on the instance Can be moved between instances and Elastic Network Adapters

Elastic Network Interfaces

An elastic network interface (referred to as a network interface in this documentation) is a logical networking component in a VPC that represents a virtual network card.

A network interface can include the following attributes:

- A primary private IPv4 address from the IPv4 address range of your VPC

- One or more secondary private IPv4 addresses from the IPv4 address range of your VPC
- One Elastic IP address (IPv4) per private IPv4 address
- One public IPv4 address
- One or more IPv6 addresses
- One or more security groups
- A MAC address
- A source/destination check flag
- A description

You can create and configure network interfaces in your account and attach them to instances in your VPC.

You cannot team by adding ENIs to an instance.

eth0 is the primary network interface and cannot be moved or detached.

By default, eth0 is the only Elastic Network Interface (ENI) created with an EC2 instance when launched.

You can add additional interfaces to EC2 instances (number dependent on instances family/type).

An ENI is bound to an AZ and you can specify which subnet/AZ you want the ENI to be added in.

You can specify which IP address within the subnet to configure or leave it be auto-assigned.

You can only add one extra ENI when launching but more can be attached later.

ENIs can be "hot attached" to running instances.

ENIs can be "warm-attached" when the instance is stopped.

ENIs can be "cold-attached" when the instance is launched.

If you add a second interface AWS will not assign a public IP address to eth0 (you would need to add an Elastic IP).

Default interfaces are terminated with instance termination.

Manually added interfaces are not terminated by default.

You can change the termination behavior.

ENHANCED NETWORKING – ELASTIC NETWORK ADAPTER (ENA)

Enhanced networking provides higher bandwidth, higher packet-per-second (PPS) performance, and consistently lower inter-instance latencies.

Enhanced networking is enabled using an Elastic Network Adapter (ENA).

If your packets-per-second rate appears to have reached its ceiling, you should consider moving to enhanced networking because you have likely reached the upper thresholds of the VIF driver.

AWS currently supports enhanced networking capabilities using SR-IOV.

SR-IOV provides direct access to network adapters, provides higher performance (packets-per-second) and lower latency.

Must launch an HVM AMI with the appropriate drivers.

Only available for certain instance types.

Only supported in VPC.

ELASTIC FABRIC ADAPTER (EFA)

An Elastic Fabric Adapter is an AWS Elastic Network Adapter (ENA) with added capabilities.

An EFA can still handle IP traffic, but also supports an important access model commonly called OS bypass.

This model allows the application (most commonly through some user-space middleware) access the network interface without having to get the operating system involved with each message.

Elastic Fabric Adapter (EFA) is a network interface for Amazon EC2 instances that enables customers to run applications requiring high levels of inter-node communications at scale on AWS.

Its custom-built operating system (OS) bypass hardware interface enhances the performance of inter-instance communications, which is critical to scaling these applications.

With EFA, High Performance Computing (HPC) applications using the Message Passing Interface (MPI) and Machine Learning (ML) applications using NVIDIA Collective Communications Library (NCCL) can scale to thousands of CPUs or GPUs.

As a result, you get the application performance of on-premises HPC clusters with the on-demand elasticity and flexibility of the AWS cloud.

EFA is available as an optional EC2 networking feature that you can enable on any supported EC2 instance at no additional cost.

ENI VS ENA VS EFA

When to use ENI:

- This is the basic adapter type for when you don't have any high performance requirements.
- Can use with all instance types.

When to use ENA:

- Good for use cases that require higher bandwidth and lower inter-instance latency.
- Supported for limited instance types (HVM only).

When to use EFA:

- High Performance Computing.
- MPI and ML use cases.
- Tightly coupled applications.
- Can use with all instance types.

PLACEMENT GROUPS

Placement groups are a logical grouping of instances in one of the following configurations.

Cluster – clusters instances into a low-latency group in a single AZ:

- A cluster placement group is a logical grouping of instances within a single Availability Zone.

- Cluster placement groups are recommended for applications that benefit from low network latency, high network throughput, or both, and if the majority of the network traffic is between the instances in the group.

Spread – spreads instances across underlying hardware (can span AZs):

- A spread placement group is a group of instances that are each placed on distinct underlying hardware.
- Spread placement groups are recommended for applications that have a small number of critical instances that should be kept separate from each other.

Partition — divides each group into logical segments called partitions:

- Amazon EC2 ensures that each partition within a placement group has its own set of racks.
- Each rack has its own network and power source. No two partitions within a placement group share the same racks, allowing you to isolate the impact of hardware failure within your application.
- Partition placement groups can be used to deploy large distributed and replicated workloads, such as HDFS, HBase, and Cassandra, across distinct racks.

The table below describes some key differences between clustered and spread placement groups:

	Clustered	Spread
What	Instances are placed into a low-latency group within a single AZ	Instances are spread across underlying hardware
When	Need low network latency and/or high network throughput	Reduce the risk of simultaneous instance failure if underlying hardware fails
Pros	Get the most out of enhanced networking Instances	Can span multiple AZs
Cons	Finite capacity: recommend launching all you might need up front	Maximum of 7 instances running per group, per AZ

Launching instances in a spread placement group reduces the risk of simultaneous failures that might occur when instances share the same underlying hardware.

Recommended for applications that benefit from low latency and high bandwidth.

Recommended to use an instance type that supports enhanced networking.

Instances within a placement group can communicate with each other using private or public IP addresses.

Best performance is achieved when using private IP addresses.

Using public IP addresses, the performance is limited to 5Gbps or less.

Low-latency 10 Gbps or 25 Gbps network.

Recommended to keep instance types homogenous within a placement group.

Can use reserved instances at an instance level but cannot reserve capacity for the placement group.

The name you specify for a placement group must be unique within your AWS account for the Region.

You can't merge placement groups.

An instance can be launched in one placement group at a time; it cannot span multiple placement groups.

On-Demand Capacity Reservation and zonal Reserved Instances provide a capacity reservation for EC2 instances in a specific Availability Zone. The capacity reservation can be used by instances in a placement group. However, it is not possible to explicitly reserve capacity for a placement group.

Instances with a tenancy of host cannot be launched in placement groups.

IAM ROLES

IAM roles are more secure than storing access keys and secret access keys on EC2 instances.

IAM roles are easier to manage.

You can attach an IAM role to an instance at launch time or at any time after by using the AWS CLI, SDK, or the EC2 console.

IAM roles can be attached, modified, or replaced at any time.

Only one IAM role can be attached to an EC2 instance at a time.

IAM roles are universal and can be used in any region.

BASTION/JUMP HOSTS

You can configure EC2 instances as bastion hosts (aka jump boxes) in order to access your VPC instances for management.

Can use the SSH or RDP protocols to connect to your bastion host.

Need to configure a security group with the relevant permissions.

Can use auto-assigned public IPs or Elastic IPs.

Can use security groups to restrict the IP addresses/CIDRs that can access the bastion host.

Use auto-scaling groups for HA (set to 1 instance to just replace if it fails).

Best practice is to deploy Linux bastion hosts in two AZs, use auto-scaling and Elastic IP addresses.

EC2 MIGRATION

VM Import/Export is a tool for migrating VMware, Microsoft, XEN VMs to the Cloud.

Can also be used to convert EC2 instances to VMware, Microsoft or XEN VMs.

Supported for:

- Windows and Linux.
- VMware ESX VMDKs and (OVA images for export only).
- Citrix XEN VHD.

- Microsoft Hyper-V VHD.

Can only be used via the API or CLI (not the console).

Stop the VM before generating VMDK or VHD images.

AWS has a VM connector plugin for vCenter:

- Allows migration of VMs to S3.
- Then converts into a EC2 AMI.
- Progress can be tracked in vCenter.

MONITORING

EC2 status checks are performed every minute and each returns a pass or a fail status.

If all checks pass, the overall status of the instance is **OK.**

If one or more checks fail, the overall status is **impaired.**

System status checks detect (StatusCheckFailed_System) problems with your instance that require **AWS** involvement to repair.

Instance status checks (StatusCheckFailed_Instance) detect problems that require **your** involvement to repair.

Status checks are built into Amazon EC2, so they cannot be disabled or deleted.

You can, however, create or delete alarms that are triggered based on the result of the status checks.

You can create Amazon CloudWatch alarms that monitor Amazon EC2 instances and automatically perform an action if the status check fails.

Actions can include:

- Recover the instance (only supported on specific instance types and can be used only with StatusCheckFailed_System).
- Stop the instance (only applicable to EBS-backed volumes).
- Terminate the instance (cannot terminate if termination protection is enabled).
- Reboot the instance.

It is a best practice to use EC2 to reboot instance rather than the OS (create a CloudWatch record).

CloudWatch Monitoring frequency:

- Standard monitoring = 5 mins
- Detailed monitoring = 1 min (chargeable)

TAGS

A tag is a label that you assign to an AWS resource.

Used to manage AWS assets.

Tags are just arbitrary name/value pairs that you can assign to virtually all AWS assets to serve as metadata.

Each tag consists of a key and an optional value, both of which you define.

Tagging strategies can be used for cost allocation, security, automation, and many other uses. For example, you can use a tag in an IAM policy to implement access control.

Enforcing standardized tagging can be done via AWS Config rules or custom scripts. For example, EC2 instances not properly tagged are stopped or terminated daily.

Most resources can have up to 50 tags.

RESOURCE GROUPS

Resource groups are mappings of AWS assets defined by tags.

Create custom consoles to consolidate metrics, alarms and config details around given tags.

HIGH AVAILABILITY APPROACHES FOR COMPUTE

Up-to-date AMIs are critical for rapid fail-over.

AMIs can be copied to other regions for safety or DR staging.

Horizontally scalable architectures are preferred because risk can be spread across multiple smaller machines versus one large machine.

Reserved instances are the only way to guarantee that resources will be available when needed.

Auto Scaling and Elastic Load Balancing work together to provide automated recovery by maintaining minimum instances.

Route 53 health checks also provide "self-healing" redirection of traffic.

MIGRATION

AWS Server Migration Service (SMS) is an agent-less service which makes it easier and faster for you to migrate thousands of on-premises workloads to AWS.

AWS SMS allows you to automate, schedule, and track incremental replications of live server volumes, making it easier for you to coordinate large-scale server migrations.

Automates migration of on-premises VMware vSphere or Microsoft Hyper-V/SCVMM virtual machines to AWS.

Replicates VMs to AWS, syncing volumes and creating periodic AMIs.

Minimizes cutover downtime by syncing VMs incrementally.

Supports Windows and Linux VMs only (just like AWS).

The Server Migration Connector is downloaded as a virtual appliance into your on-premises vSphere or Hyper-V environments.

AMAZON EBS

GENERAL

EBS is the Elastic Block Store.

EBS volumes are network attached storage that can be attached to EC2 instances.

EBS volume data persists independently of the life of the instance.

EBS volumes do not need to be attached to an instance.

You can attach multiple EBS volumes to an instance.

You cannot attach an EBS volume to multiple instances (use Elastic File Store instead).

EBS volume data is replicated across multiple servers in an AZ.

EBS volumes must be in the same AZ as the instances they are attached to.

EBS is designed for an annual failure rate of 0.1%-0.2% & an SLA of 99.95%.

Termination protection is turned off by default and must be manually enabled (keeps the volume/data when the instance is terminated).

Root EBS volumes are deleted on termination by default.

Extra non-boot volumes are not deleted on termination by default.

The behavior can be changed by altering the "DeleteOnTermination" attribute.

You can now create AMIs with encrypted root/boot volumes as well as data volumes (you can also use separate CMKs per volume).

Volume sizes and types can be upgraded without downtime (except for magnetic standard).

Elastic Volumes allow you to increase volume size, adjust performance, or change the volume type while the volume is in use.

To migrate volumes between AZ's create a snapshot then create a volume in another AZ from the snapshot (possible to change size and type).

Auto-enable IO setting prevents the stopping of IO to a disk when AWS detects inconsistencies.

The root device is created under /dev/sda1 or /dev/xvda.

Magnetic EBS is for workloads that need throughput rather than IOPS.

Throughput optimized EBS volumes cannot be a boot volume.

Each instance that you launch has an associated root device volume, either an Amazon EBS volume or an instance store volume.

You can use block device mapping to specify additional EBS volumes or instance store volumes to attach to an instance when it's launched.

You can also attach additional EBS volumes to a running instance.

You cannot decrease an EBS volume size.

When changing volumes, the new volume must be at least the size of the current volume's snapshot.

Images can be made public but not if they're encrypted.

AMIs can be shared with other accounts.

You can have up to 5,000 EBS volumes by default.

You can have up to 10,000 snapshots by default.

INSTANCE STORE

An instance store provides *temporary* (non-persistent) block-level storage for your instance.

This is different to EBS which provides persistent storage but is also a block storage service that can be a root or additional volume.

Instance store storage is located on disks that are physically attached to the host computer.

Instance store is ideal for temporary storage of information that changes frequently, such as buffers, caches, scratch data, and other temporary content, or for data that is replicated across a fleet of instances, such as a load-balanced pool of web servers.

You can specify instance store volumes for an instance only when you launch it.

You can't detach an instance store volume from one instance and attach it to a different instance.

The instance type determines the size of the instance store available and the type of hardware used for the instance store volumes.

Instance store volumes are included as part of the instance's usage cost.

Some instance types use NVMe or SATA-based solid state drives (SSD) to deliver high random I/O performance.

This is a good option when you need storage with very low latency, but you don't need the data to persist when the instance terminates, or you can take advantage of fault-tolerant architectures.

EXAM TIP: Instance stores offer very high performance and low latency. As long as you can afford to lose an instance, i.e. you are replicating your data, these can be a good solution for high performance/low latency requirements. Look out for questions that mention distributed or replicated databases that need high I/O. Also, remember that the cost of instance stores is included in the instance charges so it can also be more cost-effective than EBS Provisioned IOPS.

EBS VS INSTANCE STORE

EBS-backed means the root volume is an EBS volume and storage is persistent.

Instance store-backed means the root volume is an instance store volume and storage is not persistent.

On an EBS-backed instance, the default action is for the root EBS volume to be deleted upon termination.

Instance store volumes are sometimes called Ephemeral storage (non-persistent).

Instance store backed instances cannot be stopped. If the underlying host fails, the data will be lost.

Instance store volume root devices are created from AMI templates stored on S3.

EBS backed instances can be stopped. You will not lose the data on this instance if it is stopped (persistent).

EBS volumes can be detached and reattached to other EC2 instances.

EBS volume root devices are launched from AMI's that are backed by EBS snapshots.

Instance store volumes cannot be detached/reattached.

When rebooting the instances for both types data will not be lost.

By default, both root volumes will be deleted on termination unless you configured otherwise.

EBS VOLUME TYPES

SSD, General Purpose – GP2

- Baseline of 3 IOPS per GiB with a minimum of 100 IOPS.
- Burst up to 3000 IOPS (for volumes >= 334GB).
- Up to 16,000 IOPS per volume.
- AWS designs gp2 volumes to deliver 90% of the provisioned performance 99% of the time. A gp2 volume can range in size from 1 GiB to 16 TiB.

SSD, Provisioned IOPS – I01

- More than 16,000 IOPS.
- Up to 64,000 IOPS per volume.
- Up to 50 IOPS per GiB.
- Amazon EBS delivers the provisioned IOPS performance 99.9 percent of the time.

HDD, Throughput Optimized – (ST1):

- Frequently accessed, throughput intensive workloads with large datasets and large I/O sizes, such as MapReduce, Kafka, log processing, data warehouse, and ETL workloads.
- Throughput measured in MB/s, and includes the ability to burst up to 250 MB/s per TB, with a baseline throughput of 40 MB/s per TB and a maximum throughput of 500 MB/s per volume.
- Cannot be a boot volume.

HDD, Cold – (SC1):

- Lowest cost storage – cannot be a boot volume.
- Less frequently accessed workloads with large, cold datasets.
- These volumes can burst up to 80 MB/s per TB, with a baseline throughput of 12 MB/s per TB and a maximum throughput of 250 MB/s per volume.

HDD, Magnetic – Standard – cheap, infrequently accessed storage – lowest cost storage that can be a boot volume.

EBS optimized instances:

- Dedicated capacity for Amazon EBS I/O.
- EBS-optimized instances are designed for use with all EBS volume types.
- Max bandwidth: 400 Mbps – 12000 Mbps.
- IOPS: 3000 – 65000.
- GP-SSD within 10% of baseline and burst performance 99.9% of the time.
- PIOPS within 10% of baseline and burst performance 99.9% of the time.
- Additional hourly fee.
- Available for select instance types.
- Some instance types have EBS-optimized enabled by default.

	Solid State Drives (SSD)		Hard Disk Drives (HDD)	
Volume Type	EBS Provisioned IOPS SSD (io1)	EBS General Purpose SSD (gp2)	Throughput Optimized HDD (st1)	Cold HDD (sc1)
Short Description	Highest performance SSD volume designed for latency-sensitive transactional workloads	General Purpose SSD volume that balances price performance for a wide variety of transactional workloads	Low cost HDD volume designed for frequently accessed, throughput intensive workloads	Lowest cost HDD volume designed for less frequently accessed workloads
Use Cases	I/O-Intensive NoSQL and relational databases	Boot volumes, low-latency interactive apps, dev & test	Big data, data warehouses, log processing	Colder data requiring fewer scans per day
API Name	io1	gp2	st1	sc1
Volume Size	4GB - 16TB	1 GB - 16 TB	500 GB - 16 TB	500 GB - 16 TB
Max IOPS/Volume	64,000	16,000	500	250
Max Throughput/Volume	1,000 MB/s	250 MB/s	500 MB/s	250 MB/s
Max IOPS/Instance	80,000	80,000	80,000	80,000
Max Throughput/Instance	1,750 MB/s	1,750 MB/s	1,750 MB/s	1,750 MB/s

SNAPSHOTS

Snapshots capture a point-in-time state of an instance.

Cost-effective and easy backup strategy.

Share data sets with other users or accounts.

Can be used to migrate a system to a new AZ or region.

Can be used to convert an unencrypted volume to an encrypted volume.

Snapshots are stored on Amazon S3.

Does not provide granular backup (not a replacement for backup software).

If you make periodic snapshots of a volume, the snapshots are incremental, which means that only the blocks on the device that have changed after your last snapshot are saved in the new snapshot.

Even though snapshots are saved incrementally, the snapshot deletion process is designed so that you need to retain only the most recent snapshot in order to restore the volume.

Snapshots can only be accessed through the EC2 APIs.

EBS volumes are AZ specific but snapshots are region specific.

Volumes can be created from EBS snapshots that are the same size or larger.

Snapshots can be taken of non-root EBS volumes while running.

To take consistent snapshots writes must be stopped (paused) until the snapshot is complete – if not possible the volume needs to be detached, or if it's an EBS root volume the instance must be stopped.

To lower storage costs on S3 a full snapshot and subsequent incremental updates can be created.

You are charged for data traffic to S3 and storage costs on S3.

You are billed only for the changed blocks.

Deleting a snapshot removes only the data not needed by any other snapshot.

You can resize volumes through restoring snapshots with different sizes (configured when taking the snapshot).

Snapshots can be copied between regions (and be encrypted). Images are then created from the snapshot in the other region which creates an AMI that can be used to boot an instance.

You can create volumes from snapshots and choose the availability zone within the region.

ENCRYPTION

You can encrypt both the boot and data volumes of an EC2 instance. When you create an encrypted EBS volume and attach it to a supported instance type, the following types of data are encrypted:

- Data at rest inside the volume.
- All data moving between the volume and the instance.
- All snapshots created from the volume.
- All volumes created from those snapshots.

Encryption is supported by all EBS volume types.

Expect the same IOPS performance on encrypted volumes as on unencrypted volumes.

All instance families support encryption.

Amazon EBS encryption is available on the instance types listed below:

- General purpose: A1, M3, M4, M5, M5a, M5ad, M5d, T2, T3, and T3a.
- Compute optimized: C3, C4, C5, C5d, and C5n.
- Memory optimized: cr1.8xlarge, R3, R4, R5, R5a, R5ad, R5d, u-6tb1.metal, u-9tb1.metal, u-12tb1.metal, X1, X1e, and z1d.
- Storage optimized: D2, h1.2xlarge, h1.4xlarge, I2, and I3.
- Accelerated computing: F1, G2, G3, G4, P2, and P3.

EBS encrypts your volume with a data key using the industry-standard AES-256 algorithm.

Your data key is stored on-disk with your encrypted data, but not before EBS encrypts it with your CMK. Your data key never appears on disk in plaintext. .

The same data key is shared by snapshots of the volume and any subsequent volumes created from those snapshots.

Snapshots of encrypted volumes are encrypted automatically.

EBS volumes restored from encrypted snapshots are encrypted automatically.

EBS volumes created from encrypted snapshots are also encrypted.

You can share snapshots, but if they're encrypted it must be with a custom CMK key.

There is no direct way to change the encryption state of a volume.

Either create an encrypted volume and copy data to it or take a snapshot, encrypt it, and create a new encrypted volume from the snapshot.

To encrypt a volume or snapshot you need an encryption key, these are customer managed keys (CMK) and they are managed by the AWS Key Management Service (KMS).

A default CMK key is generated for the first encrypted volumes.

Subsequent encrypted volumes will use their own unique key (AES 256 bit).

The CMK used to encrypt a volume is used by any snapshots and volumes created from snapshots.

You cannot share encrypted volumes created using a default CMK key.

You cannot change the CMK key that is used to encrypt a volume.

You must create a copy of the snapshot and change encryption keys as part of the copy.

This is required in order to be able to share the encrypted volume.

By default, only the account owner can create volumes from snapshots.

You can share unencrypted snapshots with the AWS community by making them public.

You can also share unencrypted snapshots with other AWS accounts by making them private and selecting the accounts to share them with.

You cannot make encrypted snapshots public.

You can share encrypted snapshots with other AWS accounts using a non-default CMK key and configuring cross-account permissions to give the account access to the key, mark as private and configure the account to share with.

The receiving account must copy the snapshot before they can then create volumes from the snapshot.

It is recommended that the receiving account re-encrypt the shared and encrypted snapshot using their own CMK key.

The following information applies to snapshots:

- Snapshots are created asynchronously and are incremental.
- You can copy unencrypted snapshots (optionally encrypt).
- You can copy an encrypted snapshot (optionally re-encrypt with a different key).
- Snapshot copies receive a new unique ID.
- You can copy within or between regions.
- You cannot move snapshots, only copy them.
- You cannot take a copy of a snapshot when it is in a "pending" state, it muse be "complete".
- S3 Server Side Encryption (SSE) protects data in transit while copying.
- User defined tags are not copied.
- You can have up to 5 snapshot copy requests running in a single destination per account.
- You can copy Import/Export service, AWS Marketplace, and AWS Storage Gateway snapshots.
- If you try to copy an encrypted snapshot without having access to the encryption keys it will fail silently (cross-account permissions are required).

Copying snapshots may be required for:

- Creating services in other regions.
- DR – the ability to restore from snapshot in another region.
- Migration to another region.
- Applying encryption.

- Data retention.

To take application-consistent snapshots of RAID arrays:

- Stop the application from writing to disk.
- Flush all caches to the disk.
- Freeze the filesystem.
- Unmount the RAID array.
- Shut down the associated EC2 instance.

AMIS

An Amazon Machine Image (AMI) is a special type of virtual appliance that is used to create a virtual machine within the Amazon Elastic Compute Cloud ("EC2").

An AMI includes the following:

- A template for the root volume for the instance (for example, an operating system, an application server, and applications).
- Launch permissions that control which AWS accounts can use the AMI to launch instances.
- A block device mapping that specifies the volumes to attach to the instance when it's launched.

AMIs are either instance store-backed or EBS-backed.

Instance store-backed:

- Launch an EC2 instance from an AWS instance store-backed AMI.
- Update the root volume as required.
- Create the AMI which will upload to a user-specified S3 bucket (user bucket).
- Register the AMI with EC2 (creates another EC2 controlled S3 image).
- To make changes update the source then deregister and reregister.
- Upon launch the image is copied to the EC2 host.
- Deregister an image when the AMI is not needed anymore (does not affect existing instances created from the AMI).
- Instance store-backed volumes can only be created at launch time.

EBS-backed:

- Must stop the instance to create a consistent image and then create the AMI.
- AWS registers the AMIs manually.
- During creation AWS creates snapshots of all attached volumes – there is no need to specify a bucket but you will be charged for storage on S3.
- You cannot delete the snapshot of the root volume as long as the AMI is registered (deregister and delete).
- You can now create AMIs with encrypted root/boot volumes as well as data volumes (can also use separate CMKs per volume).

Copying AMIs:

- You can copy an Amazon Machine Image (AMI) within or across an AWS region using the AWS Management Console, the AWS AWS Command Line Interface or SDKs, or the Amazon EC2 API, all of which support theCopyImage action.
- You can copy both Amazon EBS-backed AMIs and instance store-backed AMIs.
- You can copy encrypted AMIs and AMIs with encrypted snapshots.

EBS COPYING, SHARING AND ENCRYPTION METHODS

The following diagram aims to articulate the various possible options for copying EBS volumes, sharing AMIs and snapshots and applying encryption:

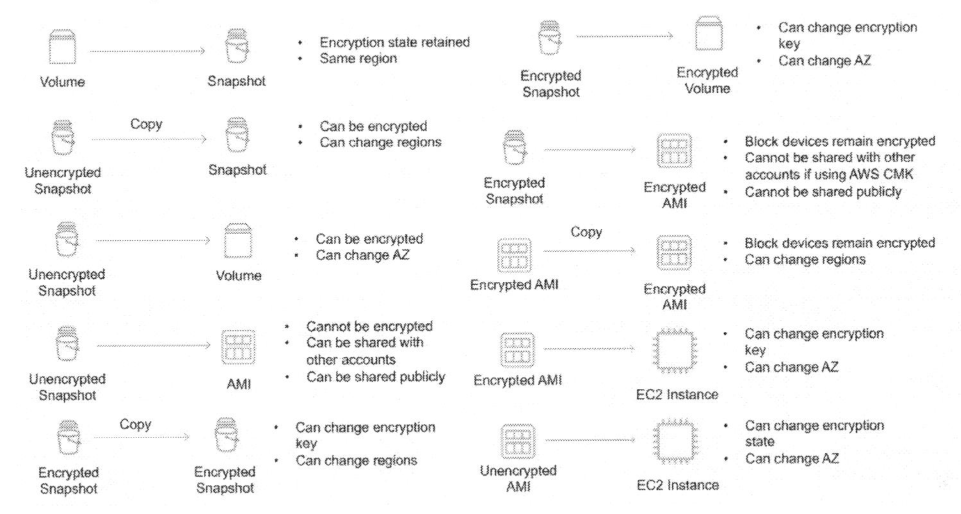

RAID

RAID can be used to increase IOPS.

RAID 0 = 0 striping – data is written across multiple disks and increases performance but no redundancy.

RAID 1 = 1 mirroring – creates 2 copies of the data but does not increase performance, only redundancy.

RAID 10 = 10 combination of RAID 1 and 2 resulting in increase performance and redundancy (at the cost of additional disks).

You can configure multiple striped gp2 or standard volumes (typically RAID 0).

You can configure multiple striped PIOPS volumes (typically RAID 0).

RAID is configured through the guest OS.

EBS optimized EC2 instances are another way of increasing performance.

Ensure the EC2 instance can handle the bandwidth required for the increased performance.

Use EBS optimized instances or instances with a 10 Gbps network interface.

Not recommended to use RAID for root/boot volumes.

EBS LIMITS (PER REGION)

Name	Default Limit
Provisioned IOPS	300,000
Provisioned IOPS (SSD) volume storage (TiB)	300
General Purpose (SSD) volume storage (TiB)	300
Magnetic volume storage (TiB)	300
Max Cold HDD (SC1) Storage in (TiB)	300
Max Throughput Optimized HDD (ST1) Storage (TiB)	300

ELASTIC LOAD BALANCING

GENERAL ELB CONCEPTS

Elastic Load Balancing automatically distributes incoming application traffic across multiple targets, such as Amazon EC2 instances, containers, and IP addresses.

There are three types of Elastic Load Balancer (ELB) on AWS:

- Classic Load Balancer (CLB) – this is the oldest of the three and provides basic load balancing at both layer 4 and layer 7.
- Application Load Balancer (ALB) – layer 7 load balancer that routes connections based on the content of the request.
- Network Load Balancer (NLB) – layer 4 load balancer that routes connections based on IP protocol data.

Note: The Classic Load Balancer may be phased out over time and Amazon are promoting the ALB and NLB for most use cases within VPC.

The following image provides an overview of some of the key differences between the three types of ELB:

Instance Protocol:
HTTP, HTTPS

Load Balancer Protocol:
HTTP, HTTPS

Application Load Balancer

Internet Client

Application Load Balancer

- Operates at the request level
- Routes based on the content of the request (layer 7)
- Supports path-based routing, host-based routing, query string parameter-based routing, and source IP address-based routing
- Supports IP addresses, Lambda Functions and containers as targets

Internet Client

Network Load Balancer

- Operates at the connection level
- Routes connections based on IP protocol data (layer 4)
- Offers ultra high performance, low latency and TLS offloading at scale
- Can have static IP / Elastic IP
- Supports UDP and static IP addresses as targets

Instance Protocol:
TCP, SSL, HTTP, HTTPS

Load Balancer Protocol:
TCP, SSL, HTTP, HTTPS

Classic Load Balancer

Internet Client

Classic Load Balancer

- Old generation; not recommended for new applications
- Performs routing at Layer 4 and Layer 7
- Use for existing applications running in EC2-Classic

The following table provides a more detailed feature comparison:

Feature	Application Load Balancer	Network Load Balancer	Classic Load Balancer
Protocols	HTTP, HTTPS	TCP	TCP, SSL, HTTP, HTTPS
Platforms	VPC	VPC	EC2-Classic, VPC
Health Checks	✓	✓	✓
CloudWatch Metrics	✓	✓	✓
Logging	✓	✓	✓
Zonal fail-over	✓	✓	✓
Connection draining	✓	✓	✓
Load balancing to multiple ports on an instance	✓	✓	
WebSockets	✓	✓	
IP addresses as targets	✓	✓	
Lambda functions as targets	✓		
Load balancer deletion protection	✓	✓	
Path-based routing	✓		
Host-based routing	✓		
HTTP header-based routing	✓		
HTTP method-based routing	✓		
Query string parameter-based routing	✓		
Source IP address CIDR-based routing	✓		
Native HTTP/2	✓		
Configurable idle connection timeout	✓		✓

Feature	Application Load Balancer	Network Load Balancer	Classic Load Balancer
Cross-zone load balancing	✓	✓	✓
SSL offloading	✓	✓	✓
Server Name Indication (SNI)	✓		
Sticky sessions	✓		✓
Back-end server encryption	✓	✓	✓
Static IP		✓	
Elastic IP address		✓	
Preserve source IP address		✓	
Resource-based IAM permissions	✓	✓	✓
Tag-based IAM permissions	✓	✓	
Slow start	✓		
User authentication	✓		
Redirects	✓		
Fixed response	✓		
Custom security policies			✓

Elastic Load Balancing provides fault tolerance for applications by automatically balancing traffic across targets – Amazon EC2 instances, containers and IP addresses – and Availability Zones while ensuring only healthy targets receive traffic.

An ELB can distribute incoming traffic across your Amazon EC2 instances in a single Availability Zone or multiple Availability Zones.

Only 1 subnet per AZ can be enabled for each ELB.

Route 53 can be used for region load balancing with ELB instances configured in each region.

ELBs can be Internet facing or internal-only.

Internet facing ELB:

- ELB nodes have public IPs.
- Routes traffic to the private IP addresses of the EC2 instances.
- Need one public subnet in each AZ where the ELB is defined.
- ELB DNS name format: <name>-<id-number>.<region>.elb.amazonaws.com.

Internal only ELB:

- ELB nodes have private IPs.
- Routes traffic to the private IP addresses of the EC2 instances.

- ELB DNS name format: **internal**-<name>-<id-number>.<region>.elb.amazonaws.com.

Internal-only load balancers do not need an Internet gateway.

EC2 instances and containers can be registered against an ELB.

ELB nodes use IP addresses within your subnets, ensure at least a /27 subnet and make sure there are at least 8 IP addresses available in order for the ELB to scale.

An ELB forwards traffic to eth0 (primary IP address).

An ELB listener is the process that checks for connection requests:

- Listeners for CLB provide options for TCP and HTTP/HTTPS.
- Listeners for ALB only provide options for HTTP and HTTPS.
- Listeners for NLB only provide TCP as an option.

Deleting an ELB does not affect the instances registered against it (they won't be deleted; they just won't receive any more requests).

For ALB at least 2 subnets must be specified.

For NLB only one subnet must be specified (recommended to add at least 2).

For CLB you don't need to specify any subnets unless you have "Enable advanced VPC configuration" enabled in which case you must specify two.

ELB uses a DNS record TTL of 60 seconds to ensure new ELB node IP addresses are used to service clients.

By default, the ELB has an idle connection timeout of 60 seconds, set the idle timeout for applications to at least 60 seconds.

Perfect Forward Secrecy (PFS) provides additional safeguards against the eavesdropping of encrypted data, through the use of a unique random session key.

Server Order Preference lets you configure the load balancer to enforce cipher ordering, providing more control over the level of security used by clients to connect with your load balancer.

ELB does not support client certificate authentication (API Gateway does support this).

ELB SECURITY GROUPS

Security groups control the ports and protocols that can reach the front-end listener.

In non-default VPCs you can choose which security group to assign.

You must assign a security group for the ports and protocols on the front-end listener.

You need to also allow the ports and protocols for the health check ports and back-end listeners.

Security group configuration for ELB:

Inbound to ELB (allow)

- Internet-facing ELB:
    - Source: 0.0.0.0/0.
    - Protocol: TCP.
    - Port: ELB listener ports.

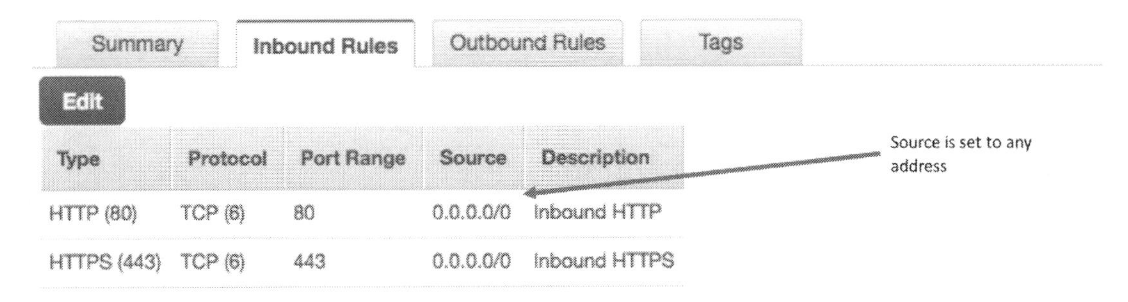

sg-6b578e13 | Internet-Facing ELB

Summary | Inbound Rules | Outbound Rules | Tags

Edit

Type	Protocol	Port Range	Source	Description
HTTP (80)	TCP (6)	80	0.0.0.0/0	Inbound HTTP
HTTPS (443)	TCP (6)	443	0.0.0.0/0	Inbound HTTPS

Internal-only ELB:

- Source: VPC CIDR.
- Protocol: TCP.
- Port: ELB Listener ports.

sg-754e970d | Internal-Only ELB

Summary | Inbound Rules | Outbound Rules | Tags

Edit

Type	Protocol	Port Range	Source	Description
HTTP (80)	TCP (6)	80	10.0.0.0/16	HTTP Listener
HTTPS (443)	TCP (6)	443	10.0.0.0/16	HTTPS Listener

Source is set to the VPC CIDR

Outbound (allow, either type of ELB):

- Destination: EC2 registered instances security group.
- Protocol: TCP.
- Port: Health Check/Listener.

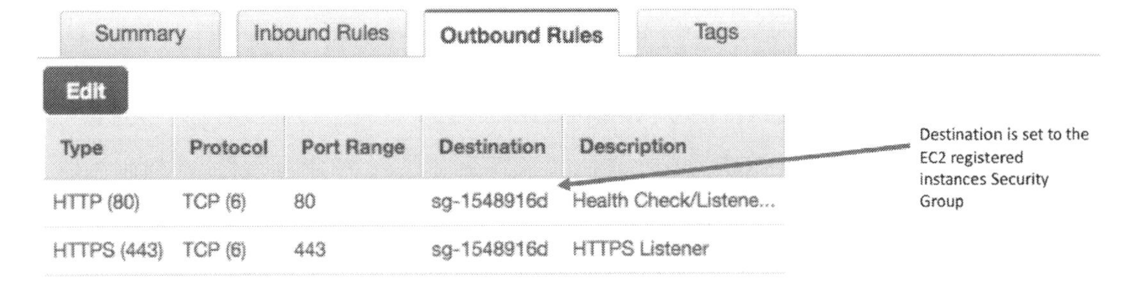

sg-6b578e13 | Internet-Facing ELB

Summary | Inbound Rules | Outbound Rules | Tags

Edit

Type	Protocol	Port Range	Destination	Description
HTTP (80)	TCP (6)	80	sg-1548916d	Health Check/Listene...
HTTPS (443)	TCP (6)	443	sg-1548916d	HTTPS Listener

Security group configuration for registered instances:

Inbound to registered instances (Allow, either type of ELB).

- Source: ELB Security Group.
- Protocol: TCP.

- Port: Health Check/Listener.

sg-1548916d | My EC2 ELB Instances

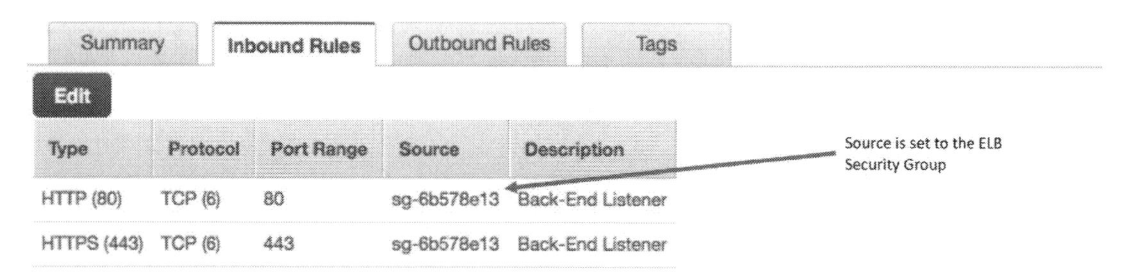

Outbound (Allow, for both types of ELB).

- Destination: ELB Security Group.
- Protocol: TCP.
- Port: Ephemeral.

sg-1548916d | My EC2 ELB Instances

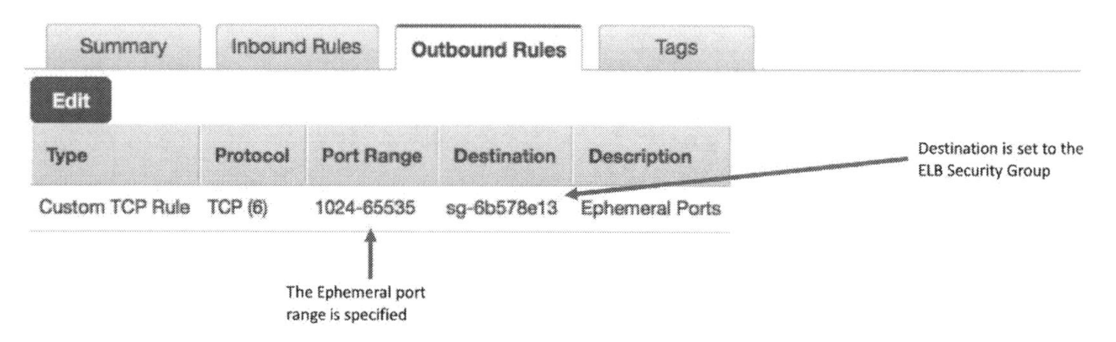

It is also important to ensure NACL settings are set correctly.

Distributed Denial of Service (DDoS) protection:

- ELB automatically distributes incoming application traffic across multiple targets, such as Amazon Elastic Compute Cloud (Amazon EC2) instances, containers, and IP addresses, and multiple Availability Zones, which minimizes the risk of overloading a single resource.
- ELB, like CloudFront, only supports valid TCP requests, so DDoS attacks such as UDP and SYN floods are not able to reach EC2 instances.
- ELB also offers a single point of management and can serve as a line of defence between the internet and your backend, private EC2 instances.

ELB MONITORING

Monitoring takes place using:

- **CloudWatch – every 1 minute**
    - ELB service only sends information when requests are active.
    - Can be used to trigger SNS notifications.
- **Access Logs**
    - Disabled by default.

- Includes information about the clients (not included in CloudWatch metrics).
- Can identify requester, IP, request type etc.
- Can be optionally stored and retained in S3.

- **CloudTrail**
  - Can be used to capture API calls to the ELB.
  - Can be stored in an S3 bucket.

LIMITS

The following table details the default limits for your account on a per-region basis:

Name	Default Limit
Application Load Balancers	20
Network Load Balancers	20
Target Groups	3000
Classic Load Balancers	20

CLASSIC LOAD BALANCER (CLB)

The Classic Load Balancer provides basic load balancing across multiple Amazon EC2 instances and operates at both the request level and connection level.

Operates at layer 4 and layer 7.

Supported protocols: TCP, SSL, HTTP, HTTPS.

CLB does not support HTTP/2.

Load balancers can listen on the following ports:

- [EC2-VPC] 1-65535.
- [EC2-Classic] 25, 80, 443, 465, 587, 1024-65535.

CLB's do not have pre-defined IPv4 addresses but are resolved using a DNS name.

Does not support Elastic IPs.

Supports IPv4 and IPv6.

Within a VPC only IPv4 is supported.

Provides SSL termination and processing.

Sticky Sessions:

- Cookie-based sticky sessions are supported.
- Session stickiness uses cookies and ensures a client is bound to an individual back-end instance for the duration of the cookie lifetime.
- Cookies can be inserted by the application or by the load balancer when configured.

- After cookies expire new requests will be routed by the load balancer normally and a new cookie will be inserted and bind subsequent sessions to the same back-end instance.
- With application-inserted cookies if the back-end instance becomes unhealthy, new requests will be routed by the load balancer normally and a new cookie will be inserted and bind subsequent sessions to the same back-end instance.
- With CLB-inserted cookies if the back-end instance becomes unhealthy, new requests will be routed by the load balancer normally BUT the session will no longer be sticky.

Must have multiple CLBs for multiple SSL certs.

Integrates with Auto Scaling, CloudWatch, CloudTrail and Route 53.

Instances monitored by CLB are reported as InService or OutofService.

Supports domain zone apex records, e.g. example.com.

Wildcard certificates are supported.

Health checks:

- Can be configured for HTTP, TCP, HTTPS, SSL.
- Ping port specifies the port for the health check.
- Ping path specifies the path to check, e.g. /index.html.
- Can define timeout, interval, unhealthy threshold, healthy threshold.

For fault tolerance it is recommended to distribute registered instances across multiple AZs (ideally evenly).

Cross-one load balancing:

- Cross-zone load balancing is enabled by default for CLB and ALB but not for NLB (when created through the console).
- Cross-zone load balancing is NOT enabled by default if the CLB is created from the CLI or API.
- You can enable or disable cross-zone load balancing on the CLB and NLB at any time.
- For the ALB, cross-zone load balancing is always on and cannot be disabled.
- When cross-zone load balancing is enabled, each load balancer node distributes traffic across the registered targets in all enabled Availability Zones.
- When cross-zone load balancing is disabled, each load balancer node distributes traffic across the registered targets in its Availability Zone only.

Connection draining is enabled by default and provides a period of time for existing connections to close cleanly.

When connection draining is in action a CLB will be in the status "InService: Instance deregistration currently in progress".

CLB can take 1 to 7 minutes to detect an increase in load and scale.

If you're anticipating a fast increase in load you can contact AWS and instruct them to pre-warm (provision) additional CLB nodes.

Listeners:

- A CLB listener is the process that checks for connection requests.
- You can configure the protocol/port on which your CLB listener listens.

- Front-end listeners check for traffic from clients to the CLB.
- Back-end listeners are configured with the protocol/port to check for traffic from the CLB to the EC2 instances.
- Front-end and back-end listeners can listen on ports 1-65535.
- Front-end and back-end listeners must be at the same layer (e.g. layer 4 or layer 7).
- There is a 1:1 mapping between front-end and back-end listeners.
- Up to 100 listeners can be configured.
- Supports L4 (TCP, SSL) and L7 (HTTP, HTTPS) listeners.

With packet interception the source IP/port will be from the ELB.

Proxy protocol for TCP/SSL carries the source (client) IP/port information.

The Proxy Protocol header helps you identify the IP address of a client when you have a load balancer that uses TCP for back-end connections.

Ensure the client doesn't go through a proxy or there will be multiple proxy headers.

Also need to ensure the EC2 instance's TCP stack can process the extra information.

X-forwarded-for for HTTP/HTTPS carries the source IP/port information.

To use an HTTPS listener the CLB must have an X.509 SSL/TLS server certificate – this will allow the CLB to terminate the secure session from the client to the CLB.

The session between the CLB and the EC2 instance can be re-encrypted.

You can use a certificate generated by AWS Certificate Manager (ACM) or your own certificate.

If you don't want interception/offloading you can use TCP listeners with certificates on the EC2 instances (traffic is secured end-to-end).

Proxy protocol only applies to L4.

X-forwarded-for only applies to L7.

To filter by source IP use NACLs for proxy protocol (L4) / X-forwarded-for (L7) headers with the EC2 instance's application performing the filtering.

Security

CLB supports a single X.509 certificate.

Two-way authentication with client certificates is not supported on the CLB – you would need to pass through the session using the proxy protocol and have an application that supports client-side certificates.

When using end-to-end encryption use TCP not SSL/HTTPS on the CLB (does not support Session Stickiness).

AWS ACM certificates include an RSA public key – ensure you include a set of ciphers that support RSA in the security policy.

The latest predefined security policy does not include support for SSLv3.

When choosing a custom security policy, you can select the ciphers and protocols (only for CLB).

SSL Security Policy includes:

- Protocol Versions (SSL/TLS)

- Supports TLS 1.0, 1.1, 1.2, SSL 3.0
- SSL Ciphers
  - Encryption algorithms
  - SSL can use different ciphers to encrypt data
- Server Order Preference
  - When enabled the first match in the cipher list with the Client list is used

If disabled (default) the first match in the client cipher list with the CLB is used

APPLICATION LOAD BALANCER (ALB)

The Application Load Balancer operates at the request level (layer 7), routing traffic to targets – EC2 instances, containers and IP addresses based on the content of the request.

You can load balance HTTP/HTTPS applications and use layer 7-specific features, such as X-Forwarded-For headers.

Supports HTTPS termination between the clients and the load balancer.

Supports management of SSL certificates through AWS IAM and AWS Certificate Manager for pre-defined security policies.

Server Name Indication (SNI) supports multiple secure websites using a single secure listener.

With Server Name Indication a client indicates the hostname to connect to.

IP addresses as targets allows load balancing any application hosted in AWS or on-premises using IP addresses of the application back-ends as targets.

Need at least 2 availability zones and you can distribute incoming traffic across your targets in multiple Availability Zones.

Automatically scales its request handling capacity in response to incoming application traffic.

Can configure an Application Load Balancer to be Internet facing or create a load balancer without public IP addresses to serve as an internal (non-Internet-facing) load balancer.

Native IPv6 support.

Internal only ALB only supports IPv4.

Content-Based Routing allows the routing of requests to a service based on the content of the request:

- Host-based routing – route client requests based on the Host field of the HTTP header allowing you to route to multiple domains from the same load balancer.
- Path-based routing – route a client request based on the URL path of the HTTP header (e.g. /images or /orders).

Provides support for micro-services and containers with load balancing across multiple ports on a single EC2 instance.

Better performance for real-time streaming.

Deletion protection can be enabled.

Request tracing (allows you to track a request by its unique ID).

Better health checks and CloudWatch metrics.

Integration with Amazon Cognito for user authentication.

Uses a round-robin load balancing algorithm.

Slow start mode allows targets to "warm up" with a ramp-up period.

Health Checks:

- Can have custom response codes in health checks (200-399).
- There are more details provided in the API and management console for health check failures.
- Reason codes are returned with failed health checks.
- Health checks do not support WebSockets.
- Fail open means if no AZ contains a healthy target, the load balancer nodes route requests to all targets.

Detailed access log information is provided and saved to an S3 bucket every 5 or 6 minutes.

ALB does not support back-end server authentication (CLB does).

ALB does not support EC2-Classic (CLB does).

Deletion protection is possible.

Deregistration delay is similar to connection draining.

Sticky Sessions:

- Session stickiness uses cookies and ensures a client is bound to an individual back-end instance for the duration of the cookie lifetime.
- ALB supports load balancer-generated cookies only.
- The name of the cookie is AWSALB.
- The contents of these cookies are encrypted using a rotating key.
- You cannot decrypt or modify load balancer-generated cookies.
- Sticky sessions are enabled at the target group level.
- You can also set the duration for the stickiness of the load balancer-generated cookie, in seconds.
- WebSockets connections are inherently sticky (following the upgrade process).

Monitoring

CloudTrail can be used to capture API calls. Only pay for the S3 storage charges.

CloudTrail records information on API calls only.

To monitor other actions such as time the request was received, the client's IP address, request paths etc. use access logs.

Access logging is optional and disabled by default.

You are only charged for the S3 storage.

ALB logs requests sent to the load balancer including requests that never made it to targets.

ALB does not log health check requests.

Logging of requests is best effort so shouldn't be relied on for auditing.

Target groups

Target groups are a logical grouping of targets (EC2 instances or ECS).

Targets are the endpoints and can be EC2 instances, ECS containers, or IP addresses.

Target groups can exist independently from the ALB.

Target groups can have up to 1000 targets.

A single target can be in multiple target groups.

Only one protocol and one port can be defined per target group.

The target type in a target group can be an EC2 instance ID, IP address (must be a valid private IP from an existing subnet) or AWS Lambda Function (ALB only).

You cannot use public IP addresses as targets.

You cannot use instance IDs and IP address targets within the same target group.

A target group can only be associated with one load balancer.

The following diagram illustrates the basic components. Notice that each listener contains a default rule, and one listener contains another rule that routes requests to a different target group. One target is registered with two target groups.

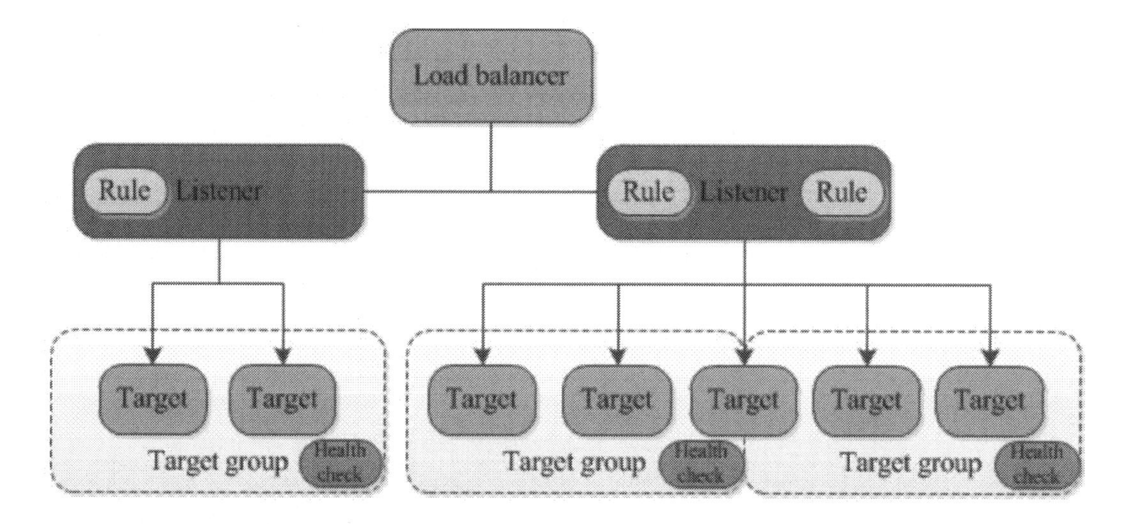

Target groups are used for registering instances against an ALB or NLB.

Target groups are a regional construct.

The following diagram shows how target groups can be used with host-based and target-based routing to route traffic to multiple websites, running on multiple ports, on a single EC2 instance:

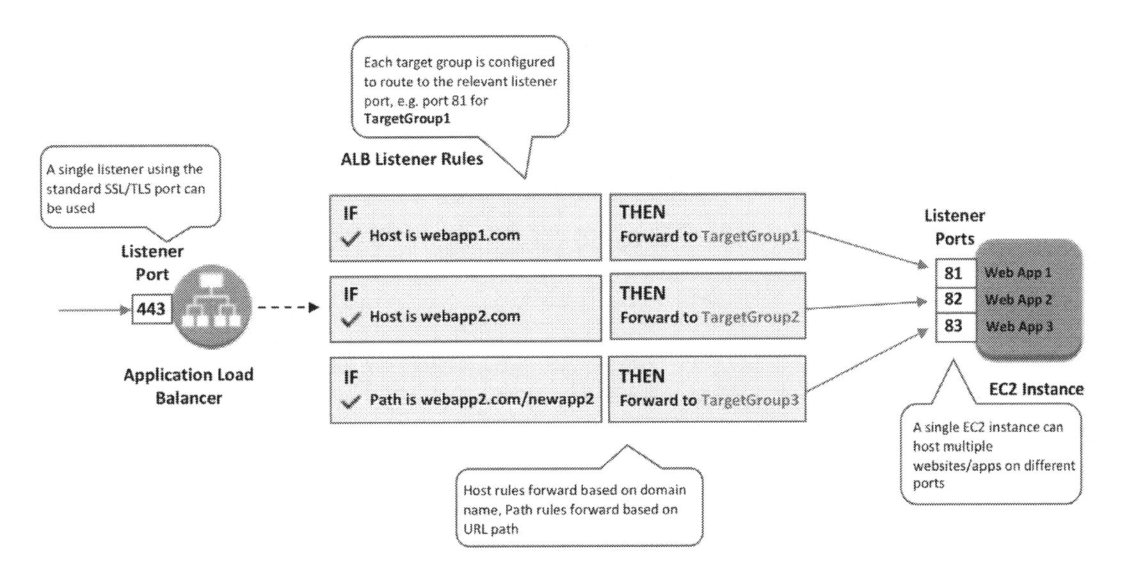

The following attributes can be defined:

- Deregistration delay – the amount of time for Elastic Load Balancing to wait before deregistering a target.
- Slow start duration – the time period, in seconds, during which the load balancer sends a newly registered target a linearly increasing share of the traffic to the target group.
- Stickiness – indicates whether sticky sessions are enabled.

The default settings for attributes are shown below:

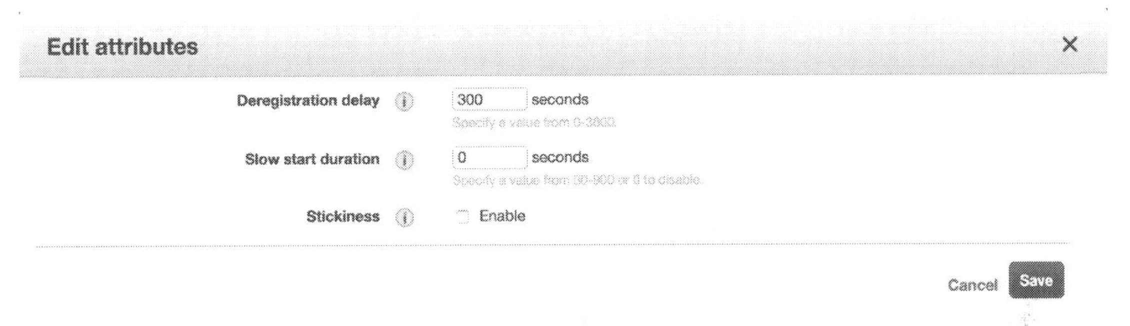

Auto Scaling groups can scale each target group individually.

You can only use Auto Scaling with the load balancer if using instance IDs in your target group.

Health checks are defined per target group.

ALB can route to multiple target groups.

You can register the same EC2 instance or IP address with the same target group multiple times using different ports (used for routing requests to micro-services).

If you register by instance ID the traffic is routed using the primary private IP address of the primary network interface.

If you register by IP address you can route traffic to an instance using any private address from one or more network interfaces.

You cannot mix different types within a target group (EC2, ECS, IP).

An EC2 instance can be registered with the same target group multiple times using multiple ports.

IP addresses can be used to register:

- Instances in a peered VPC.
- AWS resources that are addressable by IP address and port.
- On-premises resources linked to AWS through Direct Connect or a VPN connection.

Listeners and Rules

Listeners:

- Each ALB needs at least one listener and can have up to 10.
- Listeners define the port and protocol to listen on.
- Can add one or more listeners.
- Cannot have the same port in multiple listeners.

Listener rules:

- Rules determine how the load balancer routes requests to the targets in one or more target groups.
- Each rule consists of a priority, one or more actions, an optional host condition, and an optional path condition.
- Only one action can be configured per rule.
- One or more rules are required.
- Each listener has a default rule and you can optionally define additional rules.
- Up to 100 rules per ALB.
- Rules determine what action is taken when the rule matches the client request.
- Rules are defined on listeners.
- You can add rules that specify different target groups based on the content of the request (content-based routing).
- If no rules are found the default rule will be followed which directs traffic to the default target groups.

The image below shows a ruleset with a host-based and path-based entry and a default rule at the end:

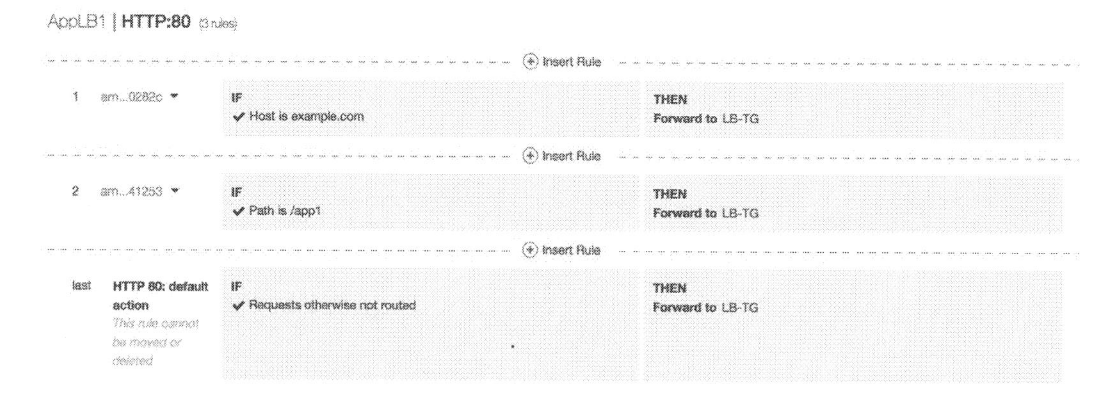

Default rules:

- When you create a listener, you define an action for the default rule.
- Default rules cannot have conditions.
- You can delete the non-default rules for a listener at any time.
- You cannot delete the default rule for a listener.
- When you delete a listener all of its rules are deleted.
- If no conditions for any of a listener's rules are met, the action for the default rule is taken.

Rule priority:

- Each rule has a priority and they are evaluated in order of lowest to highest.
- The default rule is evaluated last.
- You can change the value of a non-default rule at any time.
- You cannot change the value of the default rule.

Rule action:

- Only one target group per action.
- Each rule has a type and a target group.
- The only supported action type is forward, which forwards requests to the target group.
- You can change the target group for a rule at any time.

Rule conditions:

- There are two types of rule condition: host and path.
- When the conditions for a rule are met the action is taken.
- Each rule can have up to 2 conditions, 1 path condition and 1 host condition.
- Optional condition is the path pattern you want the ALB to evaluate in order for it to route requests.

Request routing:

- After the load balancer receives a request it evaluates the listener rules in priority order to determine which rule to apply, and then selects a target from the target group for the rule action using the round robin routing algorithm.
- Routing is performed independently for each target group even when a target is registered with multiple target groups.
- You can configure listener rules to route requests to different target groups based on the content of the application traffic.

Content-based routing:

- ALB can route requests based on the content of the request in the host field: host-based or path-based.
- Host-based is domain name-based routing e.g. example.com or app1.example.com.
- The host field contains the domain name and optionally the port number.
- Path-based is URL based routing e.g. example.com/images, example.com/app1.
- You can also create rules that combine host-based and path-based routing.

- Anything that doesn't match content routing rules will be sent to a default target group.

ALB and ECS

ECS service maintains the "desired count" of instances.

Optionally a load balancer can distribute traffic across tasks.

All containers in a single task definition are placed on a single EC2 container instance.

You can put multiple containers in the same task definition behind a CLB.

- Define multiple host ports in the service definition.
- Define these listener ports as listeners on the CLB.

ECS service can only use a single load balancer.

If your task definition requires multiple ports per container you must use a CLB with multiple listeners.

ALB cannot do multiple listeners on a single task definition.

AWS does not recommend connecting multiple services to the same CLB.

ALB allows containers to use dynamic host port mapping so that multiple tasks from the same service are allowed on the same container host.

ALB supports path-based routing and priority rules.

ALB integrates with EC2 container service using service load balancing.

If a service uses multiple ports then multiple task definitions will need to be created with multiple target groups.

Federated authentication:

- ALB now supports authentication from OIDC compliant identity providers such as Google, Facebook and Amazon.
- Implemented through an authentication action on a listener rule that integrates with Amazon Cognito to create user pools.
- AWS SAM can also be used with Amazon Cognito.

NETWORK LOAD BALANCER

Network Load Balancer operates at the connection level (Layer 4), routing connections to targets – Amazon EC2 instances, containers and IP addresses based on IP protocol data.

It is architected to handle millions of requests/sec, sudden volatile traffic patterns and provides extremely low latencies.

Network Load Balancer supports features including:

- WebSockets
- TLS termination
- Preserves the source IP of the clients
- Provides stable IP support and Zonal isolation
- Long-running connections that are very useful for WebSocket type applications

High throughput – designed to handle traffic as it grows and can load balance millions of requests/second.

Extremely low latencies for latency-sensitive applications.

Uses static IP addresses – each NLB provides a single IP address for each AZ.

Can also assign an Elastic IP to the load balancer per AZ.

The IP-per-AZ feature reduces latency with improved performance, improves availability through isolation and fault tolerance and makes the use of NLBs transparent to your client applications.

Preserves the source IP of clients and provides stable IP support and Zonal isolation.

Can load balance any application hosted in AWS or on-premises using IP addresses of the application back-ends as targets.

NLB supports connections from clients to IP-based targets in peered VPCs across different AWS Regions.

Supports both network and application target health checks.

Supports long-running/lived connections (ideal for WebSocket applications).

Supports failover between IP addresses within and across regions (uses Route 53 health checks).

Integration with Route 53 enables the removal of a failed load balancer IP address from service and subsequent redirection of traffic to an alternate Network Load Balancer in another region.

Supports cross-zone load balancing (not enabled by default when created through the console, unlike ALB and CLB).

Uses the same API as the Application Load Balancer.

Also uses Target Groups (see section above).

Target groups for Network Load Balancers support the following protocols and ports:

- **Protocols:** TCP, TLS, UDP, TCP_UDP.
- **Ports:** 1-65535.

The following table summarizes the supported combinations of listener protocol and target group settings:

Listener Protocol	Target Group Protocol	Target Group Type	Health Check Protocol
TCP	TCP | TCP_UDP	instance | ip	HTTP | HTTPS | TCP
TLS	TCP | TLS	instance | ip	HTTP | HTTPS | TCP
UDP	UDP | TCP_UDP	instance	HTTP | HTTPS | TCP
TCP_UDP	TCP_UDP	instance	HTTP | HTTPS | TCP

CloudWatch reports Network Load Balancer metrics.

Enhanced logging – can use the Flow Logs feature to record all requests sent to your load balancer.

AWS AUTO SCALING

AMAZON EC2 AUTO SCALING

AWS Auto Scaling monitors your applications and automatically adjusts capacity to maintain steady, predictable performance at the lowest possible cost.

AWS Auto Scaling refers to a collection of Auto Scaling capabilities across several AWS services.

The services within the AWS Auto Scaling family include:

- Amazon EC2 (known as Amazon EC2 Auto Scaling)
- Amazon ECS
- Amazon DynamoDB
- Amazon Aurora

GENERAL AUTO SCALING CONCEPTS

Amazon EC2 Auto Scaling helps you ensure that you have the correct number of Amazon EC2 instances available to handle the load for your application.

You create collections of EC2 instances, called Auto Scaling groups.

Automatically provides horizontal scaling (scale-out) for your instances.

Triggered by an event of scaling action to either launch or terminate instances.

Availability, cost, and system metrics can all factor into scaling.

Auto Scaling is a region-specific service.

Auto Scaling can span multiple AZs within the same AWS region.

Auto Scaling can be configured from the Console, CLI, SDKs and APIs.

There is no additional cost for Auto Scaling, you just pay for the resources (EC2 instances) provisioned.

Auto Scaling works with ELB, CloudWatch and CloudTrail.

You can determine which subnets Auto Scaling will launch new instances into.

Auto Scaling will try to distribute EC2 instances evenly across AZs.

Launch configuration is the template used to create new EC2 instances and includes parameters such as instance family, instance type, AMI, key pair and security groups.

You cannot edit a launch configuration once defined.

A launch configuration:

- Can be created from the AWS console or CLI.
- You can create a new launch configuration, or.
- You can use an existing running EC2 instance to create the launch configuration.
    - The AMI must exist on EC2.
    - EC2 instance tags and any additional block store volumes created after the instance launch will not be taken into account.
- If you want to change your launch configurations you have to create a new one, make the required changes, and use that with your auto scaling groups.

You can use a launch configuration with multiple Auto Scaling Groups (ASG).

An ASG is a logical grouping of EC2 instances managed by an Auto Scaling Policy.

An ASG can be edited once defined.

You can attach one or more classic ELBs to your existing ASG.

You can attach one or more Target Groups to your ASG to include instances behind an ALB.

The ELBs must be in the same region.

Once you do this any EC2 instance existing or added by the ASG will be automatically registered with the ASG defined ELBs.

If adding an instance to an ASG would result in exceeding the maximum capacity of the ASG the request will fail.

You can add a running instance to an ASG if the following conditions are met:

- The instance is in a running state.
- The AMI used to launch the instance still exists.
- The instance is not part of another ASG.
- The instance is in the same AZs for the ASG.

SCALING

The scaling options define the triggers and when instances should be provisioned/de-provisioned.

There are four scaling options:

- Maintain – keep a specific or minimum number of instances running.
- Manual – use maximum, minimum, or a specific number of instances.
- Scheduled – increase or decrease the number of instances based on a schedule.
- Dynamic – scale based on real-time system metrics (e.g. CloudWatch metrics).

The following table describes the scaling options available and when to use them:

Scaling Type	What it is	When to use
Maintain	Ensures the required number of instances are running	Use when you always need a known number of instances running at all times
Manual	Manually change desired capacity via the console or CLI	Use when your needs change rarely enough that you're OK to make manual changes
Scheduled	Adjust min/max instances on specific dates/times or recurring time periods	Use when you know when your busy and quiet times are. Useful for ensuring enough instances are available *before* very busy times
Dynamic	Scale in response to system load or other triggers using metrics	Useful for changing capacity based on system utilization, e.g. CPU hits 80%

The scaling options are configured through Scaling Policies which determine when, if, and how the ASG scales and shrinks.

The following table describes the scaling policy types available for dynamic scaling policies and when to use them (more detail further down the page):

Scaling	What it is	When to use
Target Tracking Policy	The scaling policy adds or removes capacity as required to keep the metric at, or close to, the specified target value	A use case is that you want to keep the aggregate CPU usage of your ASG at 70%
Simple Scaling Policy	Waits until health check and cool down period expires before re-evaluating	This is a more conservative way to add/remove instances. Useful when load is erratic. AWS recommend step scaling instead of simple in most cases
Step Scaling Policy	Increase or decrease the current capacity of your Auto Scaling group based on a set of scaling adjustments, known as step adjustments	Useful when you want to vary adjustments based on the size of the alarm breach

The diagram below depicts an Auto Scaling group with a Scaling policy set to a minimum size of 1 instance, a desired capacity of 2 instances, and a maximum size of 4 instances:

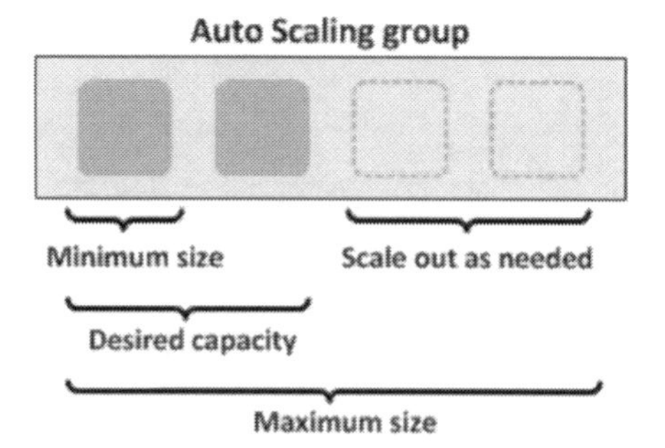

SCALING BASED ON AMAZON SQS

Can also scale based on an Amazon Simple Queue Service (SQS) queue.

This comes up as an exam question for SAA-C02.

Uses a custom metric that's sent to Amazon CloudWatch that measures the number of messages in the queue per EC2 instance in the Auto Scaling group.

Then use a target tracking policy that configures your Auto Scaling group to scale based on the custom metric and a set target value. CloudWatch alarms invoke the scaling policy.

Use a custom "backlog per instance" metric to track not just the number of messages in the queue but the number available for retrieval.

Can base off the SQS Metric "ApproximateNumberOfMessages".

ASG BEHAVIOR AND CONFIGURATION

EC2 Auto Scaling – Termination Policy:

- Termination policies control which instances are terminated first when a scale-in event occurs.
- There is a default termination policy and options for configuring your own customized termination policies.
- The default termination policy is designed to help ensure that your instances span Availability Zones evenly for high availability.
- The default policy is kept generic and flexible to cover a range of scenarios.

You can define Instance Protection which stops Auto Scaling from scaling in and terminating the instances.

If Auto Scaling fails to launch instances in an AZ it will try other AZs until successful.

The default health check grace period is 300 seconds.

Scale-out is the process in which EC2 instances are launched by the scaling policy.

Scale-in is the process in which EC2 instances are terminated by the scaling policy.

It is recommended to create a scale-in event for each scale-out event created.

Auto Scaling can perform rebalancing when it finds that the number of instances across AZs is not balanced.

Auto Scaling rebalances by launching new EC2 instances in the AZs that have fewer instances first, only then will it start terminating instances in AZs that had more instances.

Auto Scaling may go over the maximum number of instances by 10% temporarily for the purposes of rebalancing.

An imbalance may occur due to:

- Manually removing AZs/subnets from the configuration.
- Manually terminating EC2 instances.
- EC2 capacity issues.
- Spot price is reached.

Health checks:

- By default uses EC2 status checks.
- Can also use ELB health checks and custom health checks.
- ELB health checks are in addition to the EC2 status checks.
- If any health check returns an unhealthy status the instance will be terminated.
- With ELB an instance is marked as unhealthy if ELB reports it as OutOfService.
- A healthy instance enters the InService state.
- If an instance is marked as unhealthy it will be scheduled for replacement.
- If connection draining is enabled, Auto Scaling waits for in-flight requests to complete or timeout before terminating instances.
- The health check grace period allows a period of time for a new instance to warm up before performing a health check (300 seconds by default).

If using an ELB it is best to enable ELB health checks as otherwise EC2 status checks may show an instance as being healthy that the ELB has determined is unhealthy. In this case the instance will be removed from service by the ELB but will not be terminated by Auto Scaling.

Elastic IPs and EBS volumes are detached from terminated instances and will need to be manually reattached.

Using custom health checks a CLI command can be issued to set the instance's status to unhealthy, e.g.:

aws autoscaling set–instance-health –instance-id i-123abc45d –health-status Unhealthy

Once in a terminating state an EC2 instance cannot be put back into service again.

However, there is a short time period in which a CLI command can be run to change an instance to healthy.

Unlike AZ rebalancing, termination of unhealthy instances happens first, then Auto Scaling attempts to launch new instances to replace terminated instances.

You can manually remove (detach) instances from an ASG using the AWS Console or CLI.

When detaching an instance, you can optionally decrement the ASG's desired capacity (so it doesn't launch another instance).

An instance can be attached to one ASG at a time.

You can suspend and then resume one or more of the scaling processes for your Auto Scaling group.

Suspending scaling processes can be useful when you want to investigate a configuration problem or other issue with your web application and then make changes to your application, without invoking the scaling processes.

You can manually move an instance from an ASG and put it in the standby state.

Instances in standby state are still managed by Auto Scaling, are charged as normal, and do not count towards available EC2 instance for workload/application use.

Auto scaling does not perform health checks on instances in the standby state.

Standby state can be used for performing updates/changes/troubleshooting etc. without health checks being performed or replacement instances being launched.

When you delete an ASG the instances will be terminated.

You can choose to use Spot instances in launch configurations and specify a bid price.

Auto Scaling treats spot instances the same as on-demand instances.

You cannot mix Spot instances with on-demand.

If you want to change the bid price you need to create a new launch configuration.

Auto Scaling can be configured to send an SNS email when:

- An instance is launched.
- An instance is terminated.
- An instance fails to launch.
- An instance fails to terminate.

Merging ASGs

- You can merge multiple single AZ Auto Scaling Groups into a single multi-AZ ASG.
- Merging can only be performed by using the CLI.
- Process is to rezone one of the groups to cover/span the other AZs for the other ASGs.
- Then delete the other ASGs.
- Can be performed on ASGs with or without ELBs attached to them.
- The resulting ASG must be one of the pre-existing ASGs.

Cooldown Period

- The cooldown period is a configurable setting for your Auto Scaling group that helps to ensure that it doesn't launch or terminate additional instances before the previous scaling activity takes effect.
- The default cooldown period is applied when you create your Auto Scaling group.
- The default value is 300 seconds.
- You can configure the default cooldown period when you create the Auto Scaling group, using the AWS Management Console, the create-auto-scaling-group command (AWS CLI), or the CreateAutoScalingGroup API operation.
- Automatically applies to dynamic scaling and optionally to manual scaling but not supported for scheduled scaling.
- Can override the default cooldown via scaling-specific cooldown.

Scheduled:

- You cannot configure two scheduled activities at the same date/time.
- Scheduled actions can be edited from the AWS Console or CLI.

- Cooldown timer is not supported for scheduled or step on-demand scaling.

Dynamic:

- An alarm is an object that watches over a single metric, e.g. CPU/memory/network utilization.
- You need to have a scale-out and a scale-in policy configured.

Step scaling:

- Configure multiple steps/adjustments.
- Does not support cool down timers.
- Can respond to multiple alarms and initiate multiple scaling activities.
- Supports a warm-up timer which is the time it will take a newly launched instance to be ready.

The warm-up period is the period of time in which a newly created EC2 instance launched by ASG using step scaling is not considered toward the ASG metrics.

MONITORING

Basic monitoring sends EC2 metrics to CloudWatch about ASG instances every 5 minutes.

Detailed can be enabled and sends metrics every 1 minute (chargeable).

When the launch configuration is created from the console basic monitoring of EC2 instances is enabled by default.

When the launch configuration is created from the CLI detailed monitoring of EC2 instances is enabled by default.

When you enable Auto Scaling group metrics, Auto Scaling sends sampled data to CloudWatch every minute.

Configure ASG and EC2 monitoring options so they use the same time period, e.g. detailed monitoring (EC2) and 60 seconds (ASG), or basic monitoring (EC2) and 300 seconds (ASG).

LIMITS

Name	Default Limit
Auto Scaling Groups	200
Launch Configurations	200

AMAZON ECS

GENERAL ECS CONCEPTS

Amazon Elastic Container Service (ECS) is a highly scalable, high performance container management service that supports Docker containers and allows you to easily run applications on a managed cluster of Amazon EC2 instances.

Amazon ECS eliminates the need for you to install, operate, and scale your own cluster management infrastructure.

Using API calls you can launch and stop container-enabled applications, query the complete state of clusters, and access many familiar features like security groups, Elastic Load Balancing, EBS volumes and IAM roles.

Amazon ECS can be used to schedule the placement of containers across clusters based on resource needs and availability requirements.

There is no additional charge for Amazon ECS. You pay for AWS resources (e.g. EC2 instances or EBS volumes) you create to store and run your application.

Possible to use Elastic Beanstalk to handle the provisioning of an Amazon ECS cluster, balancing load, auto-scaling, monitoring, and placing your containers across your cluster.

Alternatively use ECS directly for more fine-grained control for customer application architectures.

It is possible to associate a service on Amazon ECS to an Application Load Balancer (ALB) for the Elastic Load Balancing (ELB) service.

The ALB supports a target group that contains a set of instance ports. You can specify a dynamic port in the ECS task definition which gives the container an unused port when it is scheduled on the EC2 instance.

ECS provides Blox, a collection of open source projects for container management and orchestration. Blox makes it easy to consume events from Amazon ECS, store the cluster state locally and query the local data store through APIs.

You can use any AMI that meets the Amazon ECS AMI specification.

ECS VS EKS

Amazon also provide the Elastic Container Service for Kubernetes (Amazon EKS) which can be used to deploy, manage, and scale containerized applications using Kubernetes on AWS.

The table below describes some of the differences between these services to help you understand when you might choose one over the other:

Amazon ECS	Amazon EKS
Managed, highly available, highly scalable container platform	
AWS-specific platform that supports Docker containers	Compatible with upstream Kubernetes so it's easy to lift and shift from other Kubernetes deployments
Considered simpler to learn and use	Considered more feature-rich and complex with a steep learning curve
Leverages AWS services like Route 53, ALB, and CloudWatch	A hosted Kubernetes platform that handles many things internally
"Tasks" are instances of containers that are run on underlying compute but more or less isolated	"Pods" are containers collocated with one another and can have shared access to each other
Limited extensibility	Extensible via a wide variety of third-party and community add-ons

LAUNCH TYPES

An Amazon ECS launch type determines the type of infrastructure on which your tasks and services are hosted.

There are two launch types and the table below describes some of the differences between the two launch types:

Amazon EC2	Amazon Fargate
You explicitly provision EC2 instances	The control plane asks for resources and Fargate automatically provisions
You're responsible for upgrading, patching, care of EC2 pool	Fargate provisions compute as needed
You must handle cluster optimization	Fargate handles cluster optimization
More granular control over infrastructure	Limited control, as infrastructure is automated

Fargate Launch Type

- The Fargate launch type allows you to run your containerized applications without the need to provision and manage the backend infrastructure. Just register your task definition and Fargate launches the container for you.
- Fargate Launch Type is a serverless infrastructure managed by AWS.
- Fargate only supports container images hosted on Elastic Container Registry (ECR) or Docker Hub.

EC2 Launch Type

- The EC2 launch type allows you to run your containerized applications on a cluster of Amazon EC2 instances that you manage.
- Private repositories are only supported by the EC2 Launch Type.

The following diagram shows the two launch types and summaries some key differences:

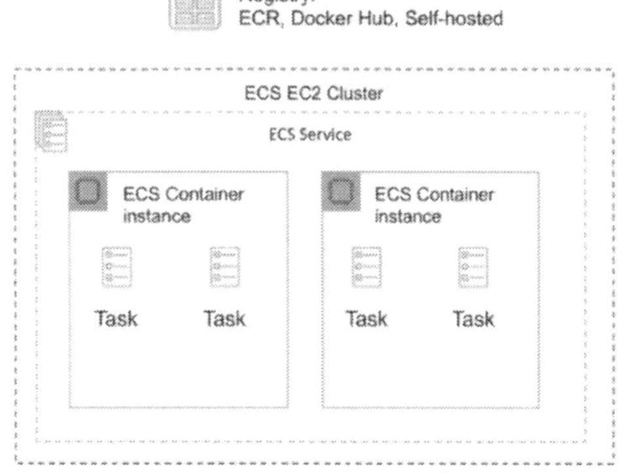

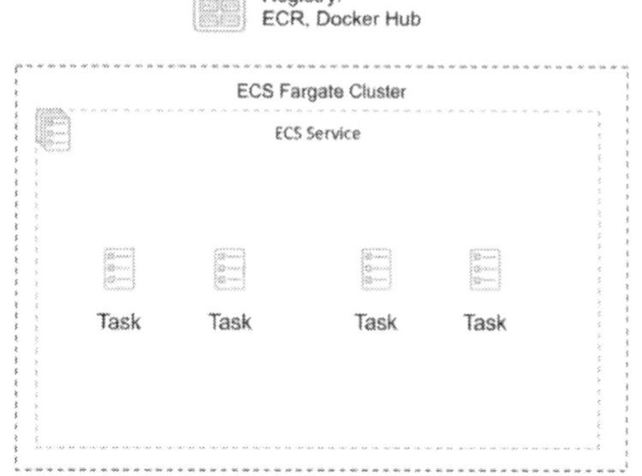

EC2 Launch Type
- You explicitly provision EC2 instances
- You're responsible for managing EC2 instances
- Charged per running EC2 instance
- EFS and EBS integration
- You handle cluster optimization
- More granular control over infrastructure

Fargate Launch Type
- Fargate automatically provisions resources
- Fargate provisions and manages compute
- Charged for running tasks
- No EFS and EBS integration
- Fargate handles cluster optimization
- Limited control, infrastructure is automated

ECS TERMS

The following table provides an overview of some of the terminology used with Amazon ECS:

Elastic Container Service (ECS) Term	Description
Cluster	Logical grouping of EC2 instances
Container instance	EC2 instance running the ECS agent
Task Definition	Blueprint that describes how a docker container should launch
Task	A running container using settings in a Task Definition
Service	Defines long running tasks - can control task count with Auto Scaling and attach an ELB

IMAGES

Containers are created from a read-only template called an image which has the instructions for creating a Docker container.

Images are built from a Dockerfile.

Only Docker containers are currently supported.

An image contains the instructions for creating a Docker container.

Images are stored in a registry such as DockerHub or AWS Elastic Container Registry (ECR).

ECR is a managed AWS Docker registry service that is secure, scalable and reliable.

ECR supports private Docker repositories with resource-based permissions using AWS IAM in order to access repositories and images.

Developers can use the Docker CLI to push, pull and manage images.

TASKS

A task definition is required to run Docker containers in Amazon ECS.

A task definition is a text file in JSON format that describes one or more containers, up to a maximum of 10.

Task definitions use Docker images to launch containers.

You specify the number of tasks to run (i.e. the number of containers).

Some of the parameters you can specify in a task definition include:

- Which Docker images to use with the containers in your task.
- How much CPU and memory to use with each container.
- Whether containers are linked together in a task.
- The Docker networking mode to use for the containers in your task.
- What (if any) ports from the container are mapped to the host container instances.
- Whether the task should continue if the container finished or fails.
- The commands the container should run when it is started.
- Environment variables that should be passed to the container when it starts.
- Data volumes that should be used with the containers in the task.
- IAM role the task should use for permissions.

You can use Amazon ECS Run task to run one or more tasks once.

CLUSTERS

ECS Clusters are a logical grouping of container instances the you can place tasks on.

A default cluster is created but you can then create multiple clusters to separate resources.

ECS allows the definition of a specified number (desired count) of tasks to run in the cluster.

Clusters can contain tasks using the Fargate and EC2 launch type.

For clusters with the EC2 launch type clusters can contain different container instance types.

Each container instance may only be part of one cluster at a time.

“Services” provide auto-scaling functions for ECS.

Clusters are region specific.

You can create IAM policies for your clusters to allow or restrict users’ access to specific clusters.

SERVICE SCHEDULER

You can schedule ECS using Service Scheduler and Custom Scheduler.

Ensures that the specified number of tasks are constantly running and reschedules tasks when a task fails.

Can ensure tasks are registered against an ELB.

CUSTOM SCHEDULER

You can create your own schedulers to meet business needs.

Leverage third party schedulers such as Blox.

The Amazon ECS schedulers leverage the same cluster state information provided by the Amazon ECS API to make appropriate placement decisions.

ECS CONTAINER AGENT

The ECS container agent allows container instances to connect to the cluster.

The container agent runs on each infrastructure resource on an ECS cluster.

The ECS container agent is included in the Amazon ECS optimized AMI and can also be installed on any EC2 instance that supports the ECS specification (only supported on EC2 instances).

Linux and Windows based.

For non-AWS Linux instances to be used on AWS you must manually install the ECS container agent.

AUTO SCALING

Service Auto Scaling

Amazon ECS service can optionally be configured to use Service Auto Scaling to adjust the desired task count up or down automatically.

Service Auto Scaling leverages the Application Auto Scaling service to provide this functionality.

Amazon ECS Service Auto Scaling supports the following types of scaling policies:

- Target Tracking Scaling Policies—Increase or decrease the number of tasks that your service runs based on a target value for a specific CloudWatch metric. This is similar to the way that your thermostat maintains the temperature of your home. You select temperature and the thermostat does the rest.
- Step Scaling Policies—Increase or decrease the number of tasks that your service runs in response to CloudWatch alarms. Step scaling is based on a set of scaling adjustments, known as step adjustments, which vary based on the size of the alarm breach.

Cluster Auto Scaling

This is a new feature released in December 2019. It is unlikely that this will appear on the SAA-C01 exam but could appear on the SAA-C02 exam.

Uses a new ECS resource type called a Capacity Provider.

A Capacity Provider can be associated with an EC2 Auto Scaling Group (ASG).

When you associate an ECS Capacity Provider with an ASG and add the Capacity Provider to an ECS cluster, the cluster can now scale your ASG automatically by using two new features of ECS:

1. **Managed scaling**, with an automatically-created scaling policy on your ASG, and a new scaling metric (Capacity Provider Reservation) that the scaling policy uses; and
2. **Managed instance termination protection**, which enables container-aware termination of instances in the ASG when scale-in happens.

SECURITY/SLA

EC2 instances use an IAM role to access ECS.

IAM can be used to control access at the container level using IAM roles.

The container agent makes calls to the ECS API on your behalf through the applied IAM roles and policies.

You need to apply IAM roles to container instances before they are launched (EC2 launch type).

AWS recommend limiting the permissions that are assigned to the container instance's IAM roles.

Assign extra permissions to tasks through separate IAM roles (IAM Roles for Tasks).

ECS tasks use an IAM role to access services and resources.

Security groups attach at the instance or container level.

You have root level access to the operating system of the EC2 instances.

The Compute SLA guarantees a Monthly Uptime Percentage of at least 99.99% for Amazon ECS.

LIMITS

Soft limits (default):

- Clusters per region = 1000.
- Instances per cluster = 1000.
- Services per cluster = 500.

Hard limits:

- One load balancer per service.
- 1000 tasks per service (the "desired" count).
- Max 10 containers per task definition.
- Max 10 tasks per instance (host).

PRICING

EC2 Launch Type:

No additional charge – you pay for the EC2 resources you launch including instances, EBS volumes and load balancers

Fargate:

You pay for the vCPU and memory allocated to the containers you run.

AWS LAMBDA

GENERAL LAMBDA CONCEPTS

AWS Lambda lets you run code as functions without provisioning or managing servers.

Lambda-based applications (also referred to as serverless applications) are composed of functions triggered by events.

With serverless computing, your application still runs on servers, but all the server management is done by AWS.

You cannot log in to the compute instances that run Lambda functions or customize the operating system or language runtime.

Lambda functions:

- Consist of code and any associated dependencies.
- Configuration information is associated with the function.
- You specify the configuration information when you create the function.
- API provided for updating configuration data.

You specify the amount of memory you need allocated to your Lambda functions.

AWS Lambda allocates CPU power proportional to the memory you specify using the same ratio as a general purpose EC2 instance type.

Functions can access:

- AWS services or non-AWS services.
- AWS services running in VPCs (e.g. RedShift, Elasticache, RDS instances).
- Non-AWS services running on EC2 instances in an AWS VPC.

To enable your Lambda function to access resources inside your private VPC, you must provide additional VPC-specific configuration information that includes VPC subnet IDs and security group IDs.

AWS Lambda uses this information to set up elastic network interfaces (ENIs) that enable your function.

Compute resources:

- You can request additional memory in 64MB increments from 128MB to 3008MB.
- Functions larger than 1536MB are allocated multiple CPU threads, and multi-threaded or multi-process code is needed to take advantage.

There is a maximum execution timeout.

- Max is 15 minutes (900 seconds), default is 3 seconds.
- You pay for the time it runs.
- Lambda terminates the function at the timeout.

Code is invoked using API calls made using AWS SDKs.

Lambda assumes an IAM role when it executes the function.

The handler name refers to the method in your code where Lambda begins execution.

The components of AWS Lambda are:

- A Lambda function which is comprised of your custom code and any dependent libraries.
- Event sources such as SNS or a custom service that triggers your function and executes its logic.
- Downstream resources such as DynamoDB or Amazon S3 buckets that your Lambda function calls once it is triggered.
- Log streams are custom logging statements that allow you to analyze the execution flow and performance of your Lambda function.

Lambda is an event-driven compute service where AWS Lambda runs code in response to events such as changes to data in an S3 bucket or a DynamoDB table.

An event source is an AWS service or developer-created application that produces events that trigger an AWS Lambda function to run.

Event sources are mapped to Lambda functions.

Event sources maintain the mapping configuration except for stream-based services (e.g. DynamoDB, Kinesis) for which the configuration is made on the Lambda side and Lambda performs the polling.

Supported AWS event sources include:

- Amazon S3.
- Amazon DynamoDB.
- Amazon Kinesis Data Streams.
- Amazon Simple Notification Service.
- Amazon Simple Email Service.
- Amazon Simple Queue Service.
- Amazon Cognito.
- AWS CloudFormation.
- Amazon CloudWatch Logs.
- Amazon CloudWatch Events.
- AWS CodeCommit.
- Scheduled Events (powered by Amazon CloudWatch Events).
- AWS Config.
- Amazon Alexa.
- Amazon Lex.
- Amazon API Gateway.
- AWS IoT Button.
- Amazon CloudFront.
- Amazon Kinesis Data Firehose.
- Other Event Sources: Invoking a Lambda Function On Demand.

Other event sources can invoke Lambda functions on-demand (application needs permissions to invoke the Lambda function).

Lambda can run code in response to HTTP requests using Amazon API gateway or API calls made using the AWS SDKs.

AWS Lambda supports code written in Node.js (JavaScript), Python, Java (Java 8 compatible), C# (.NET Core), Ruby, Go and PowerShell.

AWS Lambda stores code in Amazon S3 and encrypts it at rest.

Continuous scaling – scales out not up.

Lambda scales concurrently executing functions up to your default limit (1000).

Lambda functions are serverless and independent, 1 event = 1 function.

Functions can trigger other functions so 1 event can trigger multiple functions.

For non-stream-based event sources each published event is a unit of work, run in parallel up to your account limit (one Lambda function per event)2.

For stream-based event sources the number of shards indicates the unit of concurrency (one function per shard).

Lambda works globally.

To enable VPC support, you need to specify one or more subnets in a single VPC and a security group as part of your function configuration.

Lambda functions provide access only to a single VPC. If multiple subnets are specified, they must all be in the same VPC.

Lambda functions configured to access resources in a particular VPC will not have access to the Internet as a default configuration. If you need access to external endpoints, you will need to create a NAT in your VPC to forward this traffic and configure your security group to allow this outbound traffic.

Versioning can be used to run different versions of your code.

Each Lambda function has a unique Amazon Resource Name (ARN) which cannot be changed after publishing.

Use cases fall within the following categories:

- Using Lambda functions with AWS services as event sources.
- On-demand Lambda function invocation over HTTPS using Amazon API Gateway (custom REST API and endpoint).
- On-demand Lambda function invocation using custom applications (mobile, web apps, clients) and AWS SDKs, AWS Mobile SDKs, and the AWS Mobile SDK for Android.
- Scheduled events can be configured to run code on a scheduled basis through the AWS Lambda Console.

BUILDING LAMBDA APPS

You can deploy and manage your serverless applications using the AWS Serverless Application Model (AWS SAM).

AWS SAM is a specification that prescribes the rules for expressing serverless applications on AWS.

This specification aligns with the syntax used by AWS CloudFormation today and is supported natively within AWS CloudFormation as a set of resource types (referred to as "serverless resources").

You can automate your serverless application's release process using AWS CodePipeline and AWS CodeDeploy.

You can enable your Lambda function for tracing with AWS X-Ray.

LAMBDA@EDGE

Lambda@Edge allows you to run code across AWS locations globally without provisioning or managing servers, responding to end users at the lowest network latency.

Lambda@Edge lets you run Node.js and Python Lambda functions to customize content that CloudFront delivers, executing the functions in AWS locations closer to the viewer.

The functions run in response to CloudFront events, without provisioning or managing servers.

You can use Lambda functions to change CloudFront requests and responses at the following points:

- After CloudFront receives a request from a viewer (viewer request).
- Before CloudFront forwards the request to the origin (origin request).
- After CloudFront receives the response from the origin (origin response).
- Before CloudFront forwards the response to the viewer (viewer response).

You just upload your Node.js code to AWS Lambda and configure your function to be triggered in response to an Amazon CloudFront request.

The code is then ready to execute across AWS locations globally when a request for content is received, and scales with the volume of CloudFront requests globally.

LIMITS

Memory – minimum 128MB, maximum 3008MB in 64MB increments.

Ephemeral disk capacity (/tmp space) per invocation – 512 MB.

Number of file descriptors – 1024.

Number of processes and threads (combined) – 1024.

Maximum execution duration per request – 900 seconds.

Concurrent executions per account – 1000 (soft limit).

OPERATIONS AND MONITORING

Lambda automatically monitors Lambda functions and reports metrics through CloudWatch.

Lambda tracks the number of requests, the latency per request, and the number of requests resulting in an error.

You can view the request rates and error rates using the AWS Lambda Console, the CloudWatch console, and other AWS resources.

X-Ray is an AWS service that can be used to detect, analyze and optimize performance issues with Lambda applications.

X-Ray collects metadata from the Lambda service and any upstream and downstream services that make up your application.

Lambda is integrated with CloudTrail for capturing API calls and can deliver log files to your S3 bucket.

CHARGES

Priced based on:

- Number of requests. First 1 million are free then $0.20 per 1 million.
- Duration. Calculated from the time your code begins execution until it returns or terminates. Depends on the amount of memory allocated to a function.

AWS ELASTIC BEANSTALK

AWS Elastic Beanstalk can be used to quickly deploy and manage applications in the AWS Cloud.

Developers upload applications and Elastic Beanstalk handles the deployment details of capacity provisioning, load balancing, auto-scaling, and application health monitoring.

AWS Elastic Beanstalk leverages Elastic Load Balancing and Auto Scaling to automatically scale your application in and out based on your application's specific needs.

In addition, multiple availability zones give you an option to improve application reliability and availability by running in more than one zone.

Considered a Platform as a Service (PaaS) solution.

Supports Java, .NET, PHP, Node.js, Python, Ruby, Go, and Docker web applications.

Supports the following languages and development stacks:

- Apache Tomcat for Java applications
- Apache HTTP Server for PHP applications
- Apache HTTP Server for Python applications
- Nginx or Apache HTTP Server for Node.js applications
- Passenger or Puma for Ruby applications
- Microsoft IIS 7.5, 8.0, and 8.5 for .NET applications
- Java SE
- Docker
- Go

Integrates with VPC.

Integrates with IAM.

Can provision most database instances.

Allows full control of the underlying resources.

Stores your application files and, optionally, server log files in Amazon S3.

Application data can also be stored on S3.

Multiple environments are supported to enable versioning.

Changes from Git repositories are replicated.

Linux and Windows 2008 R2 AMI support.

Code is deployed using a WAR file or Git repository.

Use the AWS toolkit for Visual Studio and the AWS toolkit for Eclipse to deploy Elastic Beanstalk.

Fault tolerance within a single region.

By default, applications are publicly accessible.

Provides integration with CloudWatch.

Can adjust application server settings.

Can access logs without logging into application servers.

Can use CloudFormation to deploy Elastic Beanstalk.

There is no additional charge for Elastic Beanstalk – you pay only for the AWS resources needed to store and run your applications.

COMPUTE QUIZ QUESTIONS

Answers and explanations are provided below after the last question in this section.

Question 1: What do you need to securely connect using SSH to an EC2 instance launched from the Amazon Linux 2 AMI?

1. A signed cookie
2. An access key ID and secret access key
3. A key pair
4. A password

Question 2: What can you use to run a script at startup on an Amazon EC2 Linux instance?

1. User data
2. Metadata
3. AWS Batch
4. AWS Config

Question 3: Which EC2 pricing model would you use for a short-term requirement that needs to complete over a weekend?

1. Reserved Instance
2. Spot Instance
3. Dedicated Instance
4. On-Demand Instance

Question 4: An organization uses an application that uses per-socket licensing and they need full control over the placement of their EC2 instances on underlying hardware. What should they use?

1. Dedicated instances
2. Dedicated hosts
3. Spot instances
4. Reserved instances

Question 5: What type of storage is suitable for a use case that requires extremely high-performance local disks that do not need to be persistent?

1. Elastic Block Store (EBS)
2. Snapshots
3. Instance Store
4. Amazon S3

Question 6: Which type of network adapter should be used for High Performance Computing (HPC) uses cases that include tightly coupled applications?

1. Elastic Fabric Adapter (EFA)
2. Elastic Network Interface (ENI)
3. Elastic Network Adapter (ENA)

Question 7: An Architect would like to use an Elastic Load Balancer to forward traffic to different back-end applications for https://dctlabs.com/orders and https://dctlabs.com/account. Which type of ELB should be used?

1. Application Load Balancer with path-based routing
2. Application Load Balancer with host-based routing
3. Network Load Balancer with TCP port-based routing
4. Classic Load Balancer with Layer 7 routing

Question 8: How can a systems administrator copy an EBS volume from the us-west-1a availability zone to an instance in the us-west-1b availability zone?

1. Create a snapshot of the EBS volume in us-west-1a. Create a new volume in us-west-2b from the snapshot
2. Create a new EBS volume attached to the instance in us-west-2b. Attach the EBS volume to the instance in us-west-1b and copy data between volumes

Question 9: Which type of data volume provides very high performance and is ideal for storing data which is either replicated between EC2 instances or is only temporary and can be lost?

1. Elastic Block Store (EBS)
2. Instance Store

Question 10: The development department in your organization need to quickly access a platform for running Docker containers. The platform service should be fully managed. Which AWS service should you provision for them?

1. Amazon Elastic Container Service (ECS) with the EC2 launch type
2. Amazon Elastic Container Service (ECS) with the Fargate launch type
3. Amazon Elastic Kubernetes Service (EKS)
4. Amazon Elastic Container Registry (ECR)

Question 11: How can auto scaling be implemented for the ECS cluster instances?

1. This is not possible, you can only auto scale tasks using services
2. Using a Capacity Provider that is associated with an Auto Scaling Group (ASG)
3. Using AWS Auto Scaling for Amazon ECS

Question 12: You have some code that you would like to run occasionally and need to minimize costs. The completion time is typically under 10 minutes. Which solution is cost-effective and operationally efficient?

1. Run the code on an Amazon EC2 instance
2. Run the code on an Amazon ECS task
3. Run the code using AWS Batch
4. Run the code using an AWS Lambda function

Question 13: Which of the following listener / protocol combinations is INCORRECT?

1. Application Load Balancer TCP and HTTP/HTTPS
2. Classic Load Balancer TCP and HTTP/HTTPS
3. Network Load Balancer TCP

Question 14: Which type of scaling is provided by Amazon EC2 Auto Scaling?

1. Vertical
2. Horizontal

COMPUTE - ANSWERS

Question 1, Answer: 3

Explanation:

1 is incorrect. Signed cookies are not an authentication method for EC2.

2 is incorrect. An access key ID and secret access key are used for programmatic access to AWS services, not for securely connecting to Linux instances over SSH. Make sure you know the difference between these two concepts.

3 is correct. Key pairs are used to securely connect to EC2 instances. A key pair consists of a public key that AWS stores, and a private key file that you store. For Linux AMIs, the private key file allows you to securely SSH (secure shell) into your instance.

4 is incorrect. You do not need a password to connect to instances launched from the Amazon Linux 2 AMI.

Question 2, Answer: 1

Explanation:

1 is correct. User data is data that is supplied by the user at instance launch in the form of a script.

2 is incorrect. Instance metadata is data about your instance that you can use to configure or manage the running instance.

3 is incorrect. AWS Batch is used for running batch computing jobs across many instances.

4 is incorrect. AWS Config is a service that enables you to assess, audit, and evaluate the configurations of your AWS resources.

Question 3, Answer: 4

Explanation:

1 is incorrect. Reserved instances require a commitment over 1 or 3 years.

2 is incorrect. Spot instances are good for cost-sensitive workloads that can afford to be interrupted. This workload must complete so Spot instances would not be ideal.

3 is incorrect. Dedicated Instances are Amazon EC2 instances that run in a VPC on hardware that's dedicated to a single customer. This would be more expensive and there is no need for dedicated hardware in this case.

4 is correct. On-demand instances are ideal for short-term or unpredictable workloads. You don't get a discount, but you do have more flexibility with no commitments.

Question 4, Answer: 2

Explanation:

1 is incorrect. Dedicated instances provide dedicated hardware, but you don't get visibility of sockets, cores, or targeted instance placement.

2 is correct. Dedicated hosts provide dedicated hardware and they give you full visibility of sockets and cores and targeted instance placement.

3 is incorrect. With Spot instances you do not have control of instance placement on underlying hardware.

4 is incorrect. With Reserved instances you do not have control of instance placement on underlying hardware.

Question 5, Answer: 3

Explanation:

1 is incorrect. EBS volumes are persistent. You can get high performance, but they are network attached disks, not local disks.

2 is incorrect. Snapshots are used for taking a backup of EBS volumes.

3 is correct. Instance store volumes are ephemeral (non-persistent) local disks that offer very high performance.

4 is incorrect. Amazon S3 is an object storage system. It is not a local disk nor is it non-persistent.

Question 6, Answer: 1

Explanation:

1 is correct. EFA is good for High Performance Computing, MPI and ML use cases, tightly coupled applications and can be used with all instance types.

2 is incorrect. ENIs are the basic adapter type for when you don't have any high-performance requirements.

3 is incorrect. ENAs are good for use cases that require higher bandwidth and lower inter-instance latency.

Question 7, Answer: 1

Explanation:

1 is correct. To forward based on the path (e.g. /orders or /account) you can use the ALB with path-based routing.

2 is incorrect. Host-based routing uses the host name (e.g. dctlabs.com or amazon.com) rather than the path (e.g. /orders or /account).

3 is incorrect. The NLB can forward based on different ports/listeners. However all of this traffic will be coming on the single port for HTTPS (443).

4 is incorrect. The CLB is a layer 7 router but there is not concepts of path-based routing.

Question 8, Answer: 1

Explanation:

1 is correct. This is the best method for copying an EBS volume between AZs. Remember, snapshots are stored on Amazon S3 which stores data within a region, not an AZ.

2 is incorrect. You cannot attach an EBS volume to an instance in a different AZ.

Question 9, Answer: 2

Explanation:

1 is incorrect. EBS is persistent storage and though it provides high performance it may not be the best solution for data that is replicated or can be lost.

2 is correct. This is a good use case for Instance Store storage. It can also be cost-effective as it comes with the price of the EC2 instance.

Question 10, Answer: 2

Explanation:

1 is incorrect. The EC2 launch type is not a fully managed service.

2 is correct. The Fargate launch type is a fully managed service.

3 is incorrect. EKS is a managed service running the Kubernetes control plane. There are no specific requirements here for using Kubernetes so this is not the best option for quickly creating a platform for the developers.

4 is incorrect. ECR is a registry for storing container images.

Question 11, Answer: 2

Explanation:

1 is incorrect. This is no longer true since a recent feature update. Watch out for updates on the exam!

2 is correct. This is a new feature that may start appearing on the SAA-C02 version of the exam.

3 is incorrect. AWS Auto Scaling for Amazon ECS is not something that exists.

Question 12, Answer: 4

Explanation:

1 is incorrect. An EC2 instance is not cost-effective for a workload that needs to run only occasionally for 10 minutes.

2 is incorrect. An ECS task is not the most operationally effective option as you must spin up the ECS task to run the code and then manage the deletion of the task.

3 is incorrect. AWS Batch is used for running batch computing jobs on many EC2 instances. It's not cost-effective or operationally effective for this use case.

4 is correct. This is the most cost-effective and operationally effective option. Remember that the maximum execution time is 900 seconds (15 minutes) so you are well within that timeframe here.

Question 13, Answer: 1

Explanation:

1 is correct. The ALB only support layer 7 which is HTTP and HTTPS – not TCP.

2 is incorrect. This is a correct combination of listener / protocol.

3 is incorrect. This is a correct combination of listener / protocol.

Question 14, Answer: 2

Explanation:

1 is incorrect. EC2 Auto Scaling is not an example of vertical scaling.

2 is correct. EC2 Auto Scaling scales horizontally by launching or terminating EC2 instances.

STORAGE

AMAZON S3

GENERAL

Amazon S3 is object storage built to store and retrieve any amount of data from anywhere on the Internet.

It's a simple storage service that offers an extremely durable, highly available, and infinitely scalable data storage infrastructure at very low costs.

Amazon S3 is a distributed architecture and objects are redundantly stored on multiple devices across multiple facilities (AZs) in an Amazon S3 region.

Amazon S3 is a simple key-based object store.

Keys can be any string, and they can be constructed to mimic hierarchical attributes.

Alternatively, you can use S3 Object Tagging to organize your data across all of your S3 buckets and/or prefixes.

Amazon S3 provides a simple, standards-based REST web services interface that is designed to work with any Internet-development toolkit.

Files can be from 0 bytes to 5TB.

The largest object that can be uploaded in a single PUT is 5 gigabytes.

For objects larger than 100 megabytes use the Multipart Upload capability.

Updates to an object are atomic – when reading an updated object, you will either get the new object or the old one, you will never get partial or corrupt data.

There is unlimited storage available.

It is recommended to access S3 through SDKs and APIs (the console uses APIs).

Event notifications for specific actions, can send alerts or trigger actions.

Notifications can be sent to:

- SNS Topics.
- SQS Queue.
- Lambda functions.
- Need to configure SNS/SQS/Lambda before S3.
- No extra charges from S3 but you pay for SNS, SQS and Lambda.

Requester pays function causes the requester to pay (removes anonymous access).

Can provide time-limited access to objects.

Provides read after write consistency for PUTS of new objects.

Provides eventual consistency for overwrite PUTS and DELETES (takes time to propagate).

You can only store files (objects) on S3.

HTTP 200 code indicates a successful write to S3.

S3 data is made up of:

- Key (name)
- Value (data)
- Version ID
- Metadata
- Access Control Lists

Amazon S3 automatically scales to high request rates.

For example, your application can achieve at least 3,500 PUT/POST/DELETE and 5,500 GET requests per second per prefix in a bucket.

There are no limits to the number of prefixes in a bucket. It is simple to increase your read or write performance exponentially.

For read intensive requests you can also use CloudFront edge locations to offload from S3.

ADDITIONAL CAPABILITIES

Additional capabilities offered by Amazon S3 include:

Additional S3 Capability	How it Works
Transfer Acceleration	Speed up data uploads using CloudFront in reverse
Requester Pays	The requester rather than the bucket owner pays for requests and data transfer
Tags	Assign tags to objects to use in costing, billing, security etc.
Events	Trigger notifications to SNS, SQS, or Lambda when certain events happen in your bucket
Static Web Hosting	Simple and massively scalable static website hosting
BitTorrent	Use the BitTorrent protocol to retrieve any publicly available object by automatically generating a .torrent file

USE CASES

Typical use cases include:

- Backup and Storage – Provide data backup and storage services for others.
- Application Hosting – Provide services that deploy, install, and manage web applications.

- Media Hosting – Build a redundant, scalable, and highly available infrastructure that hosts video, photo, or music uploads and downloads.
- Software Delivery – Host your software applications that customers can download.
- Static Website – you can configure a static website to run from an S3 bucket.

S3 is a persistent, highly durable data store.

Persistent data stores are non-volatile storage systems that retain data when powered off.

This is in contrast to transient data stores and ephemeral data stores which lose the data when powered off.

The following table provides a description of persistent, transient and ephemeral data stores and which AWS service to use:

Storage Type	Description	Examples
Persistent Data Store	Data is durable and sticks around after reboots, restarts, or power cycles	S3, Glacier, EBS, EFS
Transient Data Store	Data is just temporarily stored and passed along to another process or persistent store	SQS, SNS
Ephemeral Data Store	Data is lost when the system is stopped	EC2 Instance Store, Memcached

BUCKETS

Files are stored in buckets:

- A bucket can be viewed as a container for objects.
- A bucket is a flat container of objects.
- It does not provide a hierarchy of objects.
- You can use an object key name to mimic folders.

100 buckets per account by default.

You can store unlimited objects in your buckets.

You can create folders in your buckets (only available through the Console).

You cannot create nested buckets.

Bucket ownership is not transferrable.

Bucket names cannot be changed after they have been created.

If a bucket is deleted its name becomes available again.

Bucket names are part of the URL used to access the bucket.

An S3 bucket is region specific.

S3 is a universal namespace so names must be unique globally.

URL is in this format: https://s3-***eu-west-1***.amazonaws.com/***<bucketname>.***

Can backup a bucket to another bucket in another account.

Can enable logging to a bucket.

Bucket naming:

- Bucket names must be at least 3 and no more than 63 character in length.
- Bucket names must start and end with a lowercase character or a number.
- Bucket names must be a series of one or more labels which are separated by a period.
- Bucket names can contain lowercase letters, numbers and hyphens.
- Bucket names cannot be formatted as an IP address.

For better performance, lower latency, and lower cost, create the bucket closer to your clients.

OBJECTS

Each object is stored and retrieved by a unique key (ID or name).

An object in S3 is uniquely identified and addressed through:

- Service end-point.
- Bucket name.
- Object key (name).
- Optionally, an object version.

Objects stored in a bucket will never leave the region in which they are stored unless you move them to another region or enable cross-region replication.

You can define permissions on objects when uploading and at any time afterwards using the AWS Management Console.

SUB-RESOURCES

- Sub-resources are subordinate to objects, they do not exist independently but are always associated with another entity such as an object or bucket.
- Sub-resources (configuration containers) associated with buckets include:
- Lifecycle – define an object's lifecycle.
- Website – configuration for hosting static websites.
- Versioning – retain multiple versions of objects as they are changed.
- Access Control Lists (ACLs) – control permissions access to the bucket.
- Bucket Policies – control access to the bucket.
- Cross Origin Resource Sharing (CORS).
- Logging
- Sub-resources associated with objects include:

- ACLs – define permissions to access the object.
- Restore – restoring an archive.

STORAGE CLASSES

There are six S3 storage classes.

- S3 Standard (durable, immediately available, frequently accessed).
- S3 Intelligent-Tiering (automatically moves data to the most cost-effective tier).
- S3 Standard-IA (durable, immediately available, infrequently accessed).
- S3 One Zone-IA (lower cost for infrequently accessed data with less resilience).
- S3 Glacier (archived data, retrieval times in minutes or hours).
- S3 Glacier Deep Archive (lowest cost storage class for long term retention).

The table below provides the details of each Amazon S3 storage class:

	S3 Standard	S3 Standard-IA	S3 One Zone-IA	Amazon Glacier
Designed for durability	99.999999999%	99.999999999%	99.999999999%	99.999999999%
Designed for availability	99.99%	99.9%	99.5%	N/A
Availability SLA	99.9%	99%	99%	N/A
Availability Zones	≥3	≥3	1	≥3
Minimum capacity charge per object	N/A	128KB	128KB	N/A
Minimum storage duration charge	N/A	30 days	30 days	90 days
Retrieval fee	N/A	Per GB retrieved	Per GB retrieved	Per GB retrieved
First byte latency	milliseconds	milliseconds	milliseconds	Select minutes or hours
Storage type	Object	Object	Object	Object
Lifecycle transitions	Yes	Yes	Yes	Yes

Objects stored in the S3 One Zone-IA storage class are stored redundantly within a single Availability Zone in the AWS Region you select.

ACCESS AND ACCESS POLICIES

There are four mechanisms for controlling access to Amazon S3 resources:

- IAM policies.
- Bucket policies.
- Access Control Lists (ACLs).
- Query string authentication (URL to an Amazon S3 object which is only valid for a limited time).

Access auditing can be configured by configuring an Amazon S3 bucket to create access log records for all requests made against it.

For capturing IAM/user identity information in logs configure AWS CloudTrail Data Events.

By default, a bucket, its objects, and related sub-resources are all private.

By default, only a resource owner can access a bucket.

The resource owner refers to the AWS account that creates the resource.

With IAM the account owner rather than the IAM user is the owner.

Within an IAM policy you can grant either programmatic access or AWS Management Console access to Amazon S3 resources.

Amazon Resource Names (ARN) are used for specifying resources in a policy.

The format for any resource on AWS is:

arn:partition:service:region:namespace:relative-id.

For S3 resources:

- aws is a common partition name.
- s3 is the service.
- You don't specify Region and namespace.
- For Amazon S3, it can be a bucket-name or a bucket-name/object-key. You can use wild card

The format for S3 resources is:

arn:aws:s3:::bucket_name.

arn:aws:s3:::bucket_name/key_name.

A bucket owner can grant cross-account permissions to another AWS account (or users in an account) to upload objects.

The AWS account that uploads the objects owns them.

The bucket owner does not have permissions on objects that other accounts own, however:

- The bucket owner pays the charges.
- The bucket owner can deny access to any objects regardless of ownership.
- The bucket owner can archive any objects or restore archived objects regardless of ownership.

Access to buckets and objects can be granted to:

- Individual users.
- AWS accounts.
- Everyone (public/anonymous).
- All authenticated users (AWS users).

Access policies define access to resources and can be associated with resources (buckets and objects) and users.

You can use the AWS Policy Generator to create a bucket policy for your Amazon S3 bucket.

The categories of policy are resource-based policies and user policies.

Resource-based policies:

- Attached to buckets and objects.
- ACL-based policies define permissions.

- ACLs can be used to grant read/write permissions to other accounts.
- Bucket policies can be used to grant other AWS accounts or IAM users permission to the bucket and objects.

User policies:

- Can use IAM to manage access to S3 resources.
- Using IAM you can create users, groups and roles and attach access policies to them granting them access to resources.
- You cannot grant anonymous permissions in an IAM user policy as the policy is attached to a user.
- User policies can grant permissions to a bucket and the objects in it.

ACLs:

- S3 ACLs enable you to manage access to buckets and objects.
- Each bucket and object has an ACL attached to it as a subresource.
- Bucket and object permissions are independent of each other.
- The ACL defines which AWS accounts (grantees) or pre-defined S3 groups are granted access and the type of access.
- A grantee can be an AWS account or one of the predefined Amazon S3 groups.
- When you create a bucket or an object, S3 creates a default ACL that grants the resource owner full control over the resource.

Cross account access:

- You grant permission to another AWS account using the email address or the canonical user ID.
- However, if you provide an email address in your grant request, Amazon S3 finds the canonical user ID for that account and adds it to the ACL.
- Grantee accounts can then then delegate the access provided by other accounts to their individual users.

PRE-DEFINED GROUPS

Authenticated Users group:

- This group represents all AWS accounts.
- Access permission to this group allows any AWS account access to the resource.
- All requests must be signed (authenticated).
- Any authenticated user can access the resource.

All Users group:

- Access permission to this group allows anyone in the world access to the resource.
- The requests can be signed (authenticated) or unsigned (anonymous).
- Unsigned requests omit the authentication header in the request.
- AWS recommends that you never grant the All Users group WRITE, WRITE_ACP, or FULL_CONTROL permissions.

Log Delivery group:

- Providing WRITE permission to this group on a bucket enables S3 to write server access logs.
- Not applicable to objects.

The following table lists the set of permissions that Amazon S3 supports in an ACL:

- The set of ACL permissions is the same for an object ACL and a bucket ACL.
- Depending on the context (bucket ACL or object ACL), these ACL permissions grant permissions for specific buckets or object operations.
- The table lists the permissions and describes what they mean in the context of objects and buckets.

Permission	When granted on a bucket	When granted on an object
READ	Allows grantee to list the objects in the bucket	Allows grantee to read the object data and its metadata
WRITE	Allows grantee to create, overwrite, and delete any object in the bucket	Not applicable
READ_ACP	Allows grantee to read the bucket ACL	Allows grantee to read the object ACL
WRITE_ACP	Allows grantee to write the ACL for the applicable bucket	Allows grantee to write the ACL for the applicable object
FULL_CONTROL	Allows grantee the READ, WRITE, READ_ACP, and WRITE_ACP permissions on the bucket	Allows grantee the READ, READ_ACP, and WRITE_ACP permissions on the object

Note the following:

- Permissions are assigned at the account level for authenticated users.
- You cannot assign permissions to individual IAM users.
- When Read is granted on a bucket it only provides the ability to list the objects in the bucket.
- When Read is granted on an object the data can be read.
- ACP means access control permissions and READ_ACP/WRITE_ACP control who can read/write the ACLs themselves.
- WRITE is only applicable to the bucket level (except for ACP).

Bucket policies are limited to 20 KB in size.

Object ACLs are limited to 100 granted permissions per ACL.

The only recommended use case for the bucket ACL is to grant write permissions to the S3 Log Delivery group.

There are limits to managing permissions using ACLs:

- You cannot grant permissions to individual users.
- You cannot grant conditional permissions.
- You cannot explicitly deny access.

When granting other AWS accounts the permissions to upload objects, permissions to these objects can only be managed by the object owner using object ACLs.

You can use bucket policies for:

- Granting users permissions to a bucket owned by your account.
- Managing object permissions (where the object owner is the same account as the bucket owner).
- Managing cross-account permissions for all Amazon S3 permissions.

You can use user policies for:

- Granting permissions for all Amazon S3 operations.
- Managing permissions for users in your account.
- Granting object permissions to users within the account.

For an IAM user to access resources in another account the following must be provided:

- Permission from the parent account through a user policy.
- Permission from the resource owner to the IAM user through a bucket policy, or the parent account through a bucket policy, bucket ACL or object ACL.

If an AWS account owns a resource it can grant permissions to another account, that account can then delegate those permissions or a subset of them to uses in the account (permissions delegation).

An account that receives permissions from another account cannot delegate permissions cross-account to a third AWS account.

CHARGES

No charge for data transferred between EC2 and S3 in the same region.

Data transfer into S3 is free of charge.

Data transferred to other regions is charged.

Data Retrieval (applies to S3 Standard-IA and S3 One Zone-IA, S3 Glacier and S3 Glacier Deep Archive).

Charges are:

- Per GB/month storage fee.
- Data transfer out of S3.
- Upload requests (PUT and GET).
- Retrieval requests (S3-IA or Glacier).

Requester pays:

- The bucket owner will only pay for object storage fees.
- The requester will pay for requests (uploads/downloads) and data transfers.
- Can only be enabled at the bucket level.

MULTIPART UPLOAD

Can be used to speed up uploads to S3.

Multipart upload uploads objects in parts independently, in parallel and in any order.

Performed using the S3 Multipart upload API.

It is recommended for objects of 100MB or larger.

Can be used for objects from 5MB up to 5TB.

Must be used for objects larger than 5GB.

If transmission of any part fails it can be retransmitted.

Improves throughput.

Can pause and resume object uploads.

Can begin upload before you know the final object size.

COPY

You can create a copy of objects up to 5GB in size in a single atomic operation.

For files larger than 5GB you must use the multipart upload API.

Can be performed using the AWS SDKs or REST API.

The copy operation can be used to:

- Generate additional copies of objects.
- Renaming objects.
- Changing the copy's storage class or encryption at rest status.
- Move objects across AWS locations/regions.
- Change object metadata.

Once uploaded to S3 some object metadata cannot be changed, copying the object can allow you to modify this information.

TRANSFER ACCELERATION

Amazon S3 Transfer Acceleration enables fast, easy, and secure transfers of files over long distances between your client and your Amazon S3 bucket.

S3 Transfer Acceleration leverages Amazon CloudFront's globally distributed AWS Edge Locations.

Used to accelerate object uploads to S3 over long distances (latency).

Transfer acceleration is as secure as a direct upload to S3.

You are charged only if there was a benefit in transfer times.

Need to enable transfer acceleration on the S3 bucket.

Cannot be disabled, can only be suspended.

May take up to 30 minutes to implement.

URL is: <bucketname>.s3-accelerate.amazonaws.com.

Bucket names must be DNS compliance and cannot have periods between labels.

Now HIPAA compliant.

You can use multipart uploads with transfer acceleration.

Must use one of the following endpoints:

- .s3-accelerate.amazonaws.com.
- .s3-accelerate.dualstack.amazonaws.com (dual-stack option).

S3 Transfer Acceleration supports all bucket level features including multipart uploads.

STATIC WEBSITES

S3 can be used to host static websites.

Cannot use dynamic content such as PHP, .Net etc.

Automatically scales.

You can use a custom domain name with S3 using a Route 53 Alias record.

When using a custom domain name the bucket name must be the same as the domain name.

Can enable redirection for the whole domain, pages or specific objects.

URL is: <bucketname>.s3-website-.amazonaws.com.

Requester pays does not work with website endpoints.

Does not support HTTPS/SSL.

Returns an HTML document.

Supports object and bucket level redirects.

Only supports GET and HEAD requests on objects.

Supports publicly readable content only.

To enable website hosting on a bucket, specify:

- An Index document (default web page)
- Error document (optional)

Key Difference	REST API Endpoint	Website Endpoint
Access Control	Supports both public and private content	Supports only publicly readable content
Error message handling	Returns an XML-formatted error response	Returns an HTML document
Redirection support	Not applicable	Supports both object-level and bucket-level redirects
Requests support	Supports all bucket and object operations	Supports only GET and HEAD requests on objects
Responses to GET and HEAD requests at the root of the bucket	Returns a list of the object keys in the bucket	Returns the Index document that is specified in the website configuration
SSL support	Supports SSL connections	Does not support SSL connections

PRE-SIGNED URLS

Pre-signed URLs can be used to provide temporary access to a specific object to those who do not have AWS credentials.

By default, all objects are private and can only be accessed by the owner.

To share an object, you can either make it public or generate a pre-signed URL.

Expiration date and time must be configured.

These can be generated using SDKs for Java and .Net and AWS explorer for Visual Studio.

Can be used for downloading and uploading S3 objects.

VERSIONING

Versioning stores all versions of an object (including all writes and even if an object is deleted).

Versioning protects against accidental object/data deletion or overwrites.

Enables "roll-back" and "un-delete" capabilities.

Versioning can also be used for data retention and archive.

Old versions count as billable size until they are permanently deleted.

Enabling versioning does not replicate existing objects.

Can be used for backup.

Once enabled versioning cannot be disabled only suspended.

Can be integrated with lifecycle rules.

Multi-factor authentication (MFA) delete can be enabled.

MFA delete can also be applied to changing versioning settings.

MFA delete applies to:

- Changing the bucket's versioning state.
- Permanently deleting an object.

Cross Region Replication requires versioning to be enabled on the source and destination buckets.

Reverting to previous versions isn't replicated.

By default, a HTTP GET retrieves the most recent version.

Only the S3 bucket owner can permanently delete objects once versioning is enabled.

When you try to delete an object with versioning enabled a DELETE marker is placed on the object.

You can delete the DELETE marker and the object will be available again.

Deletion with versioning replicates the delete marker. But deleting the delete marker is not replicated.

Bucket versioning states:

- Enabled
- Versioned
- Un-versioned

Objects that existed before enabling versioning will have a version ID of NULL.

Suspension:

- If you suspend versioning the existing objects remain as they are however new versions will not be created.
- While versioning is suspended new objects will have a version ID of NULL and uploaded objects of the same name will overwrite the existing object.

LIFECYCLE MANAGEMENT

Used to optimize storage costs, adhere to data retention policies and to keep S3 volumes well-maintained.

A *lifecycle configuration* is a set of rules that define actions that Amazon S3 applies to a group of objects. There are two types of actions:

- **Transition actions**—Define when objects transition to another storage class. For example, you might choose to transition objects to the STANDARD_IA storage class 30 days after you created them, or archive objects to the GLACIER storage class one year after creating them.

There are costs associated with the lifecycle transition requests. For pricing information, see Amazon S3 Pricing.

- **Expiration actions**—Define when objects expire. Amazon S3 deletes expired objects on your behalf.

Lifecycle configuration is an XML file applied at the bucket level as a subresource.

Can be used in conjunction with versioning or independently.

Can be applied to current and previous versions.

Can be applied to specific objects within a bucket: objects with a specific tag or objects with a specific prefix.

Supported Transitions and Related Constraints

Amazon S3 supports the following lifecycle transitions between storage classes using a lifecycle configuration:

- You can transition from the STANDARD storage class to any other storage class.
- You can transition from any storage class to the GLACIER or DEEP_ARCHIVE storage classes.
- You can transition from the STANDARD_IA storage class to the INTELLIGENT_TIERING or ONEZONE_IA storage classes.
- You can transition from the INTELLIGENT_TIERING storage class to the ONEZONE_IA storage class.
- You can transition from the GLACIER storage class to the DEEP_ARCHIVE storage class.

The following lifecycle transitions are not supported:

- You can't transition from any storage class to the STANDARD storage class.
- You can't transition from any storage class to the REDUCED_REDUNDANCY storage class.
- You can't transition from the INTELLIGENT_TIERING storage class to the STANDARD_IA storage class.
- You can't transition from the ONEZONE_IA storage class to the STANDARD_IA or INTELLIGENT_TIERING storage classes.
- You can transition from the GLACIER storage class to the DEEP_ARCHIVE storage class only.
- You can't transition from the DEEP_ARCHIVE storage class to any other storage class.

The lifecycle storage class transitions have the following constraints:

- From the STANDARD or STANDARD_IA storage class to INTELLIGENT_TIERING. The following constraints apply:
  - For larger objects, there is a cost benefit for transitioning to INTELLIGENT_TIERING. Amazon S3 does not transition objects that are smaller than 128 KB to the INTELLIGENT_TIERING storage class because it's not cost effective.
- From the STANDARD storage classes to STANDARD_IA or ONEZONE_IA. The following constraints apply:
  - For larger objects, there is a cost benefit for transitioning to STANDARD_IA or ONEZONE_IA. Amazon S3 does not transition objects that are smaller than 128 KB to the STANDARD_IA or ONEZONE_IA storage classes because it's not cost effective.
  - Objects must be stored at least 30 days in the current storage class before you can transition them to STANDARD_IA or ONEZONE_IA. For example, you cannot create a lifecycle rule to transition objects to the STANDARD_IA storage class one day after you create them.
  - Amazon S3 doesn't transition objects within the first 30 days because newer objects are often accessed more frequently or deleted sooner than is suitable for STANDARD_IA or ONEZONE_IA storage.

- If you are transitioning noncurrent objects (in versioned buckets), you can transition only objects that are at least 30 days noncurrent to STANDARD_IA or ONEZONE_IA storage.

- From the STANDARD_IA storage class to ONEZONE_IA. The following constraints apply:
  - Objects must be stored at least 30 days in the STANDARD_IA storage class before you can transition them to the ONEZONE_IA class.

ENCRYPTION

You can securely upload/download your data to Amazon S3 via SSL endpoints using the HTTPS protocol (In Transit – SSL/TLS).

Encryption options:

Encryption Option	How it Works
SSE-S3	Use S3's existing encryption key for AES-256
SSE-C	Upload your own AES-256 encryption key which S3 uses when it writes objects
SSE-KMS	Use a key generated and managed by AWS KMS
Client-Side	Encrypt objects using your own local encryption process before uploading to S3

Server side encryption options:

- **SSE-S3 – Server Side Encryption with S3 managed keys**
  - Each object is encrypted with a unique key.
  - Encryption key is encrypted with a master key.
  - AWS regularly rotate the master key.
  - Uses AES 256.
- **SSE-KMS – Server Side Encryption with AWS KMS keys**
  - KMS uses Customer Master Keys (CMKs) to encrypt.
  - Can use the automatically created CMK key.
  - OR you can select your own key (gives you control for management of keys).
  - An envelope key protects your keys.
  - Chargeable.
- **SSE-C – Server Side Encryption with client provided keys**
  - Client manages the keys, S3 manages encryption.
  - AWS does not store the encryption keys.
  - If keys are lost data cannot be decrypted.

The following diagram depicts the options for enabling encryption and shows you where the encryption is applied and where the keys are managed:

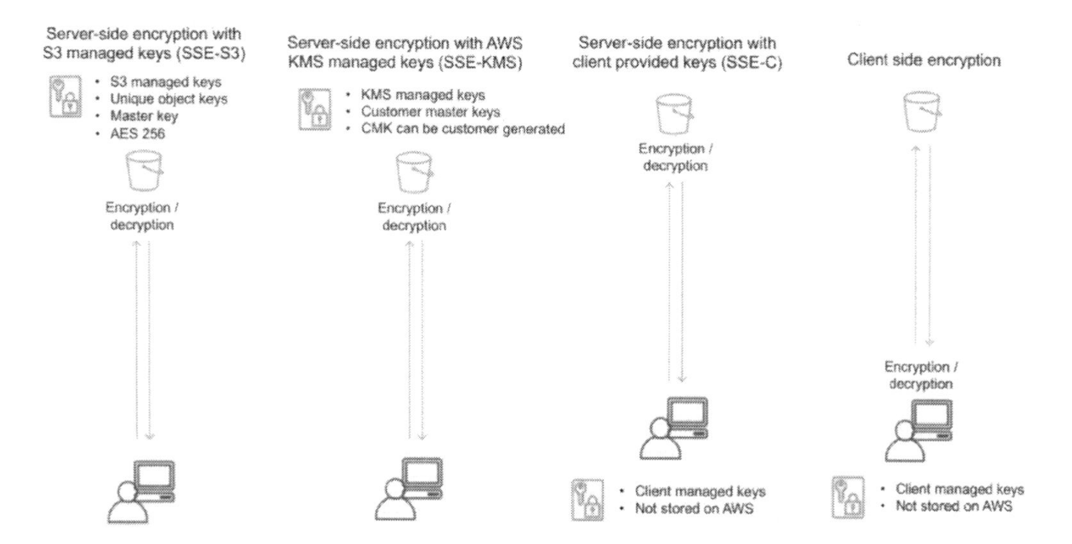

EVENT NOTIFICATIONS

Amazon S3 event notifications can be sent in response to actions in Amazon S3 like PUTs, POSTs, COPYs, or DELETEs.

Amazon S3 event notifications enable you to run workflows, send alerts, or perform other actions in response to changes in your objects stored in S3.

To enable notifications, you must first add a notification configuration that identifies the events you want Amazon S3 to publish and the destinations where you want Amazon S3 to send the notifications.

You can configure notifications to be filtered by the prefix and suffix of the key name of objects.

Amazon S3 can publish notifications for the following events:

- New object created events
- Object removal events
- Restore object events
- Reduced Redundancy Storage (RRS) object lost events
- Replication events

Amazon S3 can send event notification messages to the following destinations:

- Publish event messages to an Amazon Simple Notification Service (Amazon SNS) topic.
- Publish event messages to an Amazon Simple Queue Service (Amazon SQS) queue.
- Publish event messages to AWS Lambda by invoking a Lambda function and providing the event message as an argument.

Need to grant Amazon S3 permissions to post messages to an Amazon SNS topic or an Amazon SQS queue.

Need to also grant Amazon S3 permission to invoke an AWS Lambda function on your behalf. For information about granting these permissions.

OBJECT TAGS

S3 object tags are key-value pairs applied to S3 objects which can be created, updated or deleted at any time during the lifetime of the object.

Allow you to create Identity and Access Management (IAM) policies, setup S3 Lifecycle policies, and customize storage metrics.

Up to ten tags can be added to each S3 object and you can use either the AWS Management Console, the REST API, the AWS CLI, or the AWS SDKs to add object tags.

S3 CLOUDWATCH METRICS

You can use the AWS Management Console to enable the generation of 1-minute CloudWatch request metrics for your S3 bucket or configure filters for the metrics using a prefix or object tag.

Alternatively, you can call the S3 PUT Bucket Metrics API to enable and configure publication of S3 storage metrics.

CloudWatch Request Metrics will be available in CloudWatch within 15 minutes after they are enabled.

CloudWatch Storage Metrics are enabled by default for all buckets and reported once per day.

The S3 metrics that can be monitored include:

- S3 requests
- Bucket storage
- Bucket size
- All requests
- HTTP 4XX/5XX errors

CROSS REGION REPLICATION

CRR is an Amazon S3 feature that automatically replicates data across AWS Regions.

With CRR, every object uploaded to an S3 bucket is automatically replicated to a destination bucket in a different AWS Region that you choose.

Provides automatic, asynchronous copying of objects between buckets in different regions.

CRR is configured at the S3 bucket level.

You enable a CRR configuration on your source bucket by specifying a destination bucket in a different Region for replication.

You can use either the AWS Management Console, the REST API, the AWS CLI, or the AWS SDKs to enable CRR.

Versioning must be enabled for both the source and destination buckets.

With CRR you can only replication between regions, not within a region (see SRR below for single region replication).

Replication is 1:1 (one source bucket, to one destination bucket).

You can configure separate S3 Lifecycle rules on the source and destination buckets.

You can replicate KMS-encrypted objects by providing a destination KMS key in your replication configuration.

You can set up CRR across AWS accounts to store your replicated data in a different account in the target region.

Provides low latency access for data by copying objects to buckets that are closer to users.

To activate CRR you need to configure the replication on the source bucket:

- Define the bucket in the other region to replicate to.
- Specify to replicate all objects or a subset of objects with specific key name prefixes.

The replicas will be exact replicas and share the same key names and metadata.

You can specify a different storage class (by default the source storage class will be used).

AWS S3 will encrypt data in-transit with SSL.

AWS S3 must have permission to replicate objects.

Bucket owners must have permission to read the object and object ACL.

Can be used across accounts but the source bucket owner must have permission to replicate objects into the destination bucket.

Triggers for replication are:

- Uploading objects to the source bucket.
- DELETE of objects in the source bucket.
- Changes to the object, its metadata, or ACL.

What is replicated:

- New objects created after enabling replication.
- Changes to objects.
- Objects created using SSE-S3 using the AWS managed key.
- Object ACL updates.

What isn't replicated:

- Objects that existed before enabling replication (can use the copy API).
- Objects created with SSE-C and SSE-KMS.
- Objects to which the bucket owner does not have permissions.
- Updates to bucket-level subresources.
- Actions from lifecycle rules are not replicated.
- Objects in the source bucket that are replicated from another region are not replicated.

Deletion behavior:

- If a DELETE request is made without specifying an object version ID a delete marker will be added and replicated.
- If a DELETE request is made specifying an object version ID the object is deleted but the delete marker is not replicated.

Charges:

- Requests for upload
- Inter-region transfer
- S3 storage in both regions

SAME REGION REPLICATION (SRR)

As the name implies you can use SRR to replication objects to a destination bucket within the same region as the source bucket.

This feature was released in September 2018.

Replication is automatic and asynchronous.

New objects uploaded to an Amazon S3 bucket are configured for replication at the bucket, prefix, or object tag levels.

Replicated objects can be owned by the same AWS account as the original copy or by different accounts, to protect from accidental deletion.

Replication can be to any Amazon S3 storage class, including S3 Glacier and S3 Glacier Deep Archive to create backups and long-term archives.

When an S3 object is replicated using SRR, the metadata, Access Control Lists (ACL), and object tags associated with the object are also part of the replication.

Once SRR is configured on a source bucket, any changes to the object, metadata, ACLs, or object tags trigger a new replication to the destination bucket.

S3 ANALYTICS

Can run analytics on data stored on Amazon S3.

This includes data lakes, IoT streaming data, machine learning, and artificial intelligence.

The following strategies can be used:

S3 Analytics Strategies	Service Used
Data Lake Concept	Athena, RedShift Spectrum, QuickSight
IoT Streaming Data Repository	Kinesis Firehose
Machine Learning and AI Storage	Rekognition, Lex, MXNet
Storage Class Analysis	S3 Management Analytics

S3 PERFORMANCE GUIDELINES

AWS provide some performance guidelines for Amazon S3. These are summarized here:

Measure Performance - When optimizing performance, look at network throughput, CPU, and DRAM requirements. Depending on the mix of demands for these different resources, it might be worth evaluating different Amazon EC2 instance types.

Scale Storage Connections Horizontally - You can achieve the best performance by issuing multiple concurrent requests to Amazon S3. Spread these requests over separate connections to maximize the accessible bandwidth from Amazon S3.

Use Byte-Range Fetches - Using the Range HTTP header in a GET Object request, you can fetch a byte-range from an object, transferring only the specified portion. You can use concurrent connections to Amazon S3 to fetch different byte ranges from within the same object. This helps you achieve higher aggregate throughput versus a single whole-object request. Fetching smaller ranges of a large object also allows your application to improve retry times when requests are interrupted.

Retry Requests for Latency-Sensitive Applications - Aggressive timeouts and retries help drive consistent latency. Given the large scale of Amazon S3, if the first request is slow, a retried request is likely to take a different path and quickly succeed. The AWS SDKs have configurable timeout and retry values that you can tune to the tolerances of your specific application.

Combine Amazon S3 (Storage) and Amazon EC2 (Compute) in the Same AWS Region - Although S3 bucket names are globally unique, each bucket is stored in a Region that you select when you create the bucket. To optimize performance, we recommend that you access the bucket from Amazon EC2 instances in the same AWS Region when possible. This helps reduce network latency and data transfer costs.

Use Amazon S3 Transfer Acceleration to Minimize Latency Caused by Distance - Amazon S3 Transfer Acceleration manages fast, easy, and secure transfers of files over long geographic distances between the client and an S3 bucket. Transfer Acceleration takes advantage of the globally distributed edge locations in Amazon CloudFront. As the data arrives at an edge location, it is routed to Amazon S3 over an optimized network path. Transfer Acceleration is ideal for transferring gigabytes to terabytes of data regularly across continents. It's also useful for clients that upload to a centralized bucket from all over the world.

GLACIER

Glacier is an archiving storage solution for infrequently accessed data.

There are two storage tiers:

S3 Glacier:

- Same low latency and high throughput performance of S3 Standard.
- Designed for durability of 99.999999999% of objects in a single Availability Zone†.
- Designed for 99.5% availability over a given year.
- Backed with the Amazon S3 Service Level Agreement for availability.
- Supports SSL for data in transit and encryption of data at rest.
- S3 Lifecycle management for automatic migration of objects to other S3 Storage Classes.

S3 Glacier Deep Archive.

- Designed for durability of 99.999999999% of objects across multiple Availability Zones.
- Data is resilient in the event of one entire Availability Zone destruction.
- Supports SSL for data in transit and encryption of data at rest.
- Low-cost design is ideal for long-term archive.
- Configurable retrieval times, from minutes to hours.

- S3 PUT API for direct uploads to S3 Glacier, and S3 Lifecycle management for automatic migration of objects.

The key difference between the tiers is that Deep Archive is lower cost, but retrieval times are much longer (12 hours).

The S3 Glacier tier has configurable retrieval times from minutes to hours (you pay accordingly).

Archived objects are not available for real time access and you need to submit a retrieval request.

Glacier must complete a job before you can get its output.

Requested archival data is copied to S3 One Zone-IA.

Following retrieval, you have 24 hours to download your data.

You cannot specify Glacier as the storage class at the time you create an object.

Glacier is designed to sustain the loss of two facilities.

Glacier automatically encrypts data at rest using AES 256 symmetric keys and supports secure transfer of data over SSL.

Glacier may not be available in all AWS regions.

Glacier objects are visible through S3 only (not Glacier directly).

Glacier does not archive object metadata; you need to maintain a client-side database to maintain this information.

Archives can be 1 bytes up to 40TB.

Glacier file archives of 1 byte – 4 GB can be performed in a single operation.

Glacier file archives from 100MB up to 40TB can be uploaded to Glacier using the multipart upload API.

Uploading archives is synchronous.

Downloading archives is asynchronous.

The contents of an archive that has been uploaded cannot be modified.

You can upload data to Glacier using the CLI, SDKs or APIs – you cannot use the AWS Console.

Glacier adds 32-40KB (indexing and archive metadata) to each object when transitioning from other classes using lifecycle policies.

AWS recommends that if you have lots of small objects they are combined in an archive (e.g. zip file) before uploading.

A description can be added to archives, no other metadata can be added.

Glacier archive IDs are added upon upload and are unique for each upload.

Archive retrieval:

- Expedited is 1-5 minutes retrieval (most expensive).
- Standard is 3.5 hours retrieval (cheaper, 10GB data retrieval free per month).
- Bulk retrieval is 5-12 hours (cheapest, use for large quantities of data).

You can retrieve parts of an archive.

When data is retrieved it is copied to S3 and the archive remains in Glacier and the storage class therefore does not change.

AWS SNS can send notifications when retrieval jobs are complete.

Retrieved data is available for 24 hours by default (can be changed).

To retrieve specific objects within an archive you can specify the byte range (Range) in the HTTP GET request (need to maintain a DB of byte ranges).

Glacier Charges:

There is no charge for data transfer between EC2 and Glacier in the same region.

There is a charge if you delete data within 90 days.

When you restore you pay for:

- The Glacier archive.
- The requests.
- The restored data on S3.

AMAZON EFS

GENERAL

EFS is a fully-managed service that makes it easy to set up and scale file storage in the Amazon Cloud.

Implementation of an NFS file share and is accessed using the NFSv4.1 protocol.

Elastic storage capacity and pay for what you use (in contrast to EBS with which you pay for what you provision).

Multi-AZ metadata and data storage.

Can configure mount-points in one, or many, AZs.

Can be mounted from on-premises systems ONLY if using Direct Connect or a VPN connection.

Alternatively, use the EFS File Sync agent.

Good for big data and analytics, media processing workflows, content management, web serving, home directories etc.

Pay for what you use (no pre-provisioning required).

Can scale up to petabytes.

EFS is elastic and grows and shrinks as you add and remove data.

Can concurrently connect 1 to 1000s of EC2 instances, from multiple AZs.

A file system can be accessed concurrently from all AZs in the region where it is located.

The following diagram depicts the various options for mounting an EFS filesystem:

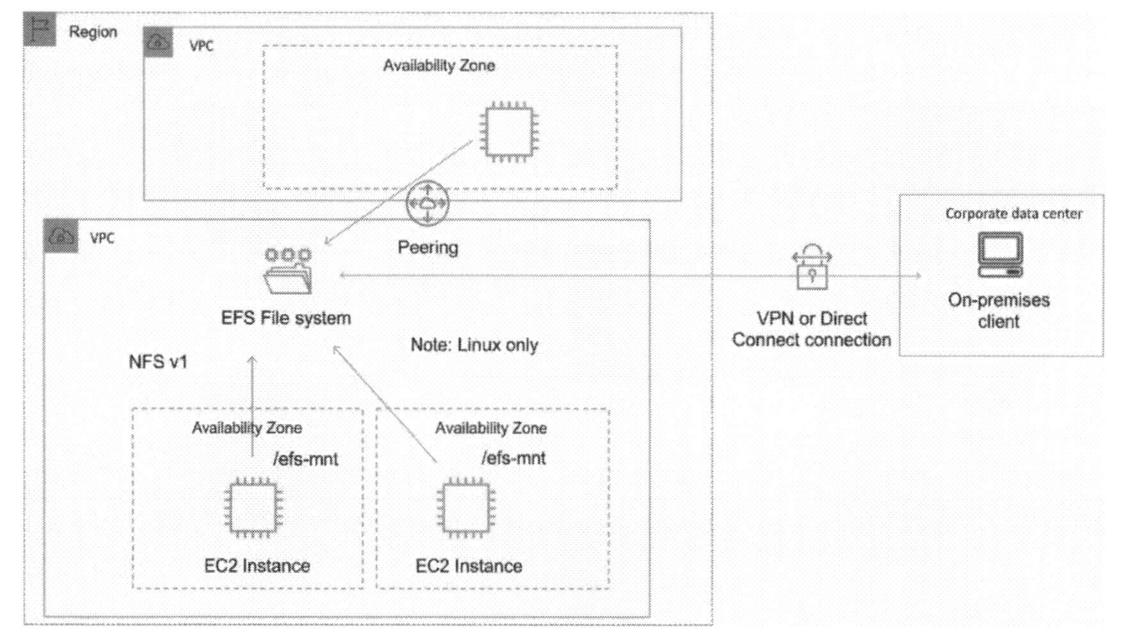

By default, you can create up to 10 file systems per account.

Access to EFS file systems from on-premises servers can be enabled via Direct Connect or AWS VPN.

You mount an EFS file system on your on-premises Linux server using the standard Linux mount command for mounting a file system via the NFSv4.1 protocol.

Can choose General Purpose or Max I/O (both SSD).

The VPC of the connecting instance must have DNS hostnames enabled.

EFS provides a file system interface, file system access semantics (such as strong consistency and file locking).

Data is stored across multiple AZ's within a region.

Read after write consistency.

Need to create mount targets and choose AZ's to include (recommended to include all AZ's).

Instances can be behind an ELB.

EC2 Classic instances must mount via ClassicLink.

EFS is compatible with all Linux-based AMIs for Amazon EC2.

Using the EFS-to-EFS Backup solution, you can schedule automatic incremental backups of your Amazon EFS file system.

The following table provides a comparison of the **storage characteristics of EFS vs EBS**:

	Amazon EFS	Amazon EBS Provisioned IOPS
Availability and durability	Data is stored redundantly across multiple AZs	Data is stored redundantly in a single AZ
Access	Up to thousands of Amazon EC2 instances, from multiple AZs, can connect concurrently to a file system	A single Amazon EC2 instance in a single AZ can connect to a file system
Use cases	Big data and analytics, media processing and workflows, content management, web serving and home directories	Boot volumes, transactional and NoSQL databases, data warehousing and ETL

PERFORMANCE

There are two performance modes:

- "General Purpose" performance mode is appropriate for most file systems.
- "Max I/O" performance mode is optimized for applications where tens, hundreds, or thousands of EC2 instances are accessing the file system.

Amazon EFS is designed to burst to allow high throughput levels for periods of time.

Amazon EFS file systems are distributed across an unconstrained number of storage servers, enabling file systems to grow elastically to petabyte scale and allowing massively parallel access from Amazon EC2 instances to your data.

This distributed data storage design means that multithreaded applications and applications that concurrently access data from multiple Amazon EC2 instances can drive substantial levels of aggregate throughput and IOPS.

The table below compares high-level performance and storage characteristics for AWS's file (EFS) and block (EBS) cloud storage offerings:

	Amazon EFS	Amazon EBS Provisioned IOPS
Per-operation latency	Low, consistent latency	Lowest, consistent latency
Throughput scale	10+ GB per second	Up to 2 GB per second

ACCESS CONTROL

When you create a file system, you create endpoints in your VPC called "mount targets".

When mounting from an EC2 instance, your file system's DNS name, which you provide in your mount command, resolves to a mount target's IP address.

You can control who can administer your file system using IAM.

You can control access to files and directories with POSIX-compliant user and group-level permissions.

POSIX permissions allow you to restrict access from hosts by user and group.

EFS Security Groups act as a firewall, and the rules you add define the traffic flow.

EFS ENCRYPTION

EFS offers the ability to encrypt data at rest and in transit.

Encryption keys are managed by the AWS Key Management Service (KMS).

Data encryption in transit uses industry standard Transport Layer Security (TLS) 1.2 to encrypt data sent between your clients and EFS file systems.

Data encrypted at rest is transparently encrypted while being written, and transparently decrypted while being read.

Enable encryption at rest in the EFS console or by using the AWS CLI or SDKs.

Encryption of data at rest and of data in transit can be configured together or separately to help meet your unique security requirements.

EFS FILE SYNC

EFS File Sync provides a fast and simple way to securely sync existing file systems into Amazon EFS.

EFS File Sync copies files and directories into Amazon EFS at speeds up to 5x faster than standard Linux copy tools, with simple setup and management in the AWS Console.

EFS File Sync securely and efficiently copies files over the internet or an AWS Direct Connect connection.

Copies file data and file system metadata such as ownership, timestamps, and access permissions.

EFS File Sync provides the following benefits:

- Efficient high-performance parallel data transfer that tolerates unreliable and high-latency networks.
- Encryption of data transferred from your IT environment to AWS.
- Data transfer rate up to five times faster than standard Linux copy tools.
- Full and incremental syncs for repetitive transfers.

The following diagram shows a high-level view of the EFS File Sync architecture:

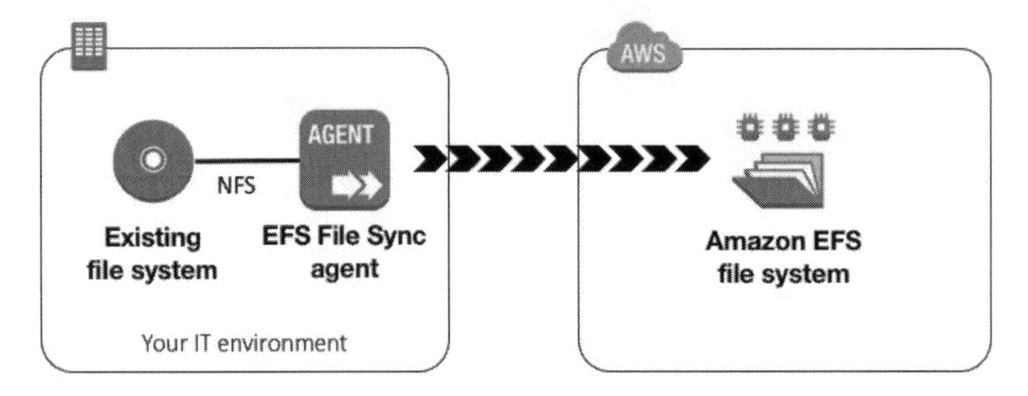

Note: EFS File Sync currently doesn't support syncing from an Amazon EFS source to an NFS destination.

When deploying Amazon EFS File Sync on EC2, the instance size must be at least xlarge for your EFS File Sync to function.

Recommended to use one of the Memory optimized r4.xlarge instance types.

Can choose to run EFS File Sync either on-premises as a virtual machine (VM), or in AWS as an EC2 instance.

Supports VMware ESXi.

COMPATIBILITY

EFS is integrated with a number of other AWS services, including CloudWatch, CloudFormation, CloudTrail, IAM, and Tagging services.

CloudWatch allows you to monitor file system activity using metrics.

CloudFormation allows you to create and manage file systems using templates.

CloudTrail allows you to record all Amazon EFS API calls in log files.

IAM allows you to control who can administer your file system.

Tagging services allows you to label your file systems with metadata that you define.

PRICING AND BILLING

You pay only for the amount of file system storage you use per month.

When using the Provisioned Throughput mode, you pay for the throughput you provision per month.

There is no minimum fee and there are no set-up charges.

With EFS File Sync, you pay per-GB for data copied to EFS.

AWS STORAGE GATEWAY

GENERAL

The AWS Storage Gateway service enables hybrid storage between on-premises environments and the AWS Cloud.

It provides low-latency performance by caching frequently accessed data on premises, while storing data securely and durably in Amazon cloud storage services.

Implemented using a virtual machine that you run on-premises (VMware or Hyper-V virtual appliance).

Provides local storage resources backed by AWS S3 and Glacier.

Often used in disaster recovery preparedness to sync data to AWS.

Useful in cloud migrations.

AWS Storage Gateway supports three storage interfaces: file, volume, and tape.

The table below shows the different gateways available and the interfaces and use cases:

New Name	Old Name	Interface	Use Case
File Gateway	None	NFS, SMB	Allow on-prem or EC2 instances to store objects in S3 via NFS or SMB mount points
Volume Gateway Stored Mode	Gateway-Stored Volumes	iSCSI	Asynchronous replication of on-prem data to S3
Volume Gateway Cached Mode	Gateway-Cached Volumes	iSCSI	Primary data stored in S3 with frequently accessed data cached locally on-prem
Tape Gateway	Gateway-Virtual Tape Library	iSCSI	Virtual media changer and tape library for use with existing backup software

Each gateway you have can provide one type of interface.

All data transferred between any type of gateway appliance and AWS storage is encrypted using SSL.

By default, all data stored by AWS Storage Gateway in S3 is encrypted server-side with Amazon S3-Managed Encryption Keys (SSE-S3).

When using the file gateway, you can optionally configure each file share to have your objects encrypted with AWS KMS-Managed Keys using SSE-KMS.

FILE GATEWAY

File gateway provides a virtual on-premises file server, which enables you to store and retrieve files as objects in Amazon S3.

Can be used for on-premises applications, and for Amazon EC2-resident applications that need file storage in S3 for object-based workloads.

Used for flat files only, stored directly on S3.

File gateway offers SMB or NFS-based access to data in Amazon S3 with local caching.

File gateway supports Amazon S3 Standard, S3 Standard – Infrequent Access (S3 Standard – IA) and S3 One Zone – IA.

File gateway supports clients connecting to the gateway using NFS v3 and v4.1.

Microsoft Windows clients that support NFS v3 can connect to file gateway.

The maximum size of an individual file is 5 TB.

VOLUME GATEWAY

The volume gateway represents the family of gateways that support block-based volumes, previously referred to as gateway-cached and gateway-stored modes.

Block storage – iSCSI based.

Cached Volume mode – the entire dataset is stored on S3 and a cache of the most frequently accessed data is cached on-site.

Stored Volume mode – the entire dataset is stored on-site and is asynchronously backed up to S3 (EBS point-in-time snapshots). Snapshots are incremental and compressed.

Each volume gateway can support up to 32 volumes.

In cached mode, each volume can be up to 32 TB for a maximum of 1 PB of data per gateway (32 volumes, each 32 TB in size).

In stored mode, each volume can be up to 16 TB for a maximum of 512 TB of data per gateway (32 volumes, each 16 TB in size).

GATEWAY VIRTUAL TAPE LIBRARY

Used for backup with popular backup software.

Each gateway is preconfigured with a media changer and tape drives. Supported by NetBackup, Backup Exec, Veeam etc.

When creating virtual tapes, you select one of the following sizes: 100 GB, 200 GB, 400 GB, 800 GB, 1.5 TB, and 2.5 TB.

A tape gateway can have up to 1,500 virtual tapes with a maximum aggregate capacity of 1 PB.

AMAZON FSX

Amazon FSx provides fully managed third-party file systems.

Amazon FSx provides you with the native compatibility of third-party file systems with feature sets for workloads such as Windows-based storage, high-performance computing (HPC), machine learning, and electronic design automation (EDA).

You don't have to worry about managing file servers and storage, as Amazon FSx automates the time-consuming administration tasks such as hardware provisioning, software configuration, patching, and backups.

Amazon FSx integrates the file systems with cloud-native AWS services, making them even more useful for a broader set of workloads.

Amazon FSx provides you with two file systems to choose from:

- Amazon FSx for Windows File Server for Windows-based applications
- Amazon FSx for Lustre for compute-intensive workloads.

AMAZON FSX FOR WINDOWS FILE SERVER

Amazon FSx for Windows File Server provides a fully managed native Microsoft Windows file system so you can easily move your Windows-based applications that require shared file storage to AWS.

Built on Windows Server, Amazon FSx provides the compatibility and features that your Microsoft applications rely on, including full support for the SMB protocol, Windows NTFS, and Microsoft Active Directory (AD) integration.

Amazon FSx uses SSD storage to provide fast performance with low latency.

This compatibility, performance, and scalability enables business-critical workloads such as home directories, media workflows, and business applications.

Amazon FSx helps you optimize TCO with Data Deduplication, reducing costs by 50-60% for general-purpose file shares.

User quotas give you the option to better monitor and control costs. You pay for only the resources used, with no upfront costs, or licensing fees.

Details and Benefits

High availability: Amazon FSx automatically replicates your data within an Availability Zone (AZ) it resides in (which you specify during creation) to protect it from component failure, continuously monitors for hardware failures, and automatically replaces infrastructure components in the event of a failure.

Multi-AZ: Amazon FSx offers a multiple availability (AZ) deployment option, designed to provide continuous availability to data, even in the event that an AZ is unavailable. Multi-AZ file systems include an active and standby file server in separate AZs, and any changes written to disk in your file system are synchronously replicated across AZs to the standby.

Supports Windows-native file system features:

- Access Control Lists (ACLs), shadow copies, and user quotas.
- NTFS file systems that can be accessed from up to thousands of compute instances using the SMB protocol.

Works with Microsoft Active Directory (AD) to easily integrate file systems with Windows environments.

Built on SSD-storage, Amazon FSx provides fast performance with up to 2 GB/second throughput per file system, hundreds of thousands of IOPS, and consistent sub-millisecond latencies.

Can choose a throughput level that is independent of your file system size.

Using DFS Namespaces, you can scale performance up to tens of gigabytes per second of throughput, with millions of IOPS, across hundreds of petabytes of data.

Amazon FSx can connect file systems to Amazon EC2, VMware Cloud on AWS, Amazon WorkSpaces, and Amazon AppStream 2.0 instances.

Amazon FSx also supports on-premises access via AWS Direct Connect or AWS VPN, and access from multiple VPCs, accounts, and regions using VPC Peering or AWS Transit Gateway.

Amazon FSx automatically encrypts your data at-rest and in-transit.

Assessed to comply with ISO, PCI-DSS, and SOC certifications, and is HIPAA eligible.

Integration with AWS CloudTrail monitors and logs your API calls letting you see actions taken by users on Amazon FSx resources.

Pay only for the resources you use, with no minimum commitments or up-front fees.

Can optimize costs by removing redundant data with Data Deduplication.

User quotas provide tracking, monitoring, and enforcing of storage consumption to help reduce costs.

AMAZON FSX FOR LUSTRE

Amazon FSx for Lustre provides a high-performance file system optimized for fast processing of workloads such as machine learning, high performance computing (HPC), video processing, financial modeling, and electronic design automation (EDA).

These workloads commonly require data to be presented via a fast and scalable file system interface, and typically have data sets stored on long-term data stores like Amazon S3.

Amazon FSx for Lustre provides a fully managed high-performance Lustre file system that allows file-based applications to access data with hundreds of gigabytes per second of data, millions of IOPS, and sub millisecond latencies.

Amazon FSx works natively with Amazon S3, letting you transparently access your S3 objects as files on Amazon FSx to run analyses for hours to months.

You can then write results back to S3, and simply delete your file system. FSx for Lustre also enables you to burst your data processing workloads from on-premises to AWS, by allowing you to access your FSx file system over Amazon Direct Connect or VPN.

You can also use FSx for Lustre as a standalone high-performance file system to burst your workloads from on-premises to the cloud.

By copying on-premises data to an FSx for Lustre file system, you can make that data available for fast processing by compute instances running on AWS.

With Amazon FSx, you pay for only the resources you use. There are no minimum commitments, upfront hardware or software costs, or additional fees.

Details and Benefits

Lustre is a popular open-source parallel file system that is designed for high-performance workloads. These workloads include HPC, machine learning, analytics, and media processing.

A parallel file system provides high throughput for processing large amounts of data and performs operations with consistently low latencies.

It does so by storing data across multiple networked servers that thousands of compute instances can interact with concurrently.

The Lustre file system provides a POSIX-compliant file system interface.

Amazon FSx can scale up to hundreds of gigabytes per second of throughput, and millions of IOPS.

Amazon FSx provides high throughput for processing large amounts of data and performs operations with consistent, sub-millisecond latencies.

Amazon FSx for Lustre supports file access to thousands of EC2 instances, enabling you to provide file storage for your high-performance workloads, like genomics, seismic exploration, and video rendering.

Amazon S3:

- Amazon FSx works natively with Amazon S3, making it easy to access your S3 data to run data processing workloads.
- Your S3 objects are presented as files in your file system, and you can write your results back to S3.
- This lets you run data processing workloads on FSx for Lustre and store your long-term data on S3 or on-premises data stores.

On-premises:

- You can use Amazon FSx for Lustre for on-premises workloads that need to burst to the cloud due to peak demands or capacity limits.

- To move your existing on-premises data into Amazon FSx, you can mount your Amazon FSx for Lustre file system from an on-premises client over AWS Direct Connect or VPN, and then use parallel copy tools to import your data to your Amazon FSx for Lustre file system.
- At any time, you can write your results back to be durably stored in your data lake.

Security:

- All Amazon FSx file system data is encrypted at rest.
- You can access your file system from your compute instances using the open-source Lustre client.
- Once mounted, you can work with the files and directories in your file system just like you would with a local file system.
- FSx for Lustre is compatible with the most popular Linux-based AMIs, including Amazon Linux, Red Hat Enterprise Linux (RHEL), CentOS, Ubuntu, and SUSE Linux.
- You access your Amazon FSx file system from endpoints in your Amazon VPC, which enables you to isolate your file system in your own virtual network.
- You can configure security group rules and control network access to your Amazon FSx file systems.
- Amazon FSx is integrated with AWS Identity and Access Management (IAM).
- This integration means that you can control the actions your AWS IAM users and groups can take to manage your file systems (such as creating and deleting file systems).
- You can also tag your Amazon FSx resources and control the actions that your IAM users and groups can take based on those tags.

STORAGE QUIZ QUESTIONS

Answers and explanations are provided below after the last question in this section.

Question 1: You would like to run some code when an object is uploaded to an Amazon S3 bucket. How can this be achieved?

1. Create an event notification on the S3 bucket that triggers a Lambda function
2. Configure Lambda to poll the S3 bucket for changes and run a function when it finds new objects
3. Create an event notification on the S3 bucket that notifies Amazon SNS to trigger a Lambda function

Question 2: Which type Amazon storage service uses standards-based REST web interfaces to manage objects?

1. Amazon Elastic File System (EFS)
2. Amazon Elastic Block Store (EBS)
3. Amazon Simple Storage Service (S3)
4. Amazon FSx for Windows File Server

Question 3: What is the maximum file size allowed in Amazon S3?

1. 5 terabytes
2. 0 bytes
3. 5 gigabytes
4. Unlimited

Question 4: What type of consistency model is provided in Amazon S3 when you upload a new version of an object?

1. Read after write consistency
2. Eventual consistency

Question 5: Which Amazon S3 capability uses Amazon CloudFront and enables fast uploads for objects?

1. Multipart upload
2. Cross region replication (CRR)
3. BitTorrent
4. Transfer acceleration

Question 6: How can you create a hierarchy that mimics a filesystem in Amazon S3?

1. Create buckets within other buckets
2. Use folders in your buckets
3. Upload objects within other objects
4. Use lifecycle rules to tier your data

Question 7: A US based organization is concerned about uploading data to Amazon S3 as data sovereignty rules mean they cannot move their data outside of the US. What would you tell them?

1. Data never leaves a region unless specifically configured to do so.
2. Data will be replicated globally so they cannot use Amazon S3.

Question 8: For compliance reasons, an organization needs to retain data for 7 years. If they need to retrieve data, they have 24 hours to do so. Which Amazon S3 storage class is most cost-effective?

1. Amazon S3 One-Zone IA
2. Amazon S3 Intelligent Tiering
3. Amazon S3 Glacier
4. Amazon S3 Glacier Deep Archive

Question 9: An Architect is designing an application that will use hundreds of EC2 instances across multiple availability zones. A shared filesystem is required that can be mounted by all instances. Which storage service is suitable for this requirement?

1. Amazon Elastic File System (EFS)
2. Amazon Elastic Block Store (EBS)
3. Amazon Instance Store
4. Amazon Simple Storage Service (S3)

Question 10: How can you control access to files and directories in Amazon EFS filesystems?

1. Using IAM
2. Using EFS security groups
3. Using Network ACLs
4. Using user and group-level permissions

Question 11: A High-Performance Computing (HPC) application requires a high-performance filesystem for running data analysis. The filesystem should transparently access source data stored as Amazon S3 objects. Which type of filesystem is ideal for this use case?

1. Amazon FSx for Windows File Server
2. Amazon Elastic File System (EFS)
3. Amazon FSx for Lustre
4. Amazon Elastic Block Store (EBS)

Question 12: Which AWS storage service provides a NTFS filesystem that can be accessed by multiple EC2 instances using the SMB protocol?

1. Amazon FSx for Windows File Server
2. Amazon Elastic File System (EFS)
3. Amazon FSx for Lustre
4. Amazon Elastic Block Store (EBS)

STORAGE - ANSWERS

Question 1, Answer: 1

Explanation:

1 is correct. The best way to achieve this is to use an event notification on the S3 bucket that triggers a function that then runs the code.

2 is incorrect. Lambda does not poll S3.

3 is incorrect. You would not use Amazon SNS in this scenario as it is an unnecessary additional step.

Question 2, Answer: 3

Explanation:

1 is incorrect. EFS is a file-based storage system that is accessed using the NFS protocol.

2 is incorrect. EBS is a block-based storage system for mounting volumes.

3 is correct. Amazon S3 is an object-based storage system that uses standards-based REST web interfaces to work with objects.

4 is incorrect. Amazon FSx for Windows File Server provides a fully managed Microsoft filesystem that is mounted using SMB.

Question 3, Answer: 1

Explanation:

1 is correct. The maximum file size for Amazon S3 objects is 5 terabytes.

2 is incorrect. This is the minimum file size possible in Amazon S3.

3 is incorrect. 5GB is not the maximum file size possible in Amazon S3.

4 is incorrect. There is a limit on the maximum file size for objects in Amazon S3.

Question 4, Answer: 2

Explanation:

1 is incorrect. You do not get read after write consistency for overwrite PUT and DELETES.

2 is correct. In Amazon S3 you get eventual consistency for overwrite PUTS and DELETES.

Question 5, Answer: 4

Explanation:

1 is incorrect. Multipart upload is recommended for uploading objects larger than 100MB but it does not use CloudFront.

2 is incorrect. CRR is used for replicating objects between buckets in different regions.

3 is incorrect. BitTorrent can be used for retrieving objects from Amazon S3. It is not used for uploading and doesn't use CloudFront.

4 is correct. Transfer Acceleration speeds up data uploads by using the CloudFront network.

Question 6, Answer: 2

Explanation:

1 is incorrect. You cannot nest buckets (create buckets inside other buckets).

2 is correct. You can mimic the hierarchy of a filesystem by creating folder in your buckets.

3 is incorrect. You cannot upload objects within other objects.

4 is incorrect. Tiering your data is done for performance not to mimic a filesystem.

Question 7, Answer: 1

Explanation:

1 is correct. S3 is a global service but buckets are created within a region. Data is never replicated outside of that region unless you configure it (e.g. through CRR).

2 is incorrect. Data is not replicated globally with Amazon S3.

Question 8, Answer: 4

Explanation:

1 is incorrect. This is not the most cost-effective option for these requirements.

2 is incorrect. This is not the most cost-effective option for these requirements.

3 is incorrect. This is not the most cost-effective option for these requirements. It is slightly more expensive than Deep Archive but faster to retrieve data (which isn't necessary for this scenario).

4 is correct. This is the most cost-effective option for these requirements as the data retrieval time is 24 hours.

Question 9, Answer: 1

Explanation:

1 is correct. EFS is a file-based storage system accessed over NFS. You can attach thousands of instances from multiple AZs to the same filesystem.

2 is incorrect. You cannot attach multiple instances to a single EBS volume or attach volumes across AZs.

3 is incorrect. Instance Stores are local storage on the EC2 host servers, you cannot attach multiple instances to the same instance store.

4 is incorrect. Amazon S3 is an object-based storage system, not a filesystem.

Question 10, Answer: 4

Explanation:

1 is incorrect. IAM can be used to control who can administer the file system but not control the access to files and directories.

2 is incorrect. EFS security groups control network traffic that is allowed to reach the filesystem.

3 is incorrect. Network ACLs are not used for file and directory permissions, they restrict traffic into and out of subnets.

4 is correct. You can control access to files and directories with POSIX-compliant user and group-level permissions.

Question 11, Answer: 3

Explanation:

1 is incorrect. FSx for Windows File Server cannot access data stored on Amazon S3.

2 is incorrect. EFS does not integrate with Amazon S3 to transparently access objects.

3 is correct. This is a good use case for Amazon FSx for Lustre.

4 is incorrect. EBS is not a filesystem nor does it directly integrate with Amazon S3 for transparent access of S3 objects.

Question 12, Answer: 1

Explanation:

1 is correct. FSx for Windows File Server provides NTFS file systems that can be accessed from up to thousands of compute instances using the SMB protocol.

2 is incorrect. EFS is not an NTFS filesystem.

3 is incorrect. FSx for Lustre does not provide an NTFS filesystem.

4 is incorrect. EBS does not provide an NTFS filesystem nor can it be accessed by multiple EC2 instances.

AWS DATABASE

AMAZON RDS

GENERAL RDS CONCEPTS

Amazon Relational Database Service (Amazon RDS) is a managed service that makes it easy to set up, operate, and scale a relational database in the cloud.

RDS is an Online Transaction Processing (OLTP) type of database.

Primary use case is a transactional database (rather than analytical).

Best for structured, relational data store requirements.

Aims to be drop-in replacement for existing on-premise instances of the same databases.

Automated backups and patching applied in customer-defined maintenance windows.

Push-button scaling, replication and redundancy.

Amazon RDS supports the following database engines:

- Amazon Aurora
- MySQL
- MariaDB
- Oracle
- SQL Server
- PostgreSQL

RDS is a managed service and you do not have access to the underlying EC2 instance (no root access).

The RDS service includes the following:

- Security and patching of the DB instances.
- Automated backup for the DB instances.
- Software updates for the DB engine.
- Easy scaling for storage and compute.
- Multi-AZ option with synchronous replication.
- Automatic failover for Multi-AZ option.
- Read replicas option for read heavy workloads.

A DB instance is a database environment in the cloud with the compute and storage resources you specify.

Database instances are accessed via endpoints.

Endpoints can be retrieved via the DB instance description in the AWS Management Console, **DescribeDBInstances** API or **describe-db-instances** command.

By default, customers are allowed to have up to a total of 40 Amazon RDS DB instances (only 10 of these can be Oracle or MS SQL unless you have your own licences).

Maintenance windows are configured to allow DB instances modifications to take place such as scaling and software patching (some operations require the DB instance to be taken offline briefly).

You can define the maintenance window or AWS will schedule a 30-minute window.

Windows integrated authentication for SQL only works with domains created using the AWS directory service – need to establish a trust with an on-premise AD directory.

Events and Notifications:

- Amazon RDS uses AWS SNS to send RDS events via SNS notifications.
- You can use API calls to the Amazon RDS service to list the RDS events in the last 14 days (DescribeEvents API).
- You can view events from the last 14 days using the CLI.
- Using the AWS Console, you can only view RDS events for the last 1 day.

USE CASES, ALTERNATIVES AND ANTI-PATTERNS

The table below provides guidance on when best to use RDS and several other AWS database/data store services:

Data Store	When to Use
Database on EC2	• Ultimate control over database • Preferred DB not available under RDS
Amazon RDS	• Need traditional relational database for OLTP • Your data is well-formed and structured • Existing apps requiring RDBMS
Amazon DynamoDB	• Name/value pair data or unpredictable data structure • In-memory performance with persistence • High I/O needs • Scale dynamically
Amazon RedShift	• Massive amounts of data • Primarily OLAP workloads
Amazon Neptune	• Relationships between objects a major portion of data value
Amazon ElastiCache	• Fast temporary storage for small amounts of data • Highly volatile data
Amazon S3	• BLOBs • Static websites

Alternative to Amazon RDS:

If your use case isn't supported on RDS, you can run databases on Amazon EC2.

Consider the following points when considering a DB on EC2:

- You can run any database you like with full control and ultimate flexibility.
- You must manage everything like backups, redundancy, patching and scaling.
- Good option if you require a database not yet supported by RDS, such as IBM DB2 or SAP HANA.
- Good option if it is not feasible to migrate to AWS-managed database.

Anti-Patterns:

Anti-patterns are certain patterns in architecture or development that are considered bad, or sub-optimal practices – i.e. there may be a better service of method to produce the best result.

The following table describes requirements that are not a good fit for RDS:

Requirement	More Suitable Service
Lots of large binary objects (BLOBs)	S3
Automated Scalability	DynamoDB
Name/Value Data Structure	DynamoDB
Data is not well structured or unpredictable	DynamoDB
Other database platforms like IBM DB2 or SAP HANA	EC2
Complete control over the database	EC2

ENCRYPTION

You can encrypt your Amazon RDS instances and snapshots at rest by enabling the encryption option for your Amazon RDS DB instance.

Encryption at rest is supported for all DB types and uses AWS KMS.

When using encryption at rest the following elements are also encrypted:

- All DB snapshots
- Backups
- DB instance storage
- Read Replicas

You cannot encrypt an existing DB, you need to create a snapshot, copy it, encrypt the copy, then build an encrypted DB from the snapshot.

Data that is encrypted at rest includes the underlying storage for a DB instance, its automated backups, Read Replicas, and snapshots.

A Read Replica of an Amazon RDS encrypted instance is also encrypted using the same key as the master instance when both are in the same region.

If the master and Read Replica are in different regions, you encrypt using the encryption key for that region.

You can't have an encrypted Read Replica of an unencrypted DB instance or an unencrypted Read Replica of an encrypted DB instance.

Encryption/decryption is handled transparently.

RDS supports SSL encryption between applications and RDS DB instances.

RDS generates a certificate for the instance.

DB SUBNET GROUPS

A DB subnet group is a collection of subnets (typically private) that you create in a VPC and that you then designate for your DB instances.

Each DB subnet group should have subnets in at least two Availability Zones in a given region.

It is recommended to configure a subnet group with subnets in each AZ (even for standalone instances).

During the creation of an RDS instance you can select the DB subnet group and the AZ within the group to place the RDS DB instance in.

You cannot pick the IP within the subnet that is allocated.

BILLING AND PROVISIONING

AWS Charge for:

- DB instance hours (partial hours are charged as full hours).
- Storage GB/month.
- I/O requests/month – for magnetic storage.
- Provisioned IOPS/month – for RDS provisioned IOPS SSD.
- Egress data transfer.
- Backup storage (DB backups and manual snapshots).

Backup storage for the automated RDS backup is free of charge up to the provisioned EBS volume size.

However, AWS replicate data across multiple AZs and so you are charged for the extra storage space on S3.

For multi-AZ you are charged for:

- Multi-AZ DB hours.
- Provisioned storage.
- Double write I/Os.

For multi-AZ you are not charged for DB data transfer during replication from primary to standby.

Oracle and Microsoft SQL licences are included or you can bring your own (BYO).

On-demand and reserved instance pricing available.

Reserved instances are defined based on the following attributes which must not be changed:

- DB engine.
- DB instance class
- Deployment type (standalone, multi-AZ_
- License model
- Region

Reserved instances:

- Can be moved between AZs in the same region.
- Are available for multi-AZ deployments.
- Can be applied to Read Replicas if DB instance class and region are the same.
- Scaling is achieved through changing the instance class for compute and modifying storage capacity for additional storage allocation.

SCALABILITY

You can only scale RDS up (compute and storage).

You cannot decrease the allocated storage for an RDS instance.

You can scale storage and change the storage type for all DB engines except MS SQL.

For MS SQL the workaround is to create a new instance from a snapshot with the new configuration.

Scaling storage can happen while the RDS instance is running without outage however there may be performance degradation.

Scaling compute will cause downtime.

You can choose to have changes take effect immediately, however the default is within the maintenance window.

Scaling requests are applied during the specified maintenance window unless "apply immediately" is used.

All RDS DB types support a maximum DB size of 64 TiB except for Microsoft SQL Server (16 TiB).

PERFORMANCE

Amazon RDS uses EBS volumes (never uses instance store) for DB and log storage.

There are three storage types available: General Purpose (SSD), Provisioned IOPS (SSD), and Magnetic.

General Purpose (SSD):

- Use for Database workloads with moderate I/O requirement
- Cost effective
- Also called gp2
- 3 IOPS/GB
- Burst up to 3000 IOPS

Provisioned IOPS (SSD):

- Use for I/O intensive workloads
- Low latency and consistent I/O
- User specified IOPS (see table below)

For provisioned IOPS storage the table below shows the range of Provisioned IOPS and storage size range for each database engine.

Database Engine	Range of Provisioned IOPS	Range of Storage
MariaDB	1,000-40,000 IOPS	100 GiB - 16 TiB
SQL Server, Enterprise and Standard editions	1,000-32,000 IOPS	200 GiB - 16 TiB
SQL Server, Web and Express editions	1,000-32,000 IOPS	100 GiB - 16 TiB
MySQL	1,000-40,000 IOPS	100 GiB - 16 TiB
Oracle	1,000-40,000 IOPS	100 GiB - 16 TiB
PostgreSQL	1,000-40,000 IOPS	100 GiB - 16 TiB

Magnetic:

- Not recommended anymore, available for backwards compatibility.
- Doesn't allow you to scale storage when using the SQL Server database engine.
- Doesn't support elastic volumes.
- Limited to a maximum size of 4 TiB.
- Limited to a maximum of 1,000 IOPS.

MULTI-AZ AND READ REPLICAS

Multi-AZ and Read Replicas are used for high availability, fault tolerance and performance scaling.

The table below compares multi-AZ deployments to Read Replicas:

Multi-AZ Deployments	Read Replicas
Synchronous replication - highly durable	Asynchronous replication - highly scalable
Only database engine on primary instance is active	All read replicas are accessible and can be used for read scaling
Automated backups are taken from standby	No backups configured by default
Always span two Availability Zones within a single Region	Can be within an Availability Zone, Cross-AZ, or Cross-Region
Database engine version upgrades happen on primary	Database engine version upgrade is independent from source instance
Automatic failover to standby when a problem is detected	Can be manually promoted to a standalone database instance

MULTI-AZ

Multi-AZ RDS creates a replica in another AZ and synchronously replicates to it (DR only).

There is an option to choose multi-AZ during the launch wizard.

AWS recommends the use of provisioned IOPS storage for multi-AZ RDS DB instances.

Each AZ runs on its own physically distinct, independent infrastructure, and is engineered to be highly reliable.

You cannot choose which AZ in the region will be chosen to create the standby DB instance.

You can view which AZ the standby DB instance is created in.

A failover may be triggered in the following circumstances:

- Loss of primary AZ or primary DB instance failure.
- Loss of network connectivity on primary.
- Compute (EC2) unit failure on primary.
- Storage (EBS) unit failure on primary.
- The primary DB instance is changed.
- Patching of the OS on the primary DB instance.
- Manual failover (reboot with failover selected on primary).

During failover RDS automatically updates configuration (including DNS endpoint) to use the second node.

Depending on the instance class it can take 1 to a few minutes to failover to a standby DB instance.

It is recommended to implement DB connection retries in your application.

Recommended to use the endpoint rather than the IP address to point applications to the RDS DB.

The method to initiate a manual RDS DB instance failover is to reboot selecting the option to failover.

A DB instance reboot is required for changes to take effect when you change the DB parameter group or when you change a static DB parameter.

The DB parameter group is a configuration container for the DB engine configuration.

You will be alerted by a DB instance event when a failover occurs.

There is no charge for data transfer between primary and secondary RDS instances.

Multi-AZ deployments for the MySQL, MariaDB, Oracle and PostgreSQL engines use Amazon's failover technology.

Multi-AZ deployments for the SQL Server engine use SQL Server Database Mirroring (DBM).

System upgrades like OS patching, DB Instance scaling and system upgrades, are applied first on the standby, before failing over and modifying the other DB Instance.

In multi-AZ configurations snapshots and automated backups are performed on the standby to avoid I/O suspension on the primary instance.

Read Replica Support for Multi-AZ:

- Amazon RDS Read Replicas for MySQL and MariaDB support Multi-AZ deployments.
- Combining Read Replicas with Multi-AZ enables you to build a resilient disaster recovery strategy and simplify your database engine upgrade process.
- A Read Replica in a different region than the source database can be used as a standby database and promoted to become the new production database in case of a regional disruption.
- This allows you to scale reads whilst also having multi-AZ for DR.
- Note that RDS for PostgreSQL does not yet support this feature.

The process for implementing maintenance activities is as follows:

- Perform operations on standby.
- Promote standby to primary.
- Perform operations on new standby (demoted primary).

You can manually upgrade a DB instance to a supported DB engine version from the AWS Console.

By default, upgrades will take effect during the next maintenance window.

You can optionally force an immediate upgrade.

In multi-AZ deployments version upgrades will be conducted on both the primary and standby at the same time causing an outage of both DB instance.

Ensure security groups and NACLs will allow your application servers to communicate with both the primary and standby instances.

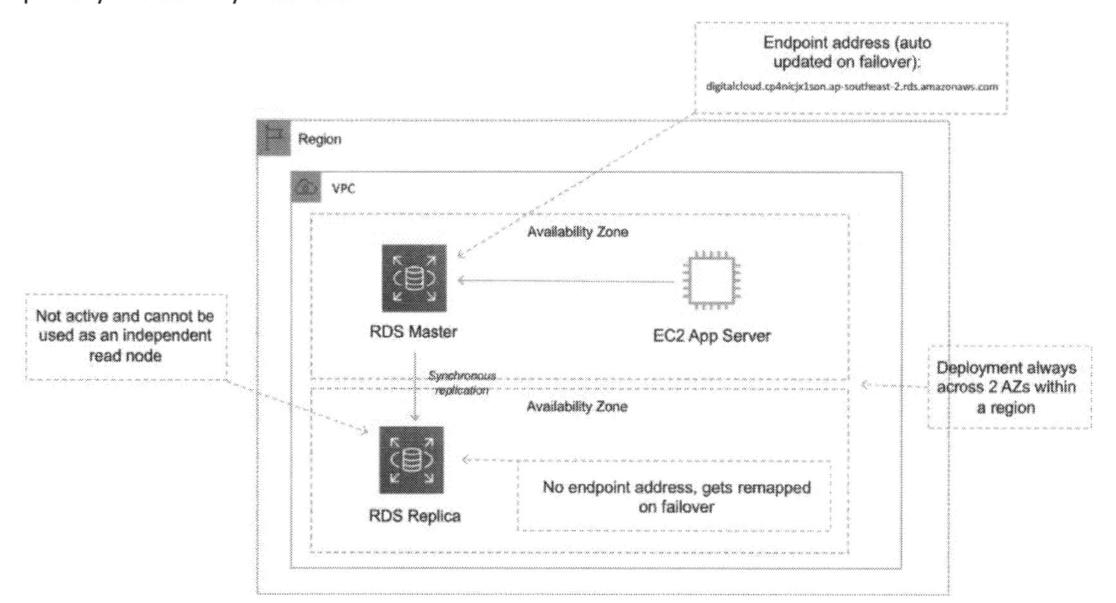

READ REPLICAS

Read replicas are used for read-heavy DBs and replication is asynchronous.

Read replicas are for workload sharing and offloading.

Read replicas provide read-only DR.

Read replicas are created from a snapshot of the master instance.

Must have automated backups enabled on the primary (retention period > 0).

Only supported for transactional database storage engines (InnoDB not MyISAM).

Read replicas are available for MySQL, PostgreSQL, MariaDB, Oracle and Aurora (not SQL Server).

For the MySQL, MariaDB, PostgreSQL, and Oracle database engines, Amazon RDS creates a second DB instance using a snapshot of the source DB instance.

It then uses the engines' native asynchronous replication to update the read replica whenever there is a change to the source DB instance.

Amazon Aurora employs an SSD-backed virtualized storage layer purpose-built for database workloads.

You can take snapshots of PostgreSQL read replicas but cannot enable automated backups.

You can enable automatic backups on MySQL and MariaDB read replicas.

You can enable writes to the MySQL and MariaDB Read Replicas.

You can have 5 read replicas of a production DB.

You cannot have more than four instances involved in a replication chain.

You can have read replicas of read replicas for MySQL and MariaDB but not for PostgreSQL.

Read replicas can be configured from the AWS Console or the API.

You can specify the AZ the read replica is deployed in.

The read replicas storage type and instance class can be different from the source but the compute should be at least the performance of the source.

You cannot change the DB engine.

In a multi-AZ failover, the read replicas are switched to the new primary.

Read replicas must be explicitly deleted.

If a source DB instance is deleted without deleting the replicas each replica becomes a standalone single-AZ DB instance.

You can promote a read replica to primary.

Promotion of read replicas takes several minutes.

Promoted read replicas retain:

- Backup retention window.
- Backup window.
- DB parameter group.

Existing read replicas continue to function as normal.

Each read replica has its own DNS endpoint.

Read replicas can have multi-AZ enabled and you can create read replicas of multi-AZ source DBs.

Read replicas can be in another region (uses asynchronous replication).

This configuration can be used for centralizing data from across different regions for analytics.

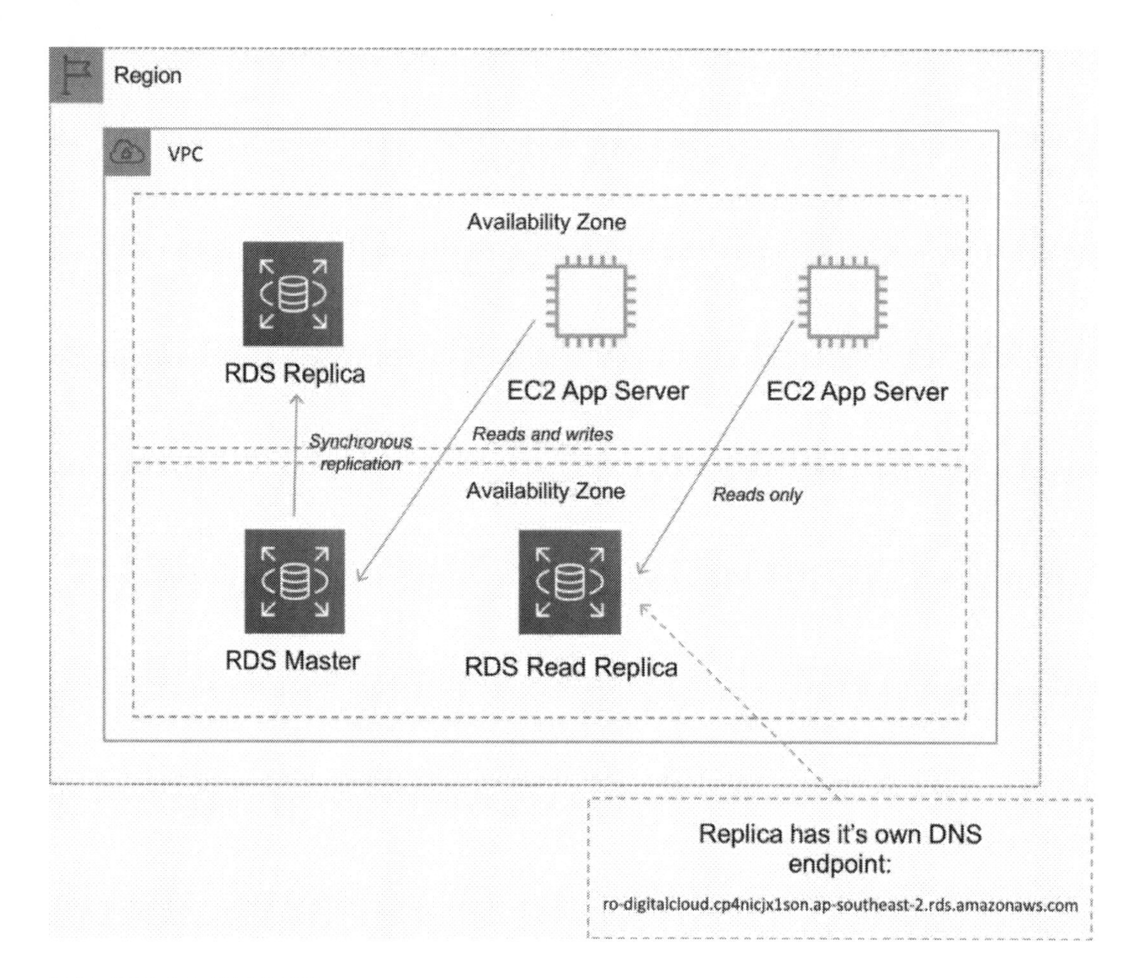

DB SNAPSHOTS

DB Snapshots are user-initiated and enable you to back up your DB instance in a known state as frequently as you wish, and then restore to that specific state.

Cannot be used for point-in-time recovery.

Snapshots are stored on S3.

Snapshots remain on S3 until manually deleted.

Backups are taken within a defined window.

I/O is briefly suspended while backups initialize and may increase latency (applicable to single-AZ RDS).

DB snapshots that are performed manually will be stored even after the RDS instance is deleted.

Restored DBs will always be a new RDS instance with a new DNS endpoint.

Can restore up to the last 5 minutes.

You cannot restore from a DB snapshot to an existing DB – a new instance is created when you restore.

Only default DB parameters and security groups are restored – you must manually associate all other DB parameters and SGs.

It is recommended to take a final snapshot before deleting an RDS instance.

Snapshots can be shared with other AWS accounts.

HIGH AVAILABILITY APPROACHES FOR DATABASES

If possible, choose DynamoDB over RDS because of inherent fault tolerance.

If DynamoDB can't be used, choose Aurora because of redundancy and automatic recovery features.

If Aurora can't be used, choose Multi-AZ RDS.

Frequent RDS snapshots can protect against data corruption or failure and they won't impact performance of Multi-AZ deployment.

Regional replication is also an option but will not be strongly consistent.

If the database runs on EC2, you have to design the HA yourself.

MIGRATION

AWS Database Migration Service helps you migrate databases to AWS quickly and securely.

Use along with the Schema Conversion Tool (SCT) to migrate databases to AWS RDS or EC2-based databases.

The source database remains fully operational during the migration, minimizing downtime to applications that rely on the database.

The AWS Database Migration Service can migrate your data to and from most widely used commercial and open-source databases.

Schema Conversion Tool can copy database schemas for homogenous migrations (same database) and convert schemas for heterogeneous migrations (different database).

DMS is used for smaller, simpler conversions and also supports MongoDB and DynamoDB.

SCT is used for larger, more complex datasets like data warehouses.

DMS has replication functions for on-premise to AWS or to Snowball or S3.

AMAZON AURORA

Amazon Aurora is a relational database service that combines the speed and availability of high-end commercial databases with the simplicity and cost-effectiveness of open source databases.

Aurora is an AWS proprietary database.

Fully managed service.

High performance, low price.

Scales in 10GB increments.

Scales up to 32vCPUs and 244GB RAM.

2 copies of data are kept in each AZ with a minimum of 3 AZ's (6 copies).

Can handle the loss of up to two copies of data without affecting DB write availability and up to three copies without affecting read availability.

The following diagram depicts how Aurora Fault Tolerance and Replicas work:

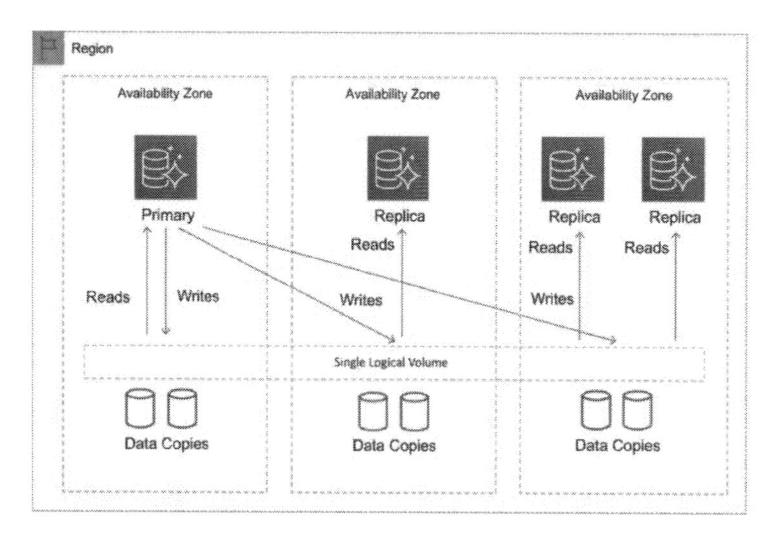

Aurora Fault Tolerance

- Fault tolerance across 3 AZs
- Single logical volume
- Aurora Replicas scale-out read requests
- Up to 15 Aurora Replicas with sub-10ms replica lag
- Aurora Replicas are independent endpoints
- Can promote Aurora Replica to be a new primary or create new primary
- Set priority (tiers) on Aurora Replicas to control order of promotion
- Can use Auto Scaling to add replicas

AURORA REPLICAS

There are two types of replication: Aurora replica (up to 15), MySQL Read Replica (up to 5).

The table below describes the differences between the two replica options:

Feature	Aurora Replica	MySQL Replica
Number of replicas	Up to 15	Up to 5
Replication type	Asynchronous (milliseconds)	Asynchronous (seconds)
Performance impact on primary	Low	High
Replica location	In-region	Cross-region
Act as failover target	Yes (no data loss)	Yes (potentially minutes of data loss)
Automated failover	Yes	No
Support for user-defined replication delay	No	Yes
Support for different data or schema vs. primary	No	Yes
Support for different data or schema vs. primary	No	Yes

You can create read replicas for an Amazon Aurora database in up to five AWS regions. This capability is available for Amazon Aurora with MySQL compatibility.

CROSS-REGION READ REPLICAS

Cross-region read replicas allow you to improve your disaster recovery posture, scale read operations in regions closer to your application users, and easily migrate from one region to another.

Cross-region replicas provide fast local reads to your users.

Each region can have an additional 15 Aurora replicas to further scale local reads.

You can choose between Global Database, which provides the best replication performance, and traditional binlog-based replication.

You can also set up your own binlog replication with external MySQL databases.

The following diagram depicts the Cross-Region Read Replica topology:

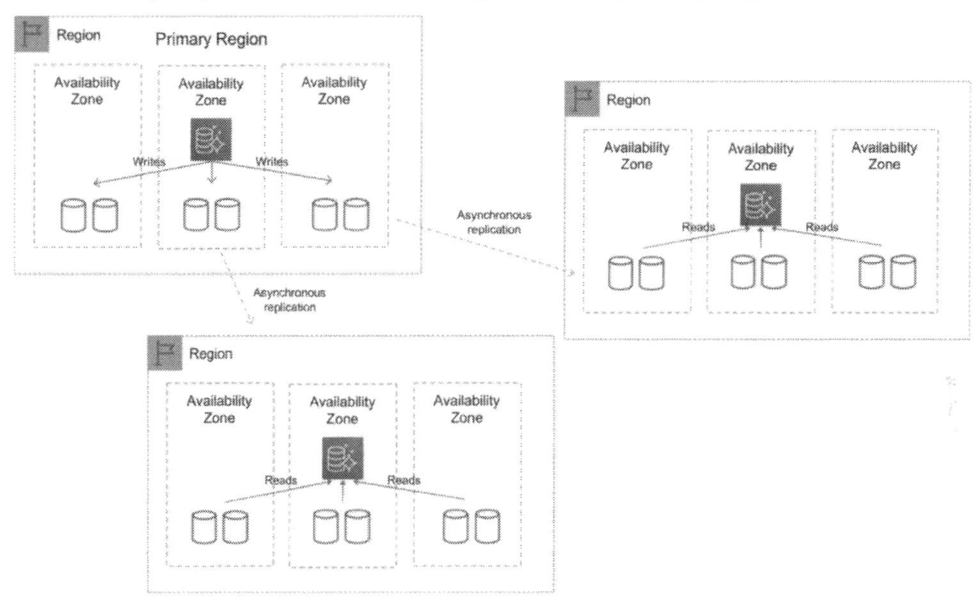

GLOBAL DATABASE

For globally distributed applications you can use Global Database, where a single Aurora database can span multiple AWS regions to enable fast local reads and quick disaster recovery.

Global Database uses storage-based replication to replicate a database across multiple AWS Regions, with typical latency of less than 1 second.

You can use a secondary region as a backup option in case you need to recover quickly from a regional degradation or outage.

A database in a secondary region can be promoted to full read/write capabilities in less than 1 minute.

The following table depicts the Aurora Global Database topology:

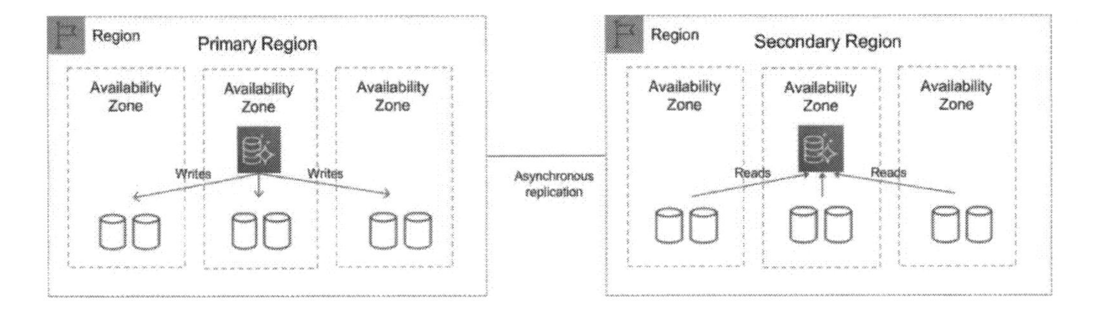

MULTI MASTER

Amazon Aurora Multi-Master is a new feature of the Aurora MySQL-compatible edition that adds the ability to scale out write performance across multiple Availability Zones, allowing applications to direct read/write workloads to multiple instances in a database cluster and operate with higher availability.

Aurora Multi-Master is designed to achieve high availability and ACID transactions across a cluster of database nodes with configurable read after write consistency.

Architecture:

- An Aurora cluster consists of a set of compute (database) nodes and a shared storage volume.
- The storage volume consists of six storage nodes placed in three Availability Zones for high availability and durability of user data.
- Every database node in the cluster is a writer node that can run read and write statements.

There is no single point of failure in the cluster.

Applications can use any writer node for their read/write and DDL needs.

A database change made by a writer node is written to six storage nodes in three Availability Zones, providing data durability and resiliency against storage node and Availability Zone failures.

The writer nodes are all functionally equal, and a failure of one writer node does not affect the availability of the other writer nodes in the cluster.

High Availability:

Aurora Multi-Master improves upon the high availability of the single-master version of Amazon Aurora because all of the nodes in the cluster are read/write nodes.

With single-master Aurora, a failure of the single writer node requires the promotion of a read replica to be the new writer.

In the case of Aurora Multi-Master, the failure of a writer node merely requires the application using the writer to open connections to another writer.

AURORA SERVERLESS

Amazon Aurora Serverless is an on-demand, auto-scaling configuration for Amazon Aurora.

Available for MySQL-compatible and PostgreSQL-compatible editions.

The database automatically starts up, shuts down, and scales capacity up or down based on application needs.

It enables you to run a database in the cloud without managing any database instances. It's a simple, cost-effective option for infrequent, intermittent, or unpredictable workloads.

You simply create a database endpoint and optionally specify the desired database capacity range and connect applications.

With Aurora Serverless, you only pay for database storage and the database capacity and I/O your database consumes while it is active.

Pay on a per-second basis for the database capacity you use when the database is active.

Can migrate between standard and serverless configurations with a few clicks in the Amazon RDS Management Console.

The table below provides a few example use cases for Amazon Aurora Serverless:

Use Case	Example
Infrequently-Used Applications	Application that is only used for a few minutes several times per day or week. Need a cost-effective database that only requires you to pay when it's active. With Aurora Serverless, you only pay for the database resources you consume.
New Applications	Deploying a new application and are unsure which instance size you need. With Aurora Serverless, you simply create an end-point and let the database auto-scale to the capacity requirements of your application.
Variable Workloads	Running a lightly-used application, with peaks of 30 minutes to several hours a few times each day or several times per year. Now you only pay for what the resources needed based on load - avoiding paying for unused resources or risking poor performance.
Unpredictable Workloads	Running workloads where there is database usage throughout the day, and also peaks of activity that are hard to predict. With Aurora Serverless, your database will auto-scale capacity to meet the needs of the application's peak load and scale back down when the surge of activity is over.
Development and Test Databases	Software development and QA teams are using databases during work hours, but don't need them on nights or weekends. With Aurora Serverless, your database automatically shuts down when not in use, and starts up much more quickly when work starts the next day.
Multitenant Applications	Web-based application with a database for each of your customers. Now you don't have to manage database capacity individually for each application in your fleet. Aurora manages individual database capacity for you, saving you valuable time.

FAULT-TOLERANT AND SELF-HEALING STORAGE

Each 10GB chunk of your database volume is replicated six ways, across three Availability Zones.

Amazon Aurora storage is fault-tolerant, transparently handling the loss of up to two copies of data without affecting database write availability and up to three copies without affecting read availability.

Amazon Aurora storage is also self-healing; data blocks and disks are continuously scanned for errors and replaced automatically.

AURORA AUTO SCALING

Aurora Auto Scaling dynamically adjusts the number of Aurora Replicas provisioned for an Aurora DB cluster using single-master replication.

Aurora Auto Scaling is available for both Aurora MySQL and Aurora PostgreSQL.

Aurora Auto Scaling enables your Aurora DB cluster to handle sudden increases in connectivity or workload.

When the connectivity or workload decreases, Aurora Auto Scaling removes unnecessary Aurora Replicas so that you don't pay for unused provisioned DB instances.

AUTOMATIC, CONTINUOUS, INCREMENTAL BACKUPS AND POINT-IN-TIME RESTORE

Amazon Aurora's backup capability enables point-in-time recovery for your instance.

This allows you to restore your database to any second during your retention period, up to the last five minutes.

Your automatic backup retention period can be configured up to thirty-five days.

Automated backups are stored in Amazon S3, which is designed for 99.999999999% durability. Amazon Aurora backups are automatic, incremental, and continuous and have no impact on database performance.

When automated backups are turned on for your DB Instance, Amazon RDS automatically performs a full daily snapshot of your data (during your preferred backup window) and captures transaction logs (as updates to your DB Instance are made).

Automated backups are enabled by default and data is stored on S3 and is equal to the size of the DB.

Amazon RDS retains backups of a DB Instance for a limited, user-specified period of time called the retention period, which by default is 7 days but can be up to 35 days.

There are two methods to backup and restore RDS DB instances:

- Amazon RDS automated backups.
- User initiated manual backups.

Both options back up the entire DB instance and not just the individual DBs.

Both options create a storage volume snapshot of the entire DB instance.

You can make copies of automated backups and manual snapshots.

Automated backups backup data to multiple AZs to provide for data durability.

Multi-AZ backups are taken from the standby instance (for MariaDB, MySQL, Oracle and PostgresSQL).

The DB instance must be in an Active state for automated backups to happen.

Only automated backups can be used for point-in-time DB instance recovery.

The granularity of point-in-time recovery is 5 minutes.

Amazon RDS creates a daily full storage volume snapshot and also captures transaction logs regularly.

You can choose the backup window.

There is no additional charge for backups but you will pay for storage costs on S3.

You can disable automated backups by setting the retention period to zero (0).

An outage occurs if you change the backup retention period from zero to a non-zero value or the other way around.

The retention period is the period AWS keeps the automated backups before deleting them.

Retention periods:

- By default the retention period is 7 days if configured from the console for all DB engines except Aurora.
- The default retention period is 1 day if configured from the API or CLI.
- The retention period for Aurora is 1 day regardless of how it is configured.
- You can increase the retention period up to 35 days.

During the backup window I/O may be suspended.

Automated backups are deleted when you delete the RDS DB instance.

Automated backups are only supported for InnoDB storage engine for MySQL (not for myISAM).

When you restore a DB instance the default DB parameters and security groups are applied – you must then apply the custom DB parameters and security groups.

You cannot restore from a DB snapshot into an existing DB instance.

Following a restore the new DB instance will have a new endpoint.

The storage type can be changed when restoring a snapshot.

AMAZON DYNAMODB

GENERAL DYNAMODB CONCEPTS

Amazon DynamoDB is a fully managed NoSQL database service that provides fast and predictable performance with seamless scalability.

Multi-AZ NoSQL data store with Cross-Region Replication option.

Push button scaling means that you can scale the DB at any time without incurring downtime.

Defaults to eventual consistency reads but can request strongly consistent read via SDK parameter.

Priced on throughput, rather than compute.

Provision read and write capacity in anticipation of need.

Autoscale capacity adjusts per configured min/max levels.

On-Demand Capacity provides flexible capacity at a small premium cost.

Can achieve ACID compliance with DynamoDB Transactions.

SSD based and uses limited indexing on attributes for performance.

DynamoDB is a Web service that uses HTTP over SSL (HTTPS) as a transport and JSON as a message serialization format.

Amazon DynamoDB stores three geographically distributed replicas of each table to enable high availability and data durability.

Data is synchronously replicated across 3 facilities (AZs) in a region.

Cross-region replication allows you to replicate across regions:

- Amazon DynamoDB global tables provides a fully managed solution for deploying a multi-region, multi-master database.
- When you create a global table, you specify the AWS regions where you want the table to be available.
- DynamoDB performs all of the necessary tasks to create identical tables in these regions, and propagate ongoing data changes to all of them.

Provides low read and write latency.

Scale storage and throughput up or down as needed without code changes or downtime.

DynamoDB is schema-less.

DynamoDB can be used for storing session state.

Provides two read models.

Eventually consistent reads (Default):

- The eventual consistency option maximises your read throughput (best read performance).
- An eventually consistent read might not reflect the results of a recently completed write.
- Consistency across all copies reached within 1 second.

Strongly consistent reads:

- A strongly consistent read returns a result that reflects all writes that received a successful response prior to the read (faster consistency).

Users/applications reading from DynamoDB tables can specify in their requests if they want strong consistency (default is eventually consistent).

Attributes consists of a name and a value or set of values.

Attributes in DynamoDB are similar to fields or columns in other database systems.

The primary key is the only required attribute for items in a table and it uniquely identifies each item.

A primary key can either be one of the following types.

Partition key:

- A simple primary key composed of one attribute known as the partition key.

Partition key and sort key:

- Referred to as a composite primary key.
- Composed of two attributes: partition key and sort key.

An item is a collection of attributes.

The aggregate size of an item cannot exceed 400KB including keys and all attributes.

Can store pointers to objects in S3, including items over 400KB.

Tables are a collection of items and items are made up of attributes (columns).

Supports key-value and document data structures.

Supports fast, in-place Atomic updates.

Stores structured data in tables, indexed by a primary key.

Supports GET/PUT operations using a user-defined primary key.

DynamoDB provides flexible querying by letting you query on non-primary key attributes using Global Secondary Indexes and Local Secondary Indexes.

You can create one or more secondary indexes on a table.

A *secondary index* lets you query the data in the table using an alternate key, in addition to queries against the primary key.

DynamoDB supports two kinds of secondary indexes:

- Global secondary index – An index with a partition key and sort key that can be different from those on the table.
- Local secondary index – An index that has the same partition key as the table, but a different sort key.

You can search using one of the following methods:

- Query operation – find items in a table or a secondary index using only the primary keys attributes.
- Scan operation – reads every item in a table or a secondary index and by default will return all items.

Use DynamoDB when relational features are not required and the DB is likely to need to scale.

Not ideal for the following situations:

- Traditional RDS apps.
- Joins and/or complex transactions.
- BLOB data.
- Large data with low I/O rate.

DYNAMODB STREAMS

DynamoDB Streams help you to keep a list of item level changes or provide a list of item level changes that have taken place in the last 24hrs.

Amazon DynamoDB is integrated with AWS Lambda so that you can create triggers—pieces of code that automatically respond to events in DynamoDB Streams.

If you enable DynamoDB Streams on a table, you can associate the stream ARN with a Lambda function that you write.

DYNAMO DAX

Amazon DynamoDB Accelerator (DAX) is a fully managed, highly available, in-memory cache for DynamoDB that delivers up to a 10x performance improvement.

Improves performance from milliseconds to microseconds, even at millions of requests per second.

DAX does all the heavy lifting required to add in-memory acceleration to your DynamoDB tables, without requiring developers to manage cache invalidation, data population, or cluster management.

You do not need to modify application logic, since DAX is compatible with existing DynamoDB API calls.

You can enable DAX with just a few clicks in the AWS Management Console or using the AWS SDK.

Just as with DynamoDB, you only pay for the capacity you provision.

Provisioned through clusters and charged by the node (runs on EC2 instances).

Pricing is per node-hour consumed and is dependent on the instance type you select.

The following diagram depicts the Amazon DynamoDB DAX service.

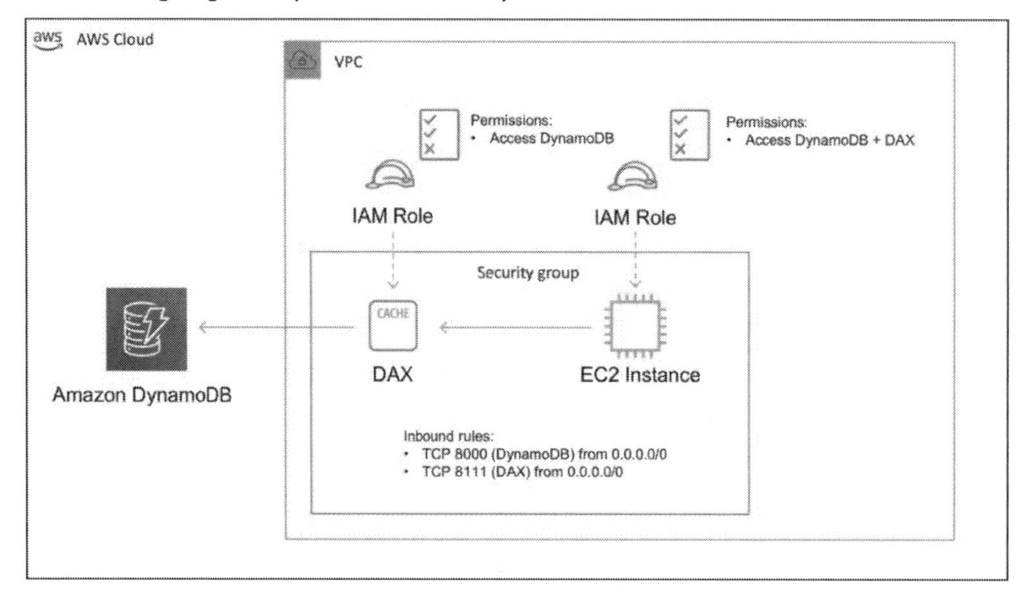

Note the following:

- You can apply an IAM role to the the DAX nodes
- You can apply Security Groups to the DAX nodes
- DynamoDB DAX sits within your VPC

BEST PRACTICES

Keep item sizes small.

If you are storing serial data in DynamoDB that will require actions based on date/time use separate tables for days, weeks, months.

Store more frequently and less frequently accessed data in separate tables.

If possible, compress larger attribute values.

Store objects larger than 400KB in S3 and use pointers (S3 Object ID) in DynamoDB.

INTEGRATIONS

ElastiCache can be used in front of DynamoDB for performance of reads on infrequently changed data.

Triggers integrate with AWS Lambda to respond to triggers.

Integration with RedShift:

- RedShift complements DynamoDB with advanced business intelligence.
- When copying data from a DynamoDB table into RedShift you can perform complex data analysis queries including joins with other tables.

- A copy operation from a DynamoDB table counts against the table's read capacity.
- After data is copied, SQL queries do not affect the data in DynamoDB.

DynamoDB is integrated with Apache Hive on EMR. Hive can allow you to:

- Read and write data in DynamoDB tables allowing you to query DynamoDB data using a SQL-like language (HiveQL).
- Copy data from a DynamoDB table to an S3 bucket and vice versa.
- Copy data from a DynamoDB table into HDFS and vice versa.
- Perform join operations on DynamoDB tables.

SCALABILITY

Push button scaling without downtime.

You can scale down only 4 times per calendar day.

AWS places some default limits on the throughput you can provision.

These are the limits unless you request a higher amount:

	On-Demand	Provisioned
Per table	40,000 read request units and 40,000 write request units	40,000 read capacity units and 40,000 write capacity units
Per account	Not applicable	80,000 read capacity units and 80,000 write capacity units
Minimum throughput for any table or global secondary index	Not applicable	1 read capacity unit and 1 write capacity unit

DynamoDB can throttle requests that exceed the provisioned throughput for a table.

DynamoDB can also throttle read requests for an Index to prevent your application from consuming too many capacity units.

When a request is throttled it fails with an HTTP 400 code (Bad Request) and a ProvisionedThroughputExceeded exception.

CROSS REGION REPLICATION WITH GLOBAL TABLES

Amazon DynamoDB global tables provide a fully managed solution for deploying a multi-region, multi-master database.

When you create a global table, you specify the AWS regions where you want the table to be available.

DynamoDB performs all of the necessary tasks to create identical tables in these regions, and propagate ongoing data changes to all of them.

DynamoDB global tables are ideal for massively scaled applications, with globally dispersed users.

Global tables provide automatic multi-master replication to AWS regions world-wide, so you can deliver low-latency data access to your users no matter where they are located.

Definitions:

- **A *global table*** is a collection of one or more replica tables, all owned by a single AWS account.
- **A *replica table*** (or *replica*, for short) is a single DynamoDB table that functions as a part of a global table. Each replica stores the same set of data items. Any given global table can only have one replica table per region.

The following diagram depicts the **Amazon DynamoDB Global Tables topology:**

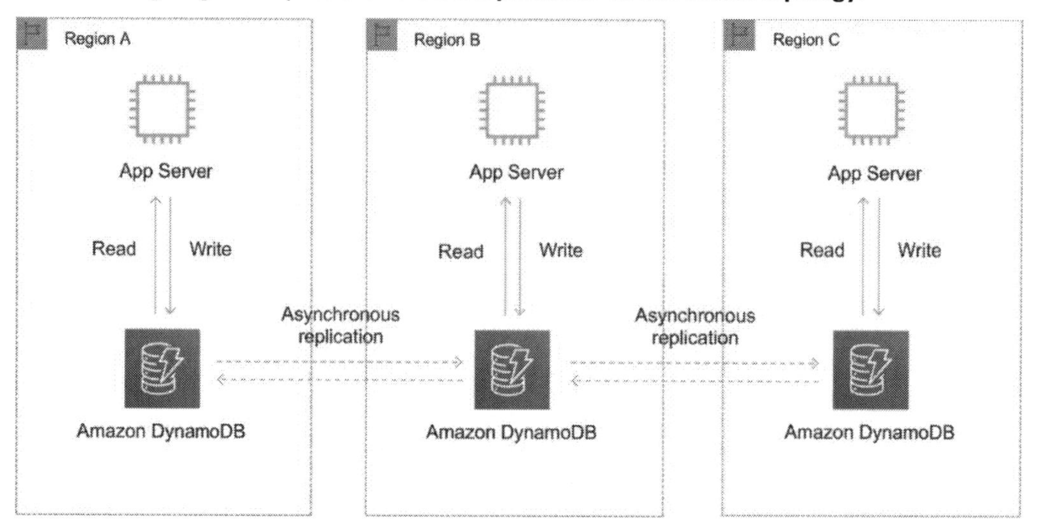

You can add replica tables to the global table, so that it can be available in additional AWS regions.

With a global table, each replica table stores the same set of data items. DynamoDB does not support partial replication of only some of the items.

An application can read and write data to any replica table. If your application only uses eventually consistent reads, and only issues reads against one AWS region, then it will work without any modification.

However, if your application requires strongly consistent reads, then it must perform all of its strongly consistent reads and writes in the same region. DynamoDB does not support strongly consistent reads across AWS regions.

It is important that each replica table and secondary index in your global table has identical write capacity settings to ensure proper replication of data.

DYNAMODB AUTO SCALING

DynamoDB auto scaling uses the AWS Application Auto Scaling service to dynamically adjust provisioned throughput capacity on your behalf, in response to actual traffic patterns.

This enables a table or a global secondary index to increase its provisioned read and write capacity to handle sudden increases in traffic, without throttling.

When the workload decreases, Application Auto Scaling decreases the throughput so that you don't pay for unused provisioned capacity.

How Application Auto Scaling works:

- You create a *scaling policy* for a table or a global secondary index.
- The scaling policy specifies whether you want to scale read capacity or write capacity (or both), and the minimum and maximum provisioned capacity unit settings for the table or index.
- The scaling policy also contains a *target utilization*—the percentage of consumed provisioned throughput at a point in time.
- Uses a *target tracking* algorithm to adjust the provisioned throughput of the table (or index) upward or downward in response to actual workloads, so that the actual capacity utilization remains at or near your target utilization.

Currently, Auto Scaling does not scale down your provisioned capacity if your table's consumed capacity becomes zero.

If you use the AWS Management Console to create a table or a global secondary index, DynamoDB auto scaling is enabled by default.

LIMITS

256 tables per account per region.

No limit on the size of a table.

Read/write capacity unit limits vary per region.

CAPACITY UNITS

One read capacity unit represents one strongly consistent read per second, or two eventually consistent reads per second for items up to 4KB.

For items larger than 4KB, DynamoDB consumes additional read capacity units.

One write capacity unit represents one write per second for an item up to 1KB.

CHARGES

DynamoDB charges for reading, writing, and storing data in your DynamoDB tables, along with any optional features you choose to enable.

There are two pricing models for DynamoDB:

- **On-demand capacity mode:** DynamoDB charges you for the data reads and writes your application performs on your tables. You do not need to specify how much read and write throughput you expect your application to perform because DynamoDB instantly accommodates your workloads as they ramp up or down.
- **Provisioned capacity mode:** you specify the number of reads and writes per second that you expect your application to require. You can use auto scaling to automatically adjust your table's capacity based on the specified utilization rate to ensure application performance while reducing cost.

Additional charges include:

- Data transfer out
- Backups per GB (continuous or on-demand)
- Global Tables

- DynamoDB Accelerator (DAX)
- DynamoDB Streams

HIGH AVAILABILITY APPROACHES FOR DATABASES

If possible, choose DynamoDB over RDS because of inherent fault tolerance.

If DynamoDB can't be used, choose Aurora because of redundancy and automatic recovery features.

If Aurora can't be used, choose Multi-AZ RDS.

Frequent RDS snapshots can protect against data corruption or failure and they won't impact performance of Multi-AZ deployment.

Regional replication is also an option but will not be strongly consistent.

If the database runs on EC2, you have to design the HA yourself.

AMAZON ELASTICACHE

GENERAL ELASTICACHE CONCEPTS

Fully managed implementations of two popular in-memory data stores – Redis and Memcached.

ElastiCache is a web service that makes it easy to deploy and run Memcached or Redis protocol-compliant server nodes in the cloud.

The in-memory caching provided by ElastiCache can be used to significantly improve latency and throughput for many read-heavy application workloads or compute-intensive workloads.

Best for scenarios where the DB load is based on Online Analytics Processing (OLAP) transactions.

Push-button scalability for memory, writes and reads.

In-memory key/value store – not persistent in the traditional sense.

Billed by node size and hours of use.

Elasticache EC2 nodes cannot be accessed from the Internet, nor can they be accessed by EC2 instances in other VPCs.

Cached information may include the results of I/O-intensive database queries or the results of computationally-intensive calculations.

Can be on-demand or reserved instances too (but not Spot instances).

Elasticache can be used for storing session state.

A node is a fixed-sized chunk of secure, network-attached RAM and is the smallest building block.

Each node runs an instance of the Memcached or Redis protocol-compliant service and has its own DNS name and port.

Failed nodes are automatically replaced.

Access to Elasticache nodes is controlled by VPC security groups and subnet groups (when deployed in a VPC).

Subnet groups are a collection of subnets designated for your Amazon ElastiCache Cluster.

You cannot move an existing Amazon ElastiCache Cluster from outside VPC into a VPC.

You need to configure subnet groups for Elasticache for the VPC that hosts the EC2 instances and the Elasticache cluster.

When not using a VPC, Amazon ElastiCache allows you to control access to your clusters through Cache Security Groups (you need to link the corresponding EC2 Security Groups).

Elasticache nodes are deployed in clusters and can span more than one subnet of the same subnet group.

A cluster is a collection of one or more nodes using the same caching engine.

Applications connect to Elasticache clusters using endpoints.

An endpoint is a node or cluster's unique address.

Maintenance windows can be defined and allow software patching to occur.

There are two types of ElastiCache engine:

- Memcached – simplest model, can run large nodes with multiple cores/threads, can be scaled in and out, can cache objects such as DBs.
- Redis – complex model, supports encryption, master / slave replication, cross AZ (HA), automatic failover and backup/restore.

USE CASES

The following table describes a few typical use cases for ElastiCache:

Use Case	Benefit
Web session store	In cases with load-balanced web servers, store web session information in Redis so if a server is lost, the session info is not lost and another web server can pick it up
Database caching	Use Memcached in front of AWS RDS to cache popular queries to offload work from RDS and return results faster to users
Leaderboards	Use Redis to provide a live leaderboard for millions of users of your mobile app
Streaming data dashboards	Provide a landing spot for streaming sensor data on the factory floor, providing live real-time dashboard displays

The table below describes the requirements that would determine whether to use the Memcached or Redis engine:

Memcached	Redis
Simple, no-frills	You need encryption
You need to scale-out and in as demand changes	You need HIPAA compliance
You need to run multiple CPU cores and threads	Support for clustering
You need to cache objects (e.g. database queries)	You need complex data types
	You need HA (replication
	Pub/Sub capability
	Geospacial Indexing
	Backup and restore

MEMCACHED

Not persistent.

Cannot be used as a data store.

Supports large nodes with multiple cores or threads.

Scales out and in, by adding and removing nodes.

Ideal front-end for data stores (RDS, Dynamo DB etc.).

Use cases:

- Cache the contents of a DB.
- Cache data from dynamically generated web pages.
- Transient session data.
- High frequency counters for admission control in high volume web apps.

Max 100 nodes per region, 1-20 nodes per cluster (soft limits).

Can integrate with SNS for node failure/recovery notification.

Supports auto-discovery for nodes added/removed from the cluster.

Scales out/in (horizontally) by adding/removing nodes.

Scales up/down (vertically) by changing the node family/type.

Does not support multi-AZ failover or replication.

Does not support snapshots.

You can place nodes in different AZs.

With ElastiCache Memcached each node represents a partition of data and nodes in a cluster can span availability zones:

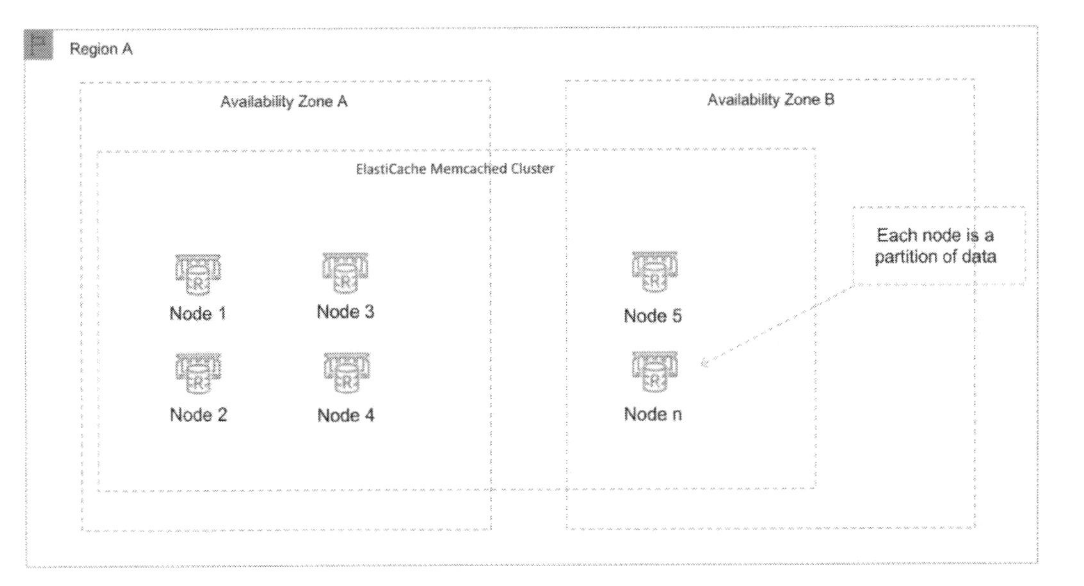

REDIS

Data is persistent.

Can be used as a datastore.

Not multi-threaded.

Scales by adding shards, not nodes.

A Redis shard is a subset of the cluster's keyspace, that can include a primary node and zero or more read-replicas.

Supports automatic and manual snapshots (S3).

Backups include cluster data and metadata.

You can restore your data by creating a new Redis cluster and populating it from a backup.

Supports master/slave replication.

During backup you cannot perform CLI or API operations on the cluster.

Automated backups are enabled by default (automatically deleted with Redis deletion).

You can only move snapshots between regions by exporting them from Elasticache before moving between regions (can then populate a new cluster with data).

Multi-AZ is possible using read replicas in another AZ in the same region.

Clustering mode disabled:

- You can only have one shard.
- One shard can have one read/write primary node and 0-5 read only replicas.
- You can distribute the replicas over multiple AZs in the same region.
- Replication from the primary node is asynchronous.

A Redis cluster with cluster mode disabled is represented in the diagram below:

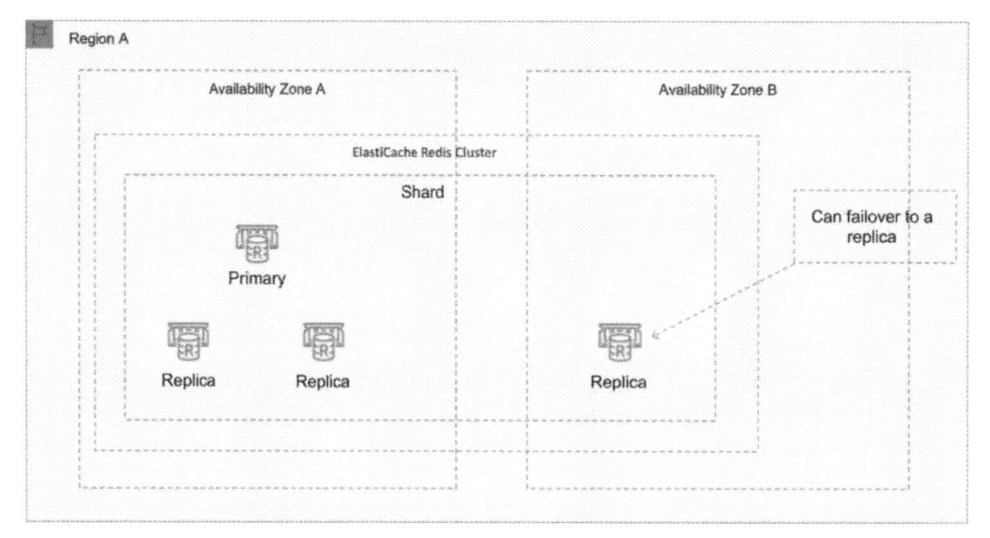

Clustering mode enabled:

- Can have up to 15 shards.
- Each shard can have one primary node and 0-5 read only replicas.
- Taking snapshots can slow down nodes, best to take from the read replicas.

A **Redis cluster with cluster mode enabled** is represented in the diagram below:

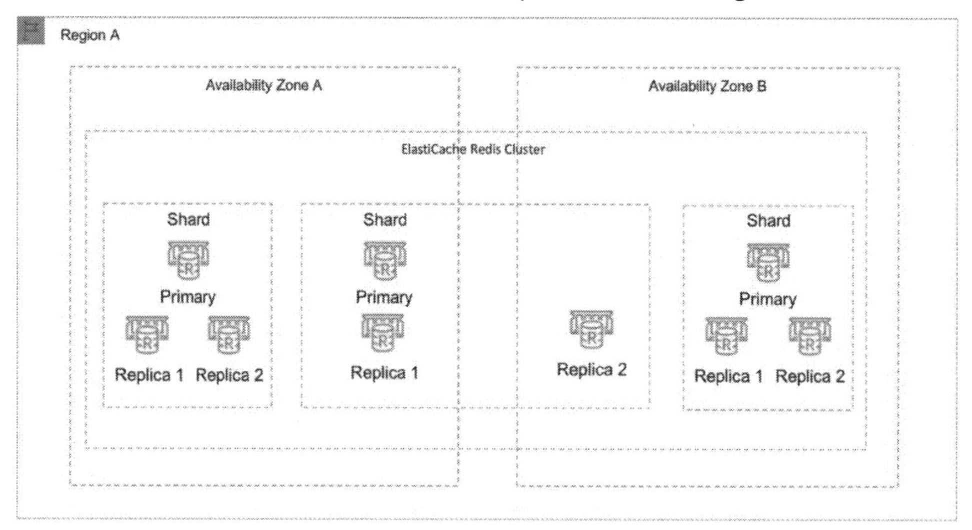

Multi-AZ failover:

- Failures are detected by Elasticache.
- Elasticache automatically promotes the replica that has the lowest replica lag.
- DNS records remain the same but point to the IP of the new primary.
- Other replicas start to sync with the new primary.

You can have a fully automated, fault tolerant Elasticache-Redis implementation by enabling both cluster mode and multi-AZ failover.

The following table compares the Memcached and Redis engines:

	Memcached	Redis (cluster mode disabled)	Redis (cluster mode enabled)
Engine versions	1.4.x	2.8.x and 3.2.x	3.2.x
Data types	Simple	Complex	Complex
Data partitioning	Yes	No	Yes
Cluster is modifiable	Yes	Yes	No
Online re-sharding	No	No	3.2.10
Encryption	No	3.2.6	3.2.6
HIPAA Compliance	No	3.2.6	3.2.6
Multi-threaded	Yes	No	No
Node type upgrade	No	Yes	No
Engine upgrading	Yes	Yes	No
High availability (replication)	No	Yes	Yes
Automatic failover	No	Optional	Required
Pub/Sub capabilities	No	Yes	Yes
Sorted sets	No	Yes	Yes
Backup and restore	No	Yes	Yes
Geospatial indexing	No	Yes	Yes

CHARGES

Pricing is per Node-hour consumed for each Node Type.

Partial Node-hours consumed are billed as full hours.

There is no charge for data transfer between Amazon EC2 and Amazon Elasticache within the same Availability Zone.

HIGH AVAILABILITY FOR ELASTICACHE

Memcached:

- Because Memcached does not support replication, a node failure will result in data loss.
- Use multiple nodes in each shard to minimize data loss on node failure.
- Launch multiple nodes across available AZs to minimize data loss on AZ failure.

Redis:

- Use multiple nodes in each shard and distribute the nodes across multiple AZs.
- Enable Multi-AZ on the replication group to permit automatic failover if the primary nodes fails.
- Schedule regular backups of your Redis cluster.

AMAZON REDSHIFT

GENERAL REDSHIFT CONCEPTS

Amazon Redshift is a fast, fully managed data warehouse that makes it simple and cost-effective to analyze all your data using standard SQL and existing Business Intelligence (BI) tools.

Clustered peta-byte scale data warehouse.

RedShift is a SQL based data warehouse used for **analytics** applications.

RedShift is an Online Analytics Processing (OLAP) type of DB.

RedShift is used for running complex analytic queries against petabytes of structured data, using sophisticated query optimization, columnar storage on high-performance local disks, and massively parallel query execution.

RedShift is ideal for **processing** large amounts of data for business intelligence.

Extremely cost-effective as compared to some other on-premises data warehouse platforms.

PostgreSQL compatible with JDBC and ODBC drivers available; compatible with most Business Intelligence tools out of the box.

Features parallel processing and columnar data stores which are optimized for complex queries.

Option to query directly from data files on S3 via RedShift Spectrum.

RedShift is 10x faster than a traditional SQL DB.

RedShift can store huge amounts of data but cannot ingest huge amounts of data in real time.

RedShift uses columnar data storage:

- Data is stored sequentially in columns instead of rows.
- Columnar based DB is ideal for data warehousing and analytics.
- Requires fewer I/Os which greatly enhances performance.

RedShift provides advanced compression:

- Data is stored sequentially in columns which allows for much better performance and less storage space.
- RedShift automatically selects the compression scheme.

RedShift provides good query performance and compression.

RedShift provides Massively Parallel Processing (MPP) by distributing data and queries across all nodes.

RedShift uses EC2 instances so you need to choose your instance type/size for scaling compute vertically, but you can also scale horizontally by adding more nodes to the cluster.

You cannot have direct access to your AWS RedShift cluster nodes as a user, but you can through applications.

HDD and SSD storage options.

The size of a single node is 160GB and clusters can be created up to a petabyte or more.

Multi-node consists of:

Leader node:

- Manages client connections and receives queries.
- Simple SQL end-point.
- Stores metadata.
- Optimizes query plan.
- Coordinates query execution.

Compute nodes:

- Stores data and performs queries and computations.
- Local columnar storage.
- Parallel/distributed execution of all queries, loads, backups, restores, resizes.
- Up to 128 compute nodes.

Amazon RedShift Spectrum is a feature of Amazon Redshift that enables you to run queries against exabytes of unstructured data in Amazon S3, with no loading or ETL required.

AVAILABILITY AND DURABILITY

RedShift uses replication and continuous backups to enhance availability and improve durability and can automatically recover from component and node failures.

Only available in one AZ but you can restore snapshots into another AZ.

Alternatively, you can run data warehouse clusters in multiple AZ's by loading data into two Amazon Redshift data warehouse clusters in separate AZs from the same set of Amazon S3 input files.

Redshift replicates your data within your data warehouse cluster and continuously backs up your data to Amazon S3.

RedShift always keeps three copies of your data:

- The original
- A replica on compute nodes (within the cluster)
- A backup copy on S3

RedShift provides continuous/incremental backups:

- Multiple copies within a cluster.
- Continuous and incremental backups to S3.
- Continuous and incremental backups across regions.
- Streaming restore.

RedShift provides fault tolerance for the following failures:

- Disk failures.
- Nodes failures.
- Network failures.
- AZ/region level disasters.

For nodes failures the data warehouse cluster will be unavailable for queries and updates until a replacement node is provisioned and added to the DB.

High availability for RedShift:

- Currently, RedShift does not support Multi-AZ deployments.
- The best HA option is to use multi-node cluster which supports data replication and node recovery.
- A single node RedShift cluster does not support data replication and you'll have to restore from a snapshot on S3 if a drive fails.

RedShift can asynchronously replicate your snapshots to S3 in another region for DR.

Single-node clusters do not support data replication (in a failure scenario you would need to restore from a snapshot).

Scaling requires a period of unavailability of a few minutes (typically during the maintenance window).

During scaling operations RedShift moves data in parallel from the compute nodes in your existing data warehouse cluster to the compute nodes in your new cluster.

By default, Amazon Redshift retains backups for 1 day. You can configure this to be as long as 35 days.

If you delete the cluster you can choose to have a final snapshot taken and retained.

Manual backups are not automatically deleted when you delete a cluster.

SECURITY

You can load encrypted data from S3.

Supports SSL Encryption in-transit between client applications and Redshift data warehouse cluster.

VPC for network isolation.

Encryption for data at rest (AES 256).

Audit logging and AWS CloudTrail integration.

RedShift takes care of key management or you can manage your own through HSM or KMS.

CHARGES

Charged for compute nodes hours, 1 unit per hour (only compute node, not leader node).

Backup storage – storage on S3.

Data transfer – no charge for data transfer between RedShift and S3 within a region but for other scenarios you may pay charges.

DATABASE QUIZ QUESTIONS

Answers and explanations are provided below after the last question in this section.

Question 1: An organization is migrating their relational databases to the AWS Cloud. They require full operating system access to install custom operational toolsets. Which AWS service should they use to host their databases?

1. Amazon EC2
2. Amazon RDS
3. Amazon DynamoDB
4. Amazon ElastiCache

Question 2: An organization is migrating databases into the AWS Cloud. They require a managed service for their MySQL database and need automatic failover to a secondary database. Which solution should they use?

1. Amazon RDS with Read Replicas
2. Amazon RDS with Multi-AZ
3. Amazon EC2 with database mirroring
4. Amazon Aurora with Global Database

Question 3: An existing Amazon RDS database needs to be encrypted. How can you enable encryption for an unencrypted Amazon RDS database?

1. Enable encryption through the AWS management console
2. Take an encrypted snapshot of the DB instance and restore the snapshot back to the instance
3. Take an encrypted snapshot of the DB instance and create a new database instance from the snapshot
4. Create a new encrypted RDS database and migrate the data across

Question 4: An Amazon RDS database is experiencing heavy demand and is slowing down. Most database calls are reads. What is the simplest way to scale the database without downtime?

1. Create a Read Replica
2. Change to an instance type with more resources
3. Offload data to DynamoDB

Question 5: A new application requires a database that can allow writes to DB instances in multiple availability zones with read after write consistency. Which solution meets these requirements?

1. Amazon Aurora Global Database
2. Amazon Aurora Replicas

3. Amazon Aurora Cross-Region Replicas
4. Amazon Aurora Multi-Master

Question 6: A customer needs a schema-less database that can seamlessly scale. Which AWS database service would you recommend?

1. Amazon DynamoDB
2. Amazon ElastiCache
3. Amazon RDS
4. Amazon Aurora

Question 7: Which DynamoDB feature integrates with AWS Lambda to automatically execute functions in response to table updates?

1. DynamoDB Global Tables
2. DynamoDB Auto Scaling
3. DynamoDB Streams
4. DynamoDB DAX

Question 8: You need to implement an in-memory caching layer in front of an Amazon RDS database. The caching layer should allow encryption and replication. Which solution meets these requirements?

1. Amazon ElastiCache Memcached
2. Amazon ElastiCache Redis
3. Amazon DynamoDB DAX

Question 9: Which Amazon ElastiCache engine provides data persistence?

1. Redis
2. Memcached

Question 10: Which of the following is a good use case for Amazon RedShift?

1. Schema-less transactional database
2. Relational data warehouse
3. Relational transactional database
4. Analytics using the Hadoop framework

DATABASE - ANSWERS

Question 1, Answer: 1

Explanation:

1 is correct. If you need to access the underlying operating system you must use Amazon EC2 for a relational database.

2 is incorrect. You do not get access to the underlying operating system with Amazon RDS.

3 is incorrect. Amazon DynamoDB is not a relational database; it is a NoSQL type of database.

4 is incorrect. Amazon ElastiCache is an in-memory caching database, it is typically placed in front of other databases. It also does not provide access to the underlying operating system.

Question 2, Answer: 2

Explanation:

1 is incorrect. A read replica will not provide automatic failover.

2 is correct. RDS Multi-AZ does provide automatic failover to a secondary database.

3 is incorrect. Amazon EC2 is not a managed service.

4 is incorrect. Amazon Aurora with Global Database is used for replicating a database across multiple regions.

Question 3, Answer: 3

Explanation:

1 is incorrect. You cannot enable encryption for an existing database.

2 is incorrect. You cannot restore the encrypted snapshot to the existing database instance.

3 is correct. You need to take an encrypted snapshot and then create a new database instance from the snapshot.

4 is incorrect. This is not the most efficient method as it involves manual copying of data.

Question 4, Answer: 1

Explanation:

1 is correct. A read replica is an easy way to quickly scale read traffic. You just need to update your application to direct reads to the replica endpoint.

2 is incorrect. This requires downtime when you change instance types.

3 is incorrect. You cannot offload data from Amazon RDS to DynamoDB.

Question 5, Answer: 4

Explanation:

1 is incorrect. Aurora Global Database spans multiple regions for disaster recovery.

2 is incorrect. Aurora Replicas scale read operations but do not allow writes to multiple DB instances.

3 is incorrect. Aurora Cross-Region Replicase scale read operations across regions. They do not allow writes to DB instances in multiple AZs.

4 is correct. Amazon Aurora Multi-Master adds the ability to scale out write performance across multiple Availability Zones and provides configurable read after write consistency.

Question 6, Answer: 1

Explanation:

1 is correct. DynamoDB is a schema-less NoSQL database that provides push-button scaling.

2 is incorrect. ElastiCache is an in-memory relational database so it is not schema-less.

3 is incorrect. Amazon RDS is a relational database (not schema-less) and uses EC2 instances so does not offer push-button scaling.

4 is incorrect. Amazon Aurora is a relational database (not schema-less) and uses EC2 instances so does not offer push-button scaling.

Question 7, Answer: 3

Explanation:

1 is incorrect. DynamoDB Global Tables provides a multi-region, multi-master database solution.

2 is incorrect. DynamoDB Auto Scaling is for scaling read and write capacity.

3 is correct. DynamoDB Streams maintains a list of item level changes and can integrate with Lambda to create triggers.

4 is incorrect. DynamoDB DAX provide microsecond latency for read requests to DynamoDB tables.

Question 8, Answer: 2

Explanation:

1 is incorrect. Memcached does not provide encryption or replication.

2 is correct. Redis provides encryption and replication.

3 is incorrect. DynamoDB DAX works with DynamoDB not Amazon RDS.

Question 9, Answer: 1

Explanation:

1 is correct. Redis provides data persistence.

2 is incorrect. Memcached does not provide data persistence.

Question 10, Answer: 2

Explanation:

1 is incorrect. RedShift is not a schema-less database, it is a relational database.

2 is correct. RedShift is a data warehouse optimized for online analytics processing (OLAP).

3 is incorrect. RedShift is optimized for online analytics processing (OLAP) use cases not online transactional processing (OLTP) use cases.

4 is incorrect. RedShift can be analyzed using SQL not Hadoop (should use EMR).

MIGRATION

AWS SNOWBALL

GENERAL

Petabyte scale data transport solution for transferring data into or out of AWS.

Uses a secure storage device for physical transportation.

AWS Snowball Client is software that is installed on a local computer and is used to identify, compress, encrypt, and transfer data.

Uses 256-bit encryption (managed with the AWS KMS) and tamper-resistant enclosures with TPM.

Snowball must be ordered from and returned to the same region.

To speed up data transfer it is recommended to run simultaneous instances of the AWS Snowball Client in multiple terminals and transfer small files as batches.

Snowball can import to S3 or export from S3.

THE SNOWBALL FAMILY

Several services are offered in the Snowball family.

The table below describes these at a high-level:

Service	What it Is
AWS Import/Export	Ship an external hard drive to AWS. Someone at AWS plugs it in and copies your data to S3
AWS Snowball	Ruggedized NAS in a box that AWS ships to you. You can copy up to 80TB of data and ship it back to AWS. They copy the data over to S3
AWS Snowball Edge	Same as Snowball, but with onboard Lambda and clustering
AWS Snowmobile	A literal shipping container full of storage (up to 100PB) and a truck to transport it

Snowball (80TB) (50TB model available only in the USA).

Snowball Edge (100TB) comes with onboard storage and compute capabilities.

Snowmobile – exabyte scale with up to 100PB per Snowmobile.

AWS Import/export is when you send your own disks into AWS – this is being deprecated in favour of Snowball.

AWS DATABASE MIGRATION SERVICE

AWS Database Migration Service helps you migrate databases to AWS quickly and securely.

The source database remains fully operational during the migration, minimizing downtime to applications that rely on the database.

The AWS Database Migration Service can migrate your data to and from most widely used commercial and open-source databases.

Supported migration paths include:

- On-premises and EC2 databases to Amazon RDS or Amazon Aurora.
- Homogeneous migrations such as Oracle to Oracle.
- Heterogeneous migrations between different database platforms, such as Oracle or Microsoft SQL Server to Amazon Aurora.

With AWS Database Migration Service, you can continuously replicate your data with high availability and consolidate databases into a petabyte-scale data warehouse by streaming data to Amazon Redshift and Amazon S3.

When migrating databases to Amazon Aurora, Amazon Redshift, Amazon DynamoDB or Amazon DocumentDB (with MongoDB compatibility) you can use DMS free for six months.

Use along with the Schema Conversion Tool (SCT) to migrate databases to AWS RDS or EC2-based databases.

The source database remains fully operational during the migration, minimizing downtime to applications that rely on the database.

The AWS Database Migration Service can migrate your data to and from most widely used commercial and open-source databases.

Schema Conversion Tool can copy database schemas for homogenous migrations (same database) and convert schemas for heterogeneous migrations (different database).

DMS is used for smaller, simpler conversions and also supports MongoDB and DynamoDB.

SCT is used for larger, more complex datasets like data warehouses.

DMS has replication functions for on-premise to AWS or to Snowball or S3.

AWS DATASYNC

AWS DataSync makes it simple and fast to move large amounts of data online between on-premises storage and Amazon S3 or Amazon Elastic File System (Amazon EFS).

Manual tasks related to data transfers can slow down migrations and burden IT operations.

DataSync eliminates or automatically handles many of these tasks, including scripting copy jobs, scheduling and monitoring transfers, validating data, and optimizing network utilization.

The DataSync software agent connects to your Network File System (NFS) and Server Message Block (SMB) storage, so you don't have to modify your applications.

DataSync can transfer hundreds of terabytes and millions of files over the internet or AWS Direct Connect links.

You can use DataSync to migrate active data sets or archives to AWS, transfer data to the cloud for timely analysis and processing, or replicate data to AWS for business continuity.

DataSync can copy data between Network File System (NFS) or Server Message Block (SMB) file servers, all Amazon Simple Storage Service (Amazon S3) storage classes, and Amazon Elastic File System (Amazon EFS) file systems.

All data is encrypted in transit with Transport Layer Security (TLS).

DataSync supports using default encryption for S3 buckets using Amazon S3-Managed Encryption Keys (SSE-S3), and Amazon EFS file system encryption of data at rest.

Task scheduling enables you to configure periodically executing a task, to detect and copy changes from your source storage system to the destination.

You can schedule your tasks using the AWS DataSync Console or AWS Command Line Interface (CLI), without needing to write and run scripts to manage repeated transfers.

The DataSync agent connects to your existing storage systems using the industry-standard NFS and SMB protocols.

The agent transfers data rapidly and deposits it your designated Amazon S3 bucket or Amazon EFS file system.

When copying data to Amazon S3, DataSync automatically converts each file to be a single S3 object in a 1:1 relationship and preserves POSIX metadata as Amazon S3 object metadata.

When you copy objects that contain file system metadata back to file formats, the original file metadata that DataSync copied to S3 is restored.

Similarly, when Amazon EFS is the destination for your data, DataSync preserves existing directory structures and file metadata.

DataSync supports VPC endpoints (powered by AWS PrivateLink) in order to move files directly into your Amazon VPC.

MIGRATION QUIZ QUESTION

Question 1:

The financial institution you are working for stores large amounts of historical transaction records. There are over 25TB of records and your manager has decided to move them into the AWS Cloud. You are planning to use Snowball as copying the data would take too long. Which of the statements below are true regarding Snowball? (choose 2)

A. Snowball can import to S3 but cannot export from S3

B. Uses a secure storage device for physical transportation

C. Can be used with multipart upload

D. Petabyte scale data transport solution for transferring data into or out of AWS

E. Snowball can be used for migration on-premise to on-premise

Question 1 answer: B,D

Explanation:

Snowball is a petabyte scale data transport solution for transferring data into or out of AWS. It uses a secure storage device for physical transportation.

The AWS Snowball Client is software that is installed on a local computer and is used to identify, compress, encrypt, and transfer data. It uses 256-bit encryption (managed with the AWS KMS) and tamper-resistant enclosures with TPM.

Snowball can import to S3 or export from S3.

Snowball cannot be used with multipart upload.

You cannot use Snowball for migration between on-premise data centers.

NETWORKING AND CONTENT DELIVERY

AMAZON VPC

GENERAL

Amazon VPC lets you provision a logically isolated section of the Amazon Web Services (AWS) cloud where you can launch AWS resources in a virtual network that you define.

Analogous to having your own DC inside AWS.

Provides complete control over the virtual networking environment including selection of IP ranges, creation of subnets, and configuration of route tables and gateways.

A VPC is logically isolated from other VPCs on AWS.

Possible to connect the corporate data center to a VPC using a hardware VPN (site-to-site).

VPCs are region wide.

A default VPC is created in each region with a subnet in each AZ.

By default, you can create up to 5 VPCs per region.

You can define dedicated tenancy for a VPC to ensure instances are launched on dedicated hardware (overrides the configuration specified at launch).

A default VPC is automatically created for each AWS account the first time Amazon EC2 resources are provisioned.

The default VPC has all-public subnets.

Public subnets are subnets that have:

- "Auto-assign public IPv4 address" set to "Yes".
- The subnet route table has an attached Internet Gateway.

Instances in the default VPC always have both a public and private IP address.

AZs names are mapped to different zones for different users (i.e. the AZ "ap-southeast-2a" may map to a different physical zone for a different user).

Components of a VPC:

- **A Virtual Private Cloud:** A logically isolated virtual network in the AWS cloud. You define a VPC's IP address space from ranges you select.
- **Subnet:** A segment of a VPC's IP address range where you can place groups of isolated resources (maps to an AZ, 1:1).
- **Internet Gateway:** The Amazon VPC side of a connection to the public Internet.
- **NAT Gateway:** A highly available, managed Network Address Translation (NAT) service for your resources in a private subnet to access the Internet.
- **Hardware VPN Connection:** A hardware-based VPN connection between your Amazon VPC and your datacenter, home network, or co-location facility.
- **Virtual Private Gateway:** The Amazon VPC side of a VPN connection.
- **Customer Gateway:** Your side of a VPN connection.

- **Router:** Routers interconnect subnets and direct traffic between Internet gateways, virtual private gateways, NAT gateways, and subnets.
- **Peering Connection:** A peering connection enables you to route traffic via private IP addresses between two peered VPCs.
- **VPC Endpoints:** Enables private connectivity to services hosted in AWS, from within your VPC without using an an Internet Gateway, VPN, Network Address Translation (NAT) devices, or firewall proxies.
- **Egress-only Internet Gateway:** A stateful gateway to provide egress only access for IPv6 traffic from the VPC to the Internet.

Options for connecting to a VPC are:

- Hardware based VPN
- Direct Connect
- VPN CloudHub
- Software VPN

ROUTING

The VPC router performs routing between AZs within a region.

The VPC router connects different AZs together and connects the VPC to the Internet Gateway.

Each subnet has a route table the router uses to forward traffic within the VPC.

Route tables also have entries to external destinations.

Up to 200 route tables per VPC.

Up to 50 route entries per route table.

Each subnet can only be associated with one route table.

Can assign one route table to multiple subnets.

If no route table is specified a subnet will be assigned to the main route table at creation time.

Cannot delete the main route table.

You can manually set another route table to become the main route table.

There is a default rule that allows all VPC subnets to communicate with one another – this cannot be deleted or modified.

Routing between subnets is always possible because of this rule – any problems communicating is more likely to be security groups or NACLs.

SUBNETS AND SUBNET SIZING

Types of subnet:

- If a subnet's traffic is routed to an internet gateway, the subnet is known as a **public subnet.**
- If a subnet doesn't have a route to the internet gateway, the subnet is known as a **private subnet.**

- If a subnet doesn't have a route to the internet gateway, but has its traffic routed to a virtual private gateway for a VPN connection, the subnet is known as a **VPN-only subnet.**

The VPC is created with a master address range (CIDR block, can be anywhere from 16-28 bits), and subnet ranges are created within that range.

New subnets are always associated with the default route table.

Once the VPC is created you cannot change the CIDR block.

You cannot create additional CIDR blocks that overlap with existing CIDR blocks.

You cannot create additional CIDR blocks in a different RFC 1918 range.

Subnets with overlapping IP address ranges cannot be created.

The first 4 and last 1 IP addresses in a subnet are reserved.

Subnets are created within availability zones (AZs).

Each subnet must reside entirely within one Availability Zone and cannot span zones.

Availability Zones are distinct locations that are engineered to be isolated from failures in other Availability Zones.

Availability Zones are connected with low latency, high throughput, and highly redundant networking.

Can create private, public or VPN subnets.

Subnets map 1:1 to AZs and cannot span AZs.

You can only attach one Internet gateway to a custom VPC.

IPv6 addresses are all public and the range is allocated by AWS.

INTERNET GATEWAYS

An Internet Gateway is a horizontally scaled, redundant, and highly available VPC component that allows communication between instances in your VPC and the internet.

An Internet Gateway serves two purposes: .

- To provide a target in your VPC route tables for internet-routable traffic.
- To perform network address translation (NAT) for instances that have been assigned public IPv4 addresses.

Internet Gateways (IGW) must be created and then attached to a VPC, be added to a route table, and then associated with the relevant subnet(s).

No availability risk or bandwidth constraints.

If your subnet is associated with a route to the Internet, then it is a public subnet.

You cannot have multiple Internet Gateways in a VPC.

IGW is horizontally scaled, redundant and HA.

IGW performs NAT between private and public IPv4 addresses.

IGW supports IPv4 and IPv6.

IGWs must be detached before they can be deleted.

Can only attach 1 IGW to a VPC at a time.

Gateway terminology:

- Internet gateway (IGW) – AWS VPC side of the connection to the public Internet.
- Virtual private gateway (VPG) – VPC endpoint on the AWS side.
- Customer gateway (CGW) – representation of the customer end of the connection.

To enable access to or from the Internet for instances in a VPC subnet, you must do the following:

- Attach an Internet Gateway to your VPC.
- Ensure that your subnet's route table points to the Internet Gateway (see below).
- Ensure that instances in your subnet have a globally unique IP address (public IPv4 address, Elastic IP address, or IPv6 address).
- Ensure that your network access control and security group rules allow the relevant traffic to flow to and from your instance.

Must update subnet route table to point to IGW, either:

- To all destinations, e.g. 0.0.0.0/0 for IPv4 or ::/0for IPv6.
- To specific public IPv4 addresses, e.g. your company's public endpoints outside of AWS.

Egress-only Internet Gateway:

- Provides outbound Internet access for IPv6 addressed instances.
- Prevents inbound access to those IPv6 instances.
- IPv6 addresses are globally unique and are therefore public by default.
- Stateful – forwards traffic from instance to Internet and then sends back the response.
- Must create a custom route for ::/0 to the Egress-Only Internet Gateway.
- Use Egress-Only Internet Gateway instead of NAT for IPv6.

VPC WIZARD

VPC with a Single Public Subnet:

- Your instances run in a private, isolated section of the AWS cloud with direct access to the Internet.
- Network access control lists and security groups can be used to provide strict control over inbound and outbound network traffic to your instances.
- Creates a /16 network with a /24 subnet. Public subnet instances use Elastic IPs or Public IPs to access the Internet.

VPC with Public and Private Subnets:

- In addition to containing a public subnet, this configuration adds a private subnet whose instances are not addressable from the Internet.
- Instances in the private subnet can establish outbound connections to the Internet via the public subnet using Network Address Translation (NAT).
- Creates a /16 network with two /24 subnets.
- Public subnet instances use Elastic IPs to access the Internet.
- Private subnet instances access the Internet via Network Address Translation (NAT).

VPC with Public and Private Subnets and Hardware VPN Access:

- This configuration adds an IPsec Virtual Private Network (VPN) connection between your Amazon VPC and your data center – effectively extending your data center to the cloud while also providing direct access to the Internet for public subnet instances in your Amazon VPC.
- Creates a /16 network with two /24 subnets.
- One subnet is directly connected to the Internet while the other subnet is connected to your corporate network via an IPsec VPN tunnel.

VPC with a Private Subnet Only and Hardware VPN Access:

- Your instances run in a private, isolated section of the AWS cloud with a private subnet whose instances are not addressable from the Internet.
- You can connect this private subnet to your corporate data center via an IPsec Virtual Private Network (VPN) tunnel.
- Creates a /16 network with a /24 subnet and provisions an IPsec VPN tunnel between your Amazon VPC and your corporate network.

NAT INSTANCES

NAT instances are managed **by** you.

Used to enable private subnet instances to access the Internet.

NAT instance must live on a public subnet with a route to an Internet Gateway.

Private instances in private subnets must have a route to the NAT instance, usually the default route destination of 0.0.0.0/0.

When creating NAT instances always disable the source/destination check on the instance.

NAT instances must be in a single public subnet.

NAT instances need to be assigned to security groups.

Security groups for NAT instances must allow HTTP/HTTPS inbound from the private subnet and outbound to 0.0.0.0/0.

There needs to be a route from a private subnet to the NAT instance for it to work.

The amount of traffic a NAT instance can support is based on the instance type.

Using a NAT instance can lead to bottlenecks (not HA).

HA can be achieved by using Auto Scaling groups, multiple subnets in different AZ's and a script to automate failover.

Performance is dependent on instance size.

Can scale up instance size or use enhanced networking.

Can scale out by using multiple NATs in multiple subnets.

Can use as a bastion (jump) host.

Can monitor traffic metrics.

Not supported for IPv6 (use Egress-Only Internet Gateway).

NAT GATEWAYS

NAT gateways are managed **for** you by AWS.

Fully-managed NAT service that replaces the need for NAT instances on EC2.

Must be created in a public subnet.

Uses an Elastic IP address for the public IP.

Private instances in private subnets must have a route to the NAT instance, usually the default route destination of 0.0.0.0/0.

Created in a specified AZ with redundancy in that zone.

For multi-AZ redundancy, create NAT Gateways in each AZ with routes for private subnets to use the local gateway.

Up to 5 Gbps bandwidth that can scale up to 45 Gbps.

Can't use a NAT Gateway to access VPC peering, VPN or Direct Connect, so be sure to include specific routes to those in your route table.

NAT gateways are highly available in each AZ into which they are deployed.

They are preferred by enterprises.

No need to patch.

Not associated with any security groups.

Automatically assigned a public IP address.

Remember to update route tables and point towards your gateway.

More secure (e.g. you cannot access with SSH and there are no security groups to maintain).

No need to disable source/destination checks.

Egress only Internet gateways operate on IPv6 whereas NAT gateways operate on IPv4.

Port forwarding is not supported.

Using the NAT Gateway as a Bastion host server is not supported.

Traffic metrics are not supported.

The table below highlights the key differences between both types of gateway:

	NAT Gateway	NAT Instance
Managed	Managed by AWS	Managed by you
Availability	Highly available within an AZ	Not highly available (would require scripting)
Bandwidth	Up to 45 Gbps	Depends on the bandwidth of the EC2 instance type selected
Maintenance	Managed by AWS	Managed by you
Performance	Optimized for NAT	Amazon Linux AMI configured to perform NAT
Public IP	Elastic IP that cannot be detached	Elastic IP that can be detached
Security Groups	Cannot associate with a Security Group	Can associate with a Security Group
Bastion Host	Not supported	Can be used as a bastion host

SECURITY GROUPS

Security groups act like a firewall at the instance level.

Specifically, security groups operate at the network interface level.

Can only assign permit rules in a security group, cannot assign deny rules.

There is an implicit deny rule at the end of the security group.

All rules are evaluated until a permit is encountered or continues until the implicit deny.

Can control ingress and egress traffic.

Security groups are stateful.

By default, custom security groups do not have inbound allow rules (all inbound traffic is denied by default).

By default, default security groups do have inbound allow rules (allowing traffic from within the group).

All outbound traffic is allowed by default in custom and default security groups.

You cannot delete the security group that's created by default within a VPC.

You can use security group names as the source or destination in other security groups.

You can use the security group name as a source in its own inbound rules.

Security group members can be within any AZ or subnet within the VPC.

Security group membership can be changed whilst instances are running.

Any changes made will take effect immediately.

Up to 5 security groups can be added per EC2 instance interface.

There is no limit on the number of EC2 instances within a security group.

You cannot block specific IP addresses using security groups, use NACLs instead.

NETWORK ACL'S

Network ACL's function at the subnet level.

The VPC router hosts the network ACL function.

With NACLs you can have permit and deny rules.

Network ACLs contain a numbered list of rules that are evaluated in order from the lowest number until the explicit deny.

Recommended to leave spacing between network ACL numbers.

Network ACLs have separate inbound and outbound rules and each rule can allow or deny traffic.

Network ACLs are stateless, so responses are subject to the rules for the direction of traffic.

NACLs only apply to traffic that is ingress or egress to the subnet not to traffic within the subnet.

A VPC automatically comes with a default network ACL which allows all inbound/outbound traffic.

A custom NACL denies all traffic both inbound and outbound by default.

All subnets must be associated with a network ACL.

You can create custom network ACL's. By default, each custom network ACL denies all inbound and outbound traffic until you add rules.

Each subnet in your VPC must be associated with a network ACL. If you don't do this manually it will be associated with the default network ACL.

You can associate a network ACL with multiple subnets; however, a subnet can only be associated with one network ACL at a time.

Network ACLs do not filter traffic between instances in the same subnet.

NACLs are the preferred option for blocking specific IPs or ranges.

Security groups cannot be used to block specific ranges of IPs.

NACL is the first line of defense, the security group is the second line.

Also recommended to have software firewalls installed on your instances.

Changes to NACLs take effect immediately.

Security Group	Network ACL
Operates at the instance (interface) level	Operates at the subnet level
Supports allow rules only	Supports allow and deny rules
Stateful	Stateless
Evaluates all rules	Processes rules in order
Applies to an instance only if associated with a group	Automatically applies to all instances in the subnets its associated with

VPC CONNECTIVITY

There are several **methods of connecting to a VPC**. These include:

- AWS Managed VPN
- AWS Direct Connect
- AWS Direct Connect plus a VPN
- AWS VPN CloudHub
- Software VPN
- Transit VPC
- VPC Peering
- AWS PrivateLink
- VPC Endpoints

Each of these will be further detailed below.

AWS MANAGED VPN

What	AWS Managed IPSec VPN Connection over your existing Internet
When	Quick and usually simple way to establish a secure tunnelled connection to a VPC; redundant link for Direct Connect or other VPC VPN
Pros	Supports static routes or BGP peering and routing
Cons	Dependent on your Internet connection
How	Create a Virtual Private Gateway (VPG) on AWS, and a Customer Gateway on the on-premises side

VPNs are quick, easy to deploy, and cost effective.

A Virtual Private Gateway (VGW) is required on the AWS side.

A Customer Gateway is required on the customer side.

The diagram below depicts an AWS Managed VPN configuration:

AWS Managed VPN

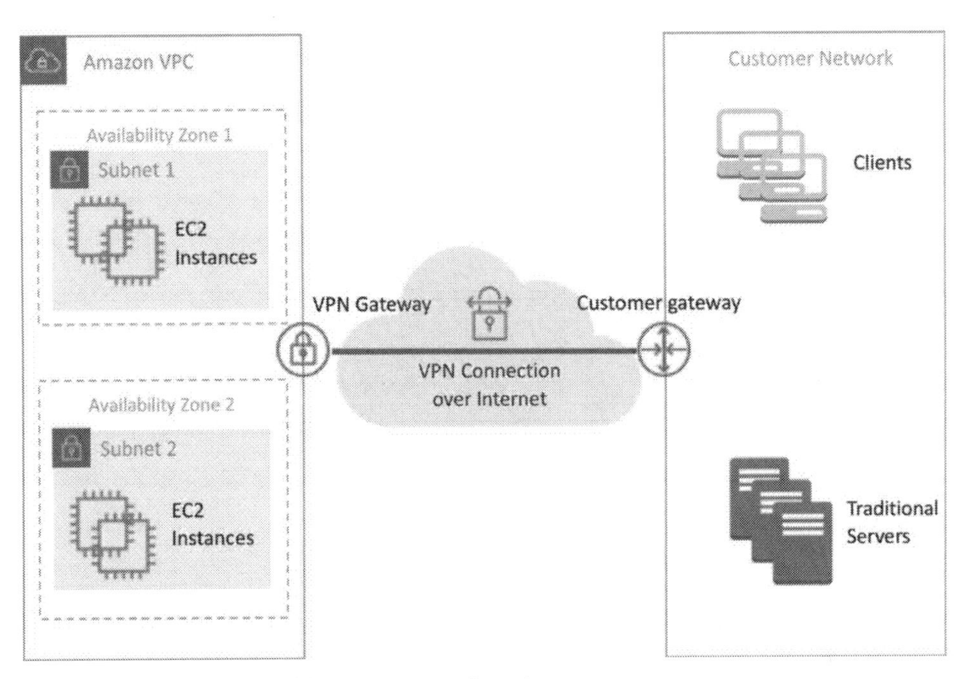

An Internet routable IP address is required on the customer gateway.

Two tunnels per connection must be configured for redundancy.

You cannot use a NAT gateway in AWS for clients coming in via a VPN.

For route propagation you need to point your VPN-only subnet's route tables at the VGW.

Must define the IP prefixes that can send/receive traffic through the VGW.

VGW does not route traffic destined outside of the received BGP advertisements, static route entries, or its attached VPC CIDR.

Cannot access Elastic IPs on your VPC via the VPN – Elastic IPs can only be connected to via the Internet.

AWS DIRECT CONNECT

What	Dedicated network connection over private lines straight into the AWS backbone
When	Requires a large network link into AWS; lots of resources and services being provided on AWS to your corporate users
Pros	More predictable network performance; potential bandwidth cost reduction; up to 10 Gbps provisioned connections; supports BGP peering and routing
Cons	May require additional telecom and hosting provider relationships and/or network circuits; costly
How	Work with your existing data networking provider; create Virtual Interfaces (VIFs) to connect to VPCs (private VIFs) or other AWS services like S3 or Glacier (public VIFs)

AWS Direct Connect makes it easy to establish a dedicated connection from an on-premises network to Amazon VPC.

Using AWS Direct Connect, you can establish private connectivity between AWS and your data center, office, or collocated environment.

This private connection can reduce network costs, increase bandwidth throughput, and provide a more consistent network experience than internet-based connections.

AWS Direct Connect lets you establish 1 Gbps or 10 Gbps dedicated network connections (or multiple connections) between AWS networks and one of the AWS Direct Connect locations.

It uses industry-standard VLANs to access Amazon Elastic Compute Cloud (Amazon EC2) instances running within an Amazon VPC using private IP addresses.

AWS Direct Connect does not encrypt your traffic that is in transit.

You can use the encryption options for the services that traverse AWS Direct Connect.

The diagram below depicts an AWS Direct Connect configuration:

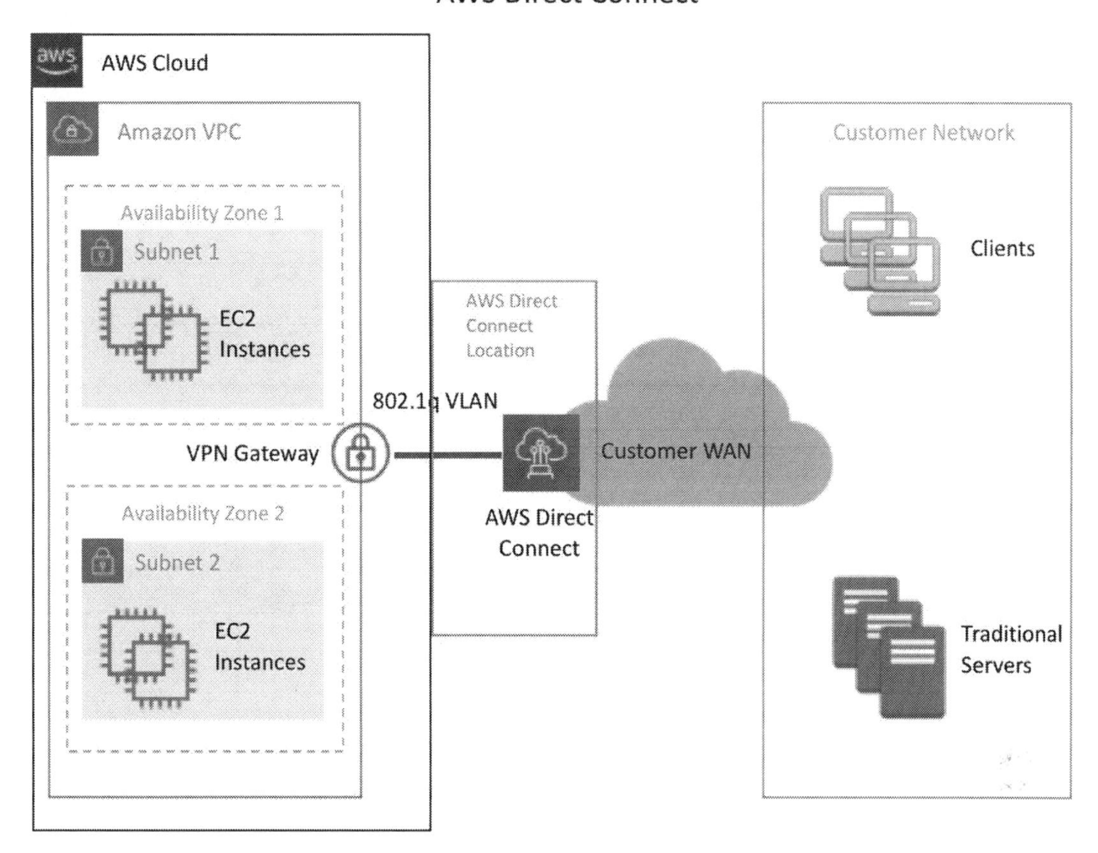

AWS DIRECT CONNECT PLUS VPN

What	IPSec VPN connection over private lines (Direct Connect)
When	Need the added security of encrypted tunnels over Direct Connect
Pros	More secure (in theory) than Direct Connect alone
Cons	More complexity introduced by VPN layer
How	Work with your existing data networking provider

With AWS Direct Connect plus VPN, you can combine one or more AWS Direct Connect dedicated network connections with the Amazon VPC VPN.

This combination provides an IPsec-encrypted private connection that also reduces network costs, increases bandwidth throughput, and provides a more consistent network experience than internet-based VPN connections.

You can use AWS Direct Connect to establish a dedicated network connection between your network create a logical connection to public AWS resources, such as an Amazon virtual private gateway IPsec endpoint.

This solution combines the AWS managed benefits of the VPN solution with low latency, increased bandwidth, more consistent benefits of the AWS Direct Connect solution, and an end-to-end, secure IPsec connection.

The diagram below depicts an AWS Direct Connect plus VPN configuration:

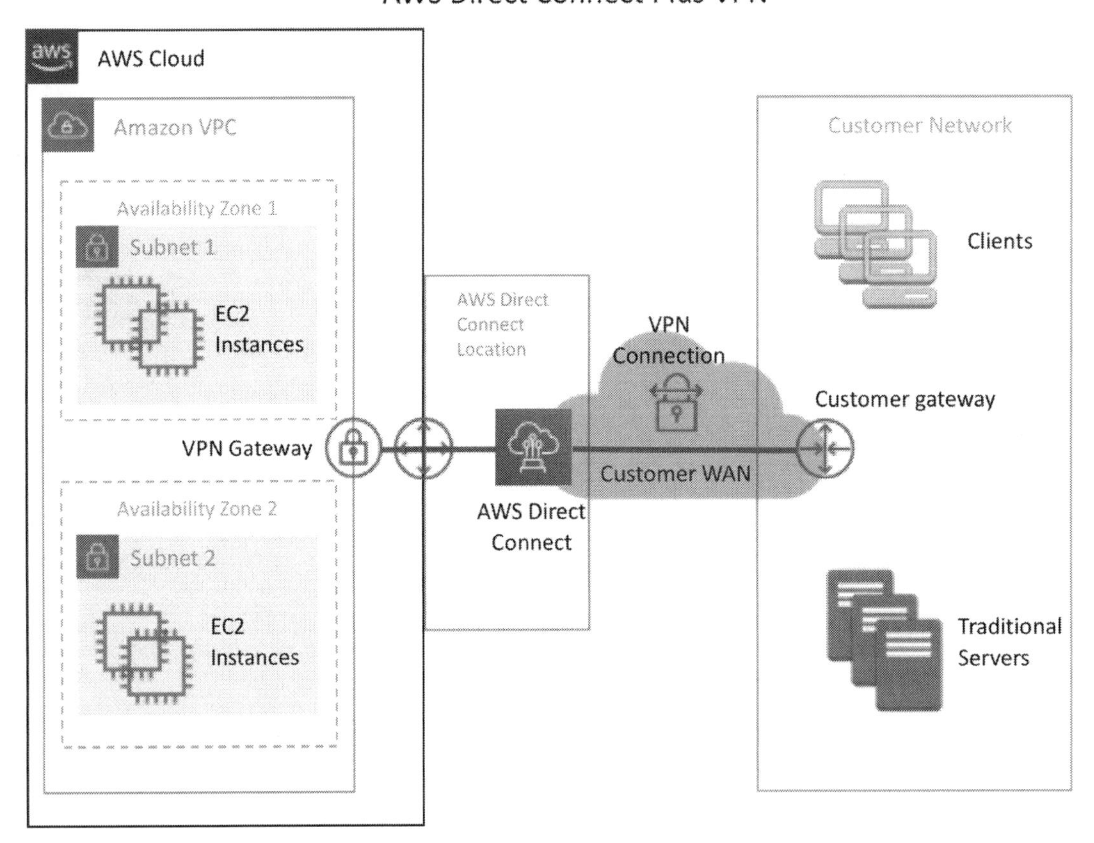

AWS VPN CLOUDHUB

What	Connect locations in a hub and spoke manner using AWSs Virtual Private Gateway
When	Link remote offices for backup or primary WAN access to AWS resources and each other
Pros	Reuses existing Internet connections; supports BGP routes to direct traffic
Cons	Dependent on Internet connection; no inherent redundancy
How	Assign multiple Customer Gateways to a Virtual Private Gateway, each with their own BGP ASN and unique IP ranges

The AWS VPN CloudHub operates on a simple hub-and-spoke model that you can use with or without a VPC.

Use this design if you have multiple branch offices and existing internet connections and would like to implement a convenient, potentially low-cost hub-and-spoke model for primary or backup connectivity between these remote offices.

VPN CloudHub is used for hardware-based VPNs and allows you to configure your branch offices to go into a VPC and then connect that to the corporate DC (hub and spoke topology with AWS as the hub).

Can have up to 10 IPSec tunnels on a VGW by default.

Uses eBGP.

Branches can talk to each other (and provides redundancy).

Can have Direct Connect connections.

Hourly rates plus data egress charges.

The diagram below depicts an AWS VPN CloudHub configuration:

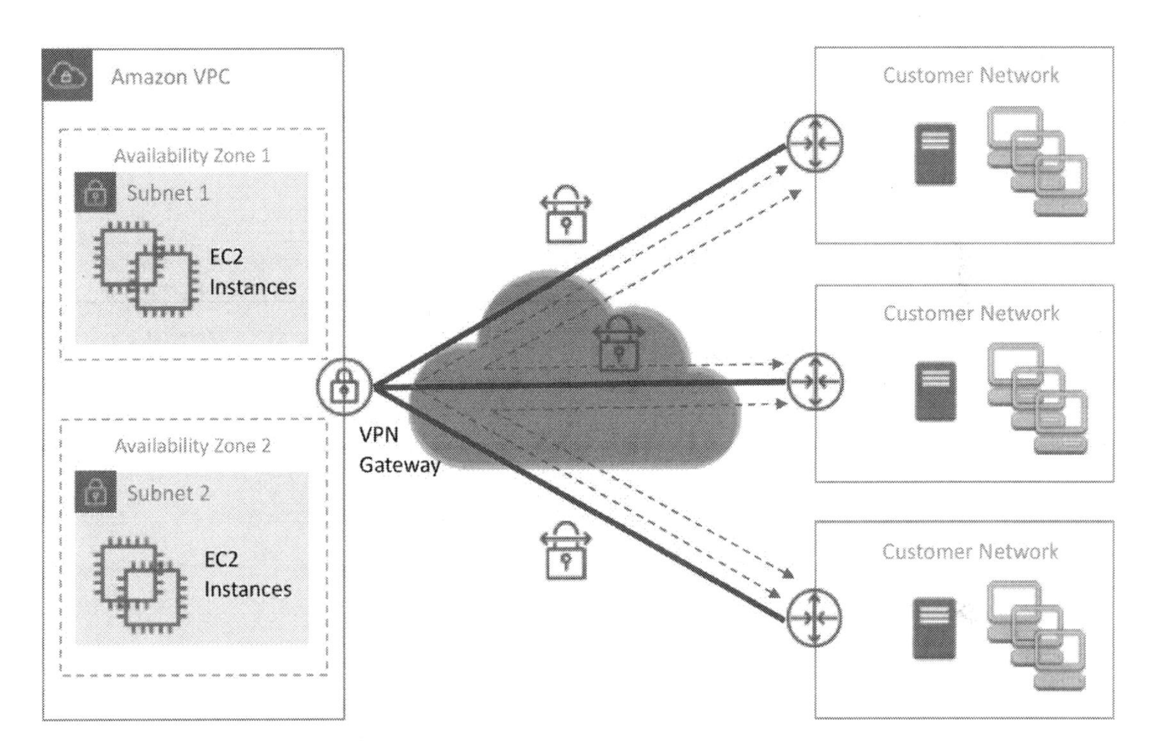

SOFTWARE VPN

What	You provide your own VPN endpoint and software
When	You must manage both ends of the VPN connection for compliance reasons or you want to use a VPN option not supported by AWS
Pros	Ultimate flexibility and manageability
Cons	You must design for any needed redundancy across the whole chain
How	Install VPN software via Marketplace appliance of on an EC2 instance

Amazon VPC offers you the flexibility to fully manage both sides of your Amazon VPC connectivity by creating a VPN connection between your remote network and a software VPN appliance running in your Amazon VPC network.

This option is recommended if you must manage both ends of the VPN connection either for compliance purposes or for leveraging gateway devices that are not currently supported by Amazon VPC's VPN solution.

The diagram below depicts a Software VPN configuration:

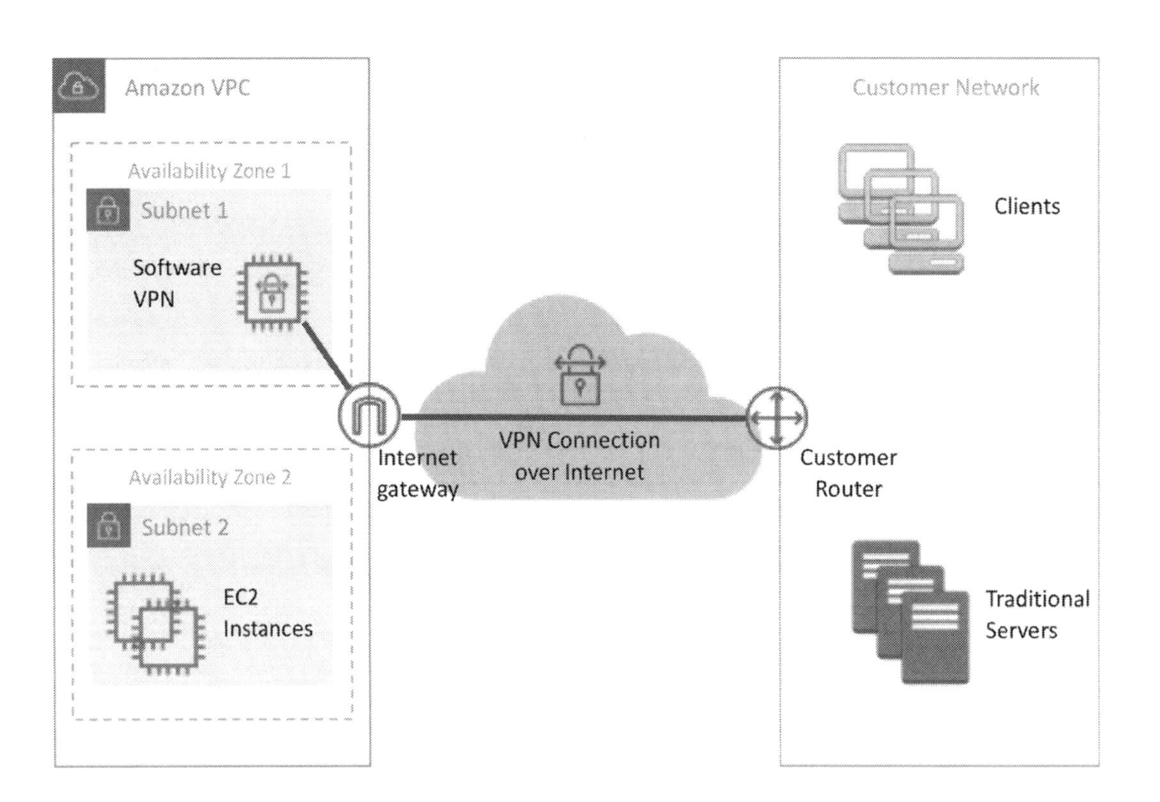

TRANSIT VPC

What	Common strategy for connecting geographically dispersed VPCs and locations in order to create a global network transit center
When	Locations and VPC-deployed assets across multiple regions that need to communicate with one another
Pros	Ultimate flexibility and manageability but also AWS-managed VPN hub-and-spoke between VPCs
Cons	You must design for any needed redundancy across the whole chain
How	Providers like Cisco, Juniper Networks, and Riverbed have offerings which work with their equipment and AWS VPC

Building on the Software VPN design mentioned above, you can create a global transit network on AWS.

A transit VPC is a common strategy for connecting multiple, geographically disperse VPCs and remote networks in order to create a global network transit center.

A transit VPC simplifies network management and minimizes the number of connections required to connect multiple VPCs and remote networks.

The diagram below depicts a Transit VPC configuration:

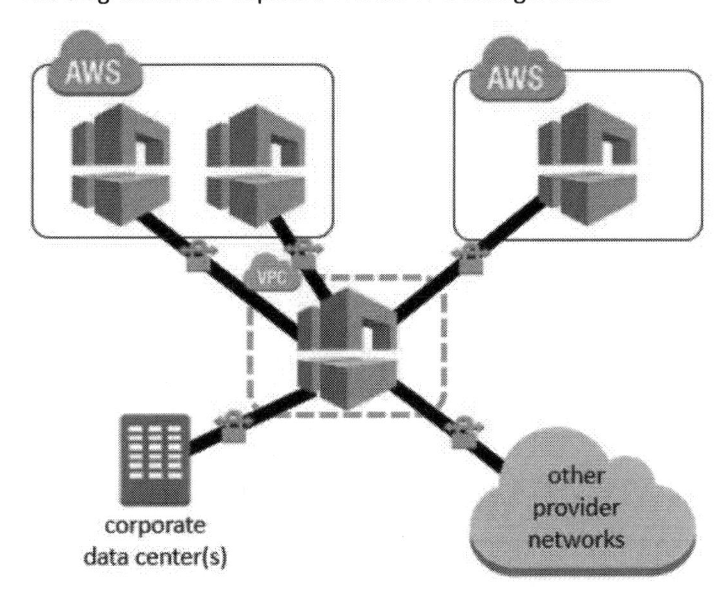

VPC PEERING

What	AWS-provided network connectivity between two VPCs
When	Multiple VPCs need to communicate or access each other's resources
Pros	Uses AWS backbone without traversing the Internet
Cons	Transitive peering is not supported
How	VPC peering request made; accepter accepts request (either within or across accounts)

A VPC peering connection is a networking connection between two VPCs that enables you to route traffic between them using private IPv4 addresses or IPv6 addresses.

Instances in either VPC can communicate with each other as if they are within the same network.

You can create a VPC peering connection between your own VPCs, or with a VPC in another AWS account.

The VPCs can be in different regions (also known as an inter-region VPC peering connection).

Data sent between VPCs in different regions is encrypted (traffic charges apply).

For inter-region VPC peering there are some limitations:

- You cannot create a security group rule that references a peer security group.
- Cannot enable DNS resolution.
- Maximum MTU is 1500 bytes (no jumbo frames support).
- Limited region support.

AWS uses the existing infrastructure of a VPC to create a VPC peering connection.

It is neither a gateway nor a VPN connection and does not rely on a separate piece of physical hardware.

There is no single point of failure for communication or a bandwidth bottleneck.

A VPC peering connection helps you to facilitate the transfer of data.

Can only have one peering connection between any two VPCs at a time.

Can peer with other accounts (within or between regions).

Cannot have overlapping CIDR ranges.

A VPC peering connection is a one to one relationship between two VPCs.

You can create multiple VPC peering connections for each VPC that you own, but transitive peering relationships are not supported.

You do not have any peering relationship with VPCs that your VPC is not directly peered with.

Limits are 50 VPC peers per VPC, up to 125 by request.

DNS is supported.

Must update route tables to configure routing.

Must update the inbound and outbound rules for VPC security group to reference security groups in the peered VPC.

When creating a VPC peering connection with another account you need to enter the account ID and VPC ID from the other account.

Need to accept the pending access request in the peered VPC.

The VPC peering connection can be added to route tables – shows as a target starting with "pcx-".

AWS PRIVATELINK

AWS PrivateLink simplifies the security of data shared with cloud-based applications by eliminating the exposure of data to the public Internet.

AWS PrivateLink provides private connectivity between VPCs, AWS services, and on-premises applications, securely on the Amazon network.

AWS PrivateLink makes it easy to connect services across different accounts and VPCs to significantly simplify the network architecture.

The table below provides more information on AWS PrivateLink and when to use it:

What	AWS-provided network connectivity between VPCs and/or AWS services using interface endpoints
When	Keep Private Subnets truly private by using the AWS backbone to reach other AWS or Marketplace services rather than the public Internet
Pros	Redundant; uses the AWS backbone
Cons	
How	Create endpoint for required AWS or Marketplace service in all required subnets; access via the provided DNS hostname

EXAM TIP: Know the difference between AWS PrivateLink and ClassicLink. ClassicLink allows you to link EC2-Classic instances to a VPC in your account, within the same region. EC2-Classic is an old platform from before VPCs were introduced and is not available to accounts created after December 2013. However, ClassicLink may come up in exam questions as a possible (incorrect) answer so you need to know what it is.

VPC ENDPOINTS

An Interface endpoint uses AWS PrivateLink and is an elastic network interface (ENI) with a private IP address that serves as an entry point for traffic destined to a supported service.

Using PrivateLink you can connect your VPC to supported AWS services, services hosted by other AWS accounts (VPC endpoint services), and supported AWS Marketplace partner services.

AWS PrivateLink access over Inter-Region VPC Peering:

- Applications in an AWS VPC can securely access AWS PrivateLink endpoints across AWS Regions using Inter-Region VPC Peering.

- AWS PrivateLink allows you to privately access services hosted on AWS in a highly available and scalable manner, without using public IPs, and without requiring the traffic to traverse the Internet.
- Customers can privately connect to a service even if the service endpoint resides in a different AWS Region.
- Traffic using Inter-Region VPC Peering stays on the global AWS backbone and never traverses the public Internet.

A gateway endpoint is a gateway that is a target for a specified route in your route table, used for traffic destined to a supported AWS service.

An interface VPC endpoint (interface endpoint) enables you to connect to services powered by AWS PrivateLink.

The table below highlights some key information about both types of endpoint:

	Interface Endpoint	**Gateway Endpoint**
What	Elastic Network Interface with a Private IP	A gateway that is a target for a specific route
How	Uses DNS entries to redirect traffic	Uses prefix lists in the route table to redirect traffic
Which services	API Gateway, CloudFormation, CloudWatch etc.	Amazon S3, DynamoDB
Security	Security Groups	VPC Endpoint Policies

By default, IAM users do not have permission to work with endpoints.

You can create an IAM user policy that grants users the permissions to create, modify, describe, and delete endpoints.

There's a long list of services that are supported by interface endpoints.

Gateway endpoints are only available for:

- Amazon DyanmoDB
- Amazon S3

EXAM TIP: Know which services use interface endpoints and gateway endpoints. The easiest way to remember this is that Gateway Endpoints are for Amazon S3 and DynamoDB only.

SHARED SERVICES VPCS

You can allow other AWS accounts to create their application resources, such as EC2 instances, Relational Database Service (RDS) databases, Redshift clusters, and Lambda functions, into shared, centrally-managed Amazon Virtual Private Clouds (VPCs).

VPC sharing enables subnets to be shared with other AWS accounts within the same AWS Organization. **Benefits include:**

- Separation of duties: centrally controlled VPC structure, routing, IP address allocation.

- Application owners continue to own resources, accounts, and security groups.
- VPC sharing participants can reference security group IDs of each other.
- Efficiencies: higher density in subnets, efficient use of VPNs and AWS Direct Connect.
- Hard limits can be avoided, for example, 50 VIFs per AWS Direct Connect connection through simplified network architecture.
- Costs can be optimized through reuse of NAT gateways, VPC interface endpoints, and intra-Availability Zone traffic.

You can create separate Amazon VPCs for each account with the account owner being responsible for connectivity and security of each Amazon VPC.

With VPC sharing, your IT team can own and manage your Amazon VPCs and your application developers no longer have to manage or configure Amazon VPCs, but they can access them as needed.

Can also share Amazon VPCs to leverage the implicit routing within a VPC for applications that require a high degree of interconnectivity and are within the same trust boundaries.

This reduces the number of VPCs that need to be created and managed, while you still benefit from using separate accounts for billing and access control.

Customers can further simplify network topologies by interconnecting shared Amazon VPCs using connectivity features, such as AWS PrivateLink, AWS Transit Gateway, and Amazon VPC peering.

Can also be used with AWS PrivateLink to secure access to resources shared such as applications behind a Network Load Balancer.

VPC FLOW LOGS

Flow Logs capture information about the IP traffic going to and from network interfaces in a VPC.

Flow log data is stored using Amazon CloudWatch Logs.

Flow logs can be created at the following levels:

- VPC.
- Subnet.
- Network interface.

You can't enable flow logs for VPC's that are peered with your VPC unless the peer VPC is in your account.

You can't tag a flow log.

You can't change the configuration of a flow log after it's been created.

After you've created a flow log, you cannot change its configuration (you need to delete and re-create).

Not all traffic is monitored, e.g. the following traffic is excluded:

- Traffic that goes to Route53.
- Traffic generated for Windows license activation.
- Traffic to and from 169.254.169.254 (instance metadata).
- Traffic to and from 169.254.169.123 for the Amazon Time Sync Service.
- DHCP traffic.

- Traffic to the reserved IP address for the default VPC router.

HIGH AVAILABILITY APPROACHES FOR NETWORKING

By creating subnets in the available AZs, you create Multi-AZ presence for your VPC.

Best practice is to create at least two VPN tunnels into your Virtual Private Gateway.

Direct Connect is not HA by default, so you need to establish a secondary connection via another Direct Connect (ideally with another provider) or use a VPN.

Route 53's health checks provide a basic level of redirecting DNS resolutions.

Elastic IPs allow you flexibility to change out backing assets without impacting name resolution.

For Multi-AZ redundancy of NAT Gateways, create gateways in each AZ with routes for private subnets to use the local gateway.

AMAZON CLOUDFRONT

GENERAL CLOUDFRONT CONCEPTS

CloudFront is a web service that gives businesses and web application developers an easy and cost-effective way to distribute content with low latency and high data transfer speeds.

CloudFront is a good choice for distribution of frequently accessed static content that benefits from edge delivery—like popular website images, videos, media files or software downloads.

Used for dynamic, static, streaming, and interactive content.

CloudFront is a global service:

- Ingress to upload objects.
- Egress to distribute content.

Amazon CloudFront provides a simple API that lets you:

- Distribute content with low latency and high data transfer rates by serving requests using a network of edge locations around the world.
- Get started without negotiating contracts and minimum commitments.

You can use a zone apex name on CloudFront.

CloudFront supports wildcard CNAME.

Supports wildcard SSL certificates, Dedicated IP, Custom SSL and SNI Custom SSL (cheaper). Supports Perfect Forward Secrecy which creates a new private key for each SSL session.

EDGE LOCATIONS AND REGIONAL EDGE CACHES

An edge location is the location where content is cached (separate to AWS regions/AZs).

Requests are automatically routed to the nearest edge location.

Edge locations are not tied to Availability Zones or regions.

Regional Edge Caches are located between origin web servers and global edge locations and have a larger cache.

Regional Edge Caches have larger cache-width than any individual edge location, so your objects remain in cache longer at these locations.

Regional Edge caches aim to get content closer to users.

Proxy methods PUT/POST/PATCH/OPTIONS/DELETE go directly to the origin from the edge locations and do not proxy through Regional Edge caches.

Dynamic content goes straight to the origin and does not flow through Regional Edge caches.

Edge locations are not just read only, you can write to them too.

The diagram below shows where Regional Edge Caches and Edge Locations are placed in relation to end users:

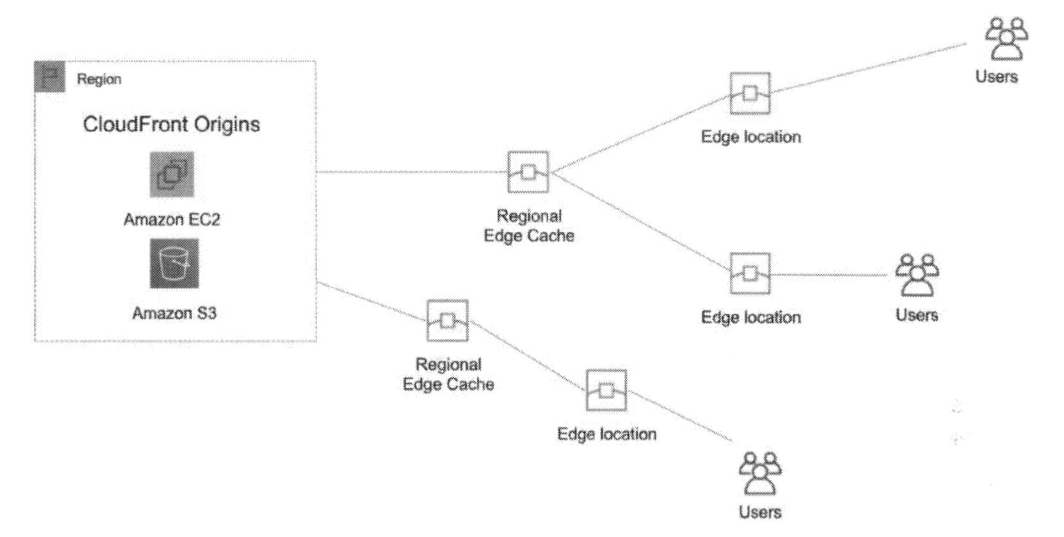

ORIGINS

An origin is the origin of the files that the CDN will distribute.

Origins can be either an S3 bucket, an EC2 instance, an Elastic Load Balancer, or Route 53 – can also be external (non-AWS).

When using Amazon S3 as an origin you place all of your objects within the bucket.

You can use an existing bucket and the bucket is not modified in any way.

By default, all newly created buckets are private.

You can setup access control to your buckets using:

- Bucket policies.
- Access Control Lists.

You can make objects publicly available or use CloudFront signed URLs.

A custom origin server is a HTTP server which can be an EC2 instance or an on-premise/non-AWS based web server.

When using an on-premise or non-AWS based web server you must specify the DNS name, ports and protocols that you want CloudFront to use when fetching objects from your origin.

Most CloudFront features are supported for custom origins except RTMP distributions (must be an S3 bucket).

When using EC2 for custom origins Amazon recommend:

- Use an AMI that automatically installs the software for a web server.
- Use ELB to handle traffic across multiple EC2 instances.
- Specify the URL of your load balancer as the domain name of the origin server.

S3 static website:

- Enter the S3 static website hosting endpoint for your bucket in the configuration.
- Example: http://<bucketname>.s3-website-<region>.amazonaws.com.

Objects are cached for 24 hours by default.

The expiration time is controlled through the TTL.

The minimum expiration time is 0.

Static websites on Amazon S3 are considered custom origins.

AWS origins are Amazon S3 buckets (not a static website).

CloudFront keeps persistent connections open with origin servers.

Files can also be uploaded to CloudFront.

High availability with Origin Failover:

- Can set up CloudFront with origin failover for scenarios that require high availability.
- Uses an origin group in which you designate a primary origin for CloudFront plus a second origin that CloudFront automatically switches to when the primary origin returns specific HTTP status code failure responses.
- Also works with Lambda@Edge functions.

DISTRIBUTIONS

To distribute content with CloudFront you need to create a distribution.

The distribution includes the configuration of the CDN including:

- Content origins.
- Access (public or restricted).
- Security (HTTP or HTTPS).
- Cookie or query-string forwarding.
- Geo-restrictions.
- Access logs (record viewer activity).

There are two types of distribution.

Web Distribution:

- Static and dynamic content including .html, .css, .php, and graphics files.
- Distributes files over HTTP and HTTPS.
- Add, update, or delete objects, and submit data from web forms.
- Use live streaming to stream an event in real time.

RTMP:

- Distribute streaming media files using Adobe Flash Media Server's RTMP protocol.
- Allows an end user to begin playing a media file before the file has finished downloading from a CloudFront edge location.
- Files must be stored in an S3 bucket.

To use CloudFront live streaming, create a web distribution.

For serving both the media player and media files you need two types of distributions:

- A web distribution for the media player.
- An RTMP distribution for the media files.

S3 buckets can be configured to create access logs and cookie logs which log all requests made to the S3 bucket.

Amazon Athena can be used to analyze access logs.

CloudFront is integrated with CloudTrail.

CloudTrail saves logs to the S3 bucket you specify.

CloudTrail captures information about all requests whether they were made using the CloudFront console, the CloudFront API, the AWS SDKs, the CloudFront CLI, or another service.

CloudTrail can be used to determine which requests were made, the source IP address, who made the request etc.

To view CloudFront requests in CloudTrail logs you must update an existing trail to include global services.

To delete a distribution, it must first be disabled (can take up to 15 minutes).

The diagram below depicts Amazon CloudFront Distributions and Origins:

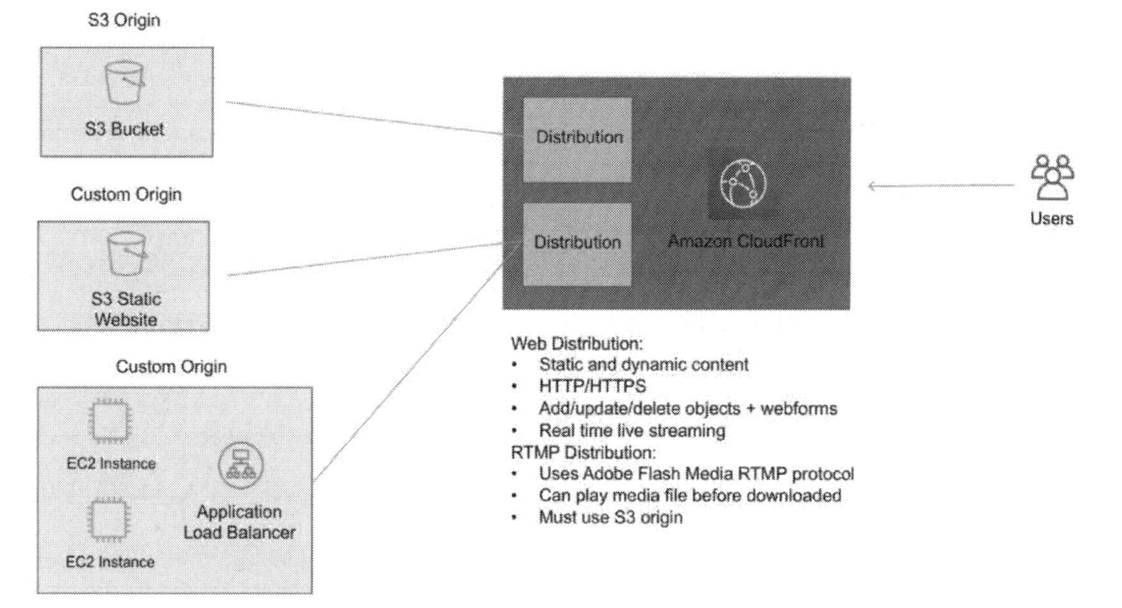

CACHE BEHAVIOR

Allows you to configure a variety of CloudFront functionality for a given URL path pattern.

For each cache behavior you can configure the following functionality:

- The path pattern (e.g. /images/*.jpg, /images*.php).
- The origin to forward requests to (if there are multiple origins).
- Whether to forward query strings.
- Whether to require signed URLs.
- Allowed HTTP methods.
- Minimum amount of time to retain the files in the CloudFront cache (regardless of the values of any cache-control headers).

The default cache behavior only allows a path pattern of /*.

Additional cache behaviors need to be defined to change the path pattern following creation of the distribution.

You can restrict access to content using the following methods:

- Restrict access to content using signed cookies or signed URLs.
- Restrict access to objects in your S3 bucket.

A special type of user called an Origin Access Identity (OAI) can be used to restrict access to content in an Amazon S3 bucket.

By using an OAI you can restrict users so they cannot access the content directly using the S3 URL, they must connect via CloudFront.

You can define the viewer protocol policy:

- HTTP and HTTPS
- Redirect HTTP to HTTPS
- HTTPS only

You can define the Allowed HTTP Methods:

- GET, HEAD
- GET, HEAD, OPTIONS
- GET, HEAD, OPTIONS, PUT, POST, PATCH, DELETE

For web distributions you can configure CloudFront to require that viewers use HTTPS.

Field-Level Encryption:

- Field-level encryption adds an additional layer of security on top of HTTPS that lets you protect specific data so that it is only visible to specific applications.
- Field-level encryption allows you to securely upload user-submitted sensitive information to your web servers.
- The sensitive information is encrypted at the edge closer to the user and remains encrypted throughout application processing.

Origin policy:

- HTTPS only.
- Match viewer – CloudFront matches the protocol with your custom origin.

- Use match viewer only if you specify Redirect HTTP to HTTPS or HTTPS only for the viewer protocol policy.
- CloudFront caches the object once even if viewers makes requests using HTTP and HTTPS.

Object invalidation:

- You can remove an object from the cache by invalidating the object.
- You cannot cancel an invalidation after submission.
- You cannot invalidate media files in the Microsoft Smooth Streaming format when you have enabled Smooth Streaming for the corresponding cache behavior.

Objects are cached for the TTL (always recorded in seconds, default is 24 hours, default max is 1 year).

Only caches for GET requests (not PUT, POST, PATCH, DELETE).

Dynamic content is cached.

Consider how often your files change when setting the TTL.

Invalidation can be used to immediately revoke cached objects – chargeable.

Deletions propagate.

RESTRICTIONS

Blacklists and whitelists can be used for geography – you can only use one at a time.

There are two options available for geo-restriction (geo-blocking):

- Use the CloudFront geo-restriction feature (use for restricting access to all files in a distribution and at the country level).
- Use a 3rd party geo-location service (use for restricting access to a subset of the files in a distribution and for finer granularity at the country level).

AWS WAF

AWS WAF is a web application firewall that lets you monitor HTTP and HTTPS requests that are forwarded to CloudFront and lets you control access to your content.

With AWS WAF you can shield access to content based on conditions in a web access control list (web ACL) such as:

- Origin IP address.
- Values in query strings.

CloudFront responds to requests with the requested content or an HTTP 403 status code (forbidden).

CloudFront can also be configured to deliver a custom error page.

Need to associate the relevant distribution with the web ACL.

SECURITY

PCI DSS compliant but recommended not to cache credit card information at edge locations.

HIPAA compliant as a HIPAA eligible service.

Distributed Denial of Service (DDoS) protection:

- CloudFront distributes traffic across multiple edge locations and filters requests to ensure that only valid HTTP(S) requests will be forwarded to backend hosts. CloudFront also supports geoblocking, which you can use to prevent requests from particular geographic locations from being served.

DOMAIN NAMES

CloudFront typically creates a domain name such as a232323.cloudfront.net.

Alternate domain names can be added using an alias record (Route 53).

For other service providers use a CNAME (cannot use the zone apex with CNAME).

Moving domain names between distributions:

- You can move subdomains yourself.
- For the root domain you need to use AWS support.

CHARGES

There is an option for reserved capacity over 12 months or longer (starts at 10TB of data transfer in a single region).

You pay for:

- Data Transfer Out to Internet.
- Data Transfer Out to Origin.
- Number of HTTP/HTTPS Requests.
- Invalidation Requests.
- Dedicated IP Custom SSL.
- Field level encryption requests.

You do not pay for:

- Data transfer between AWS regions and CloudFront.
- Regional edge cache.
- AWS ACM SSL/TLS certificates.
- Shared CloudFront certificates.

AMAZON ROUTE 53

GENERAL ROUTE 53 CONCEPTS

Amazon Route 53 is a highly available and scalable Domain Name System (DNS) service.

Route 53 offers the following functions:

- Domain name registry.
- DNS resolution.

- Health checking of resources.

Route 53 can perform any combination of these functions.

Route 53 provides a worldwide distributed DNS service.

Route 53 is located alongside all edge locations.

Health checks verify Internet connected resources are reachable, available and functional.

Route 53 can be used to route Internet traffic for domains registered with another domain registrar (any domain).

When you register a domain with Route 53 it becomes the authoritative DNS server for that domain and creates a public hosted zone.

To make Route 53 the authoritative DNS for an existing domain without transferring the domain create a Route 53 public hosted zone and change the DNS Name Servers on the existing provider to the Route 53 Name Servers.

Changes to Name Servers may not take effect for up to 48 hours due to the DNS record Time To Live (TTL) values.

You can transfer domains to Route 53 only if the Top Level Domain (TLD) is supported.

You can transfer a domain from Route 53 to another registrar by contacting AWS support.

You can transfer a domain to another account in AWS however it does not migrate the hosted zone by default (optional).

It is possible to have the domain registered in one AWS account and the hosted zone in another AWS account.

Primarily uses UDP port 53 (can use TCP).

AWS offer a 100% uptime SLA for Route 53.

You can control management access to your Amazon Route 53 hosted zone by using IAM.

There is a default limit of 50 domain names, but this can be increased by contacting support.

Private DNS is a Route 53 feature that lets you have authoritative DNS within your VPCs without exposing your DNS records (including the name of the resource and its IP address(es) to the Internet.

You can use the AWS Management Console or API to register new domain names with Route 53.

HOSTED ZONES

A hosted zone is a collection of records for a specified domain.

A hosted zone is analogous to a traditional DNS zone file; it represents a collection of records that can be managed together.

There are two types of zones:

- Public host zone – determines how traffic is routed on the Internet.
- Private hosted zone for VPC – determines how traffic is routed within VPC (resources are not accessible outside the VPC).

Amazon Route 53 automatically creates the Name Server (NS) and Start of Authority (SOA) records for the hosted zones.

Amazon Route 53 creates a set of 4 unique name servers (a delegation set) within each hosted zone.

You can create multiple hosted zones with the same name and different records.

NS servers are specified by Fully Qualified Domain Name (FQDN) but you can get the IP addresses from the command line (e.g. dig or nslookup).

For private hosted zones you can see a list of VPCs in each region and must select one.

For private hosted zones you must set the following VPC settings to "true":

- enableDnsHostname
- enableDnsSupport

You also need to create a DHCP options set.

You can extend an on-premises DNS to VPC.

You cannot extend Route 53 to on-premises instances.

You cannot automatically register EC2 instances with private hosted zones (would need to be scripted).

Health checks check the instance health by connecting to it.

Health checks can be pointed at:

- Endpoints
- Status of other health checks
- Status of a CloudWatch alarm

Endpoints can be IP addresses or domain names.

RECORDS

Amazon Route 53 currently supports the following DNS record types:

- A (address record)
- AAAA (IPv6 address record)
- CNAME (canonical name record)
- CAA (certification authority authorization)
- MX (mail exchange record)
- NAPTR (name authority pointer record
- NS (name server record)
- PTR (pointer record)
- SOA (start of authority record)
- SPF (sender policy framework)
- SRV (service locator)
- TXT (text record)
- Alias (an Amazon Route 53-specific virtual record)

The Alias record is a Route 53 specific record type.

Alias records are used to map resource record sets in your hosted zone to Amazon Elastic Load Balancing load balancers, Amazon CloudFront distributions, AWS Elastic Beanstalk environments, or Amazon S3 buckets that are configured as websites.

You can use Alias records to map custom domain names (such as api.example.com) both to API Gateway custom regional APIs and edge-optimized APIs and to Amazon VPC interface endpoints.

The Alias is pointed to the DNS name of the service.

You cannot set the TTL for Alias records for ELB, S3, or Elastic Beanstalk environment (uses the service's default).

Alias records work like a CNAME record in that you can map one DNS name (e.g. example.com) to another 'target' DNS name (e.g. elb1234.elb.amazonaws.com).

An Alias record can be used for resolving apex / naked domain names (e.g. example.com rather than sub.example.com).

A CNAME record can't be used for resolving apex / naked domain names.

Generally, use an Alias record where possible. The following table details the differences between Alias and CNAME records:

CNAME Records	Alias Records
Route 53 charges for CNAME queries	Route 53 doesn't charge for alias queries to AWS resources
You can't create a CNAME record at the top node of a DNS namespace (zone apex)	You can create an alias record at the zone apex (however you can't route to a CNAME at the zone apex)
A CNAME record redirects queries for a domain name regardless of record type	Route 53 follows the pointer in an alias record only when the record type also matches
A CNAME can point to any DNS record that is hosted anywhere	An alias record can only point to a CloudFront distribution, Elastic Beanstalk environment, ELB, S3 bucket as a static website, or to another record in the same hosted zone that you're creating the alias record in
A CNAME record is visible in the answer section of a reply from a Route 53 DNS server	An alias record is only visible in the Route 53 console or the Route 53 API
A CNAME record is followed by a recursive resolver	An alias record is only followed inside Route 53. This means that both the alias record and its target must exist in Route 53

Route 53 supports wildcard entries for all record types, except NS records.

ROUTING POLICIES

Routing policies determine how Route 53 responds to queries.

The following table highlights the key function of each type of routing policy:

Policy	What it Does
Simple	Simple DNS response providing the IP address associated with a name
Failover	If primary is down (based on health checks), routes to secondary destination
Geolocation	Uses geographic location you're in (e.g. Europe) to route you to the closest region
Geoproximity	Routes you to the closest region within a geographic area
Latency	Directs you based on the lowest latency route to resources
Multivalue answer	Returns several IP addresses and functions as a basic load balancer
Weighted	Uses the relative weights assigned to resources to determine which to route to

Simple:

- An A record is associated with one or more IP addresses
- Uses round robin
- Does not support health checks

The following diagram depicts an Amazon Route 53 Simple routing policy configuration:

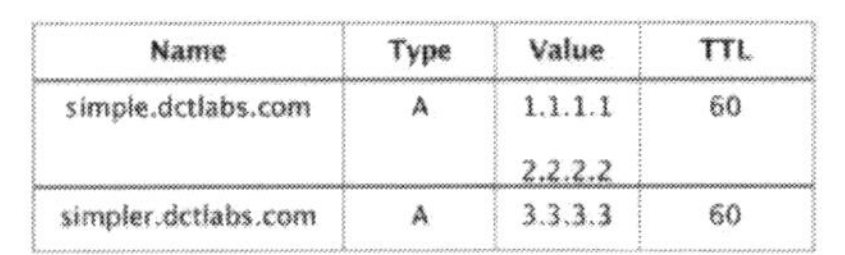

Name	Type	Value	TTL
simple.dctlabs.com	A	1.1.1.1 2.2.2.2	60
simpler.dctlabs.com	A	3.3.3.3	60

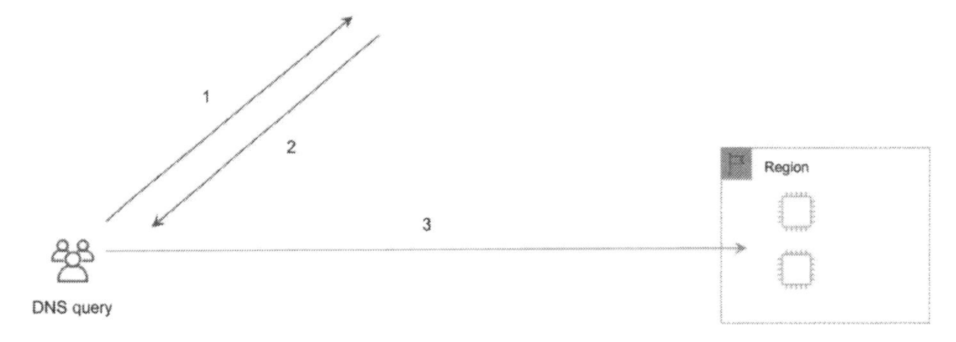

Failover:

- Failover to a secondary IP address.
- Associated with a health check.
- Used for active-passive.
- Routes only when the resource is healthy.
- Can be used with ELB.
- When used with Alias records set Evaluate Target Health to "Yes" and do not use health checks.

The following diagram depicts an Amazon Route 53 Failover routing policy configuration:

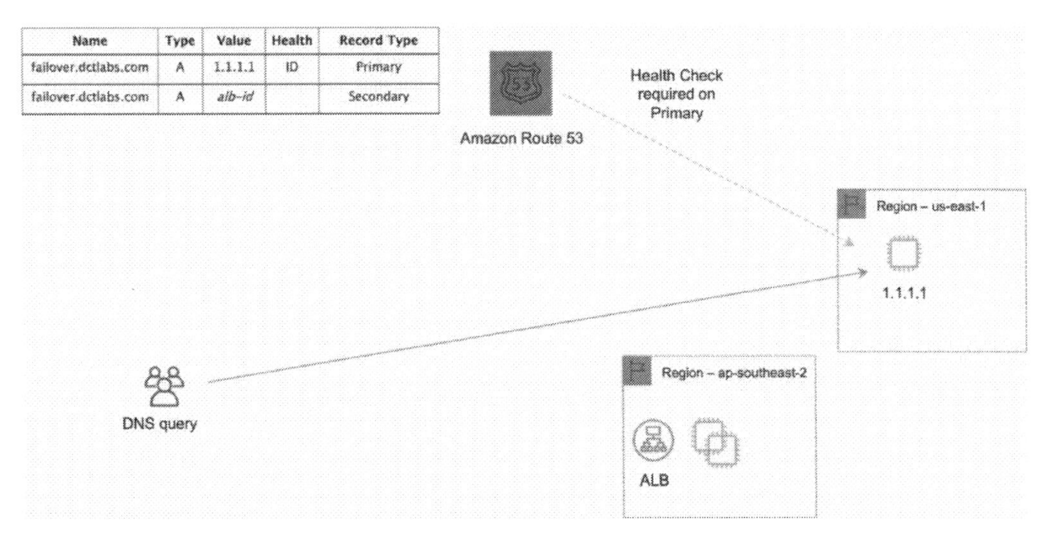

Geo-location:

- Caters to different users in different countries and different languages.
- Contains users within a particular geography and offers them a customized version of the workload based on their specific needs.
- Geolocation can be used for localizing content and presenting some or all of your website in the language of your users.
- Can also protect distribution rights.
- Can be used for spreading load evenly between regions.
- If you have multiple records for overlapping regions, Route 53 will route to the smallest geographic region.
- You can create a default record for IP addresses that do not map to a geographic location.

The following diagram depicts an Amazon Route 53 Geolocation routing policy configuration:

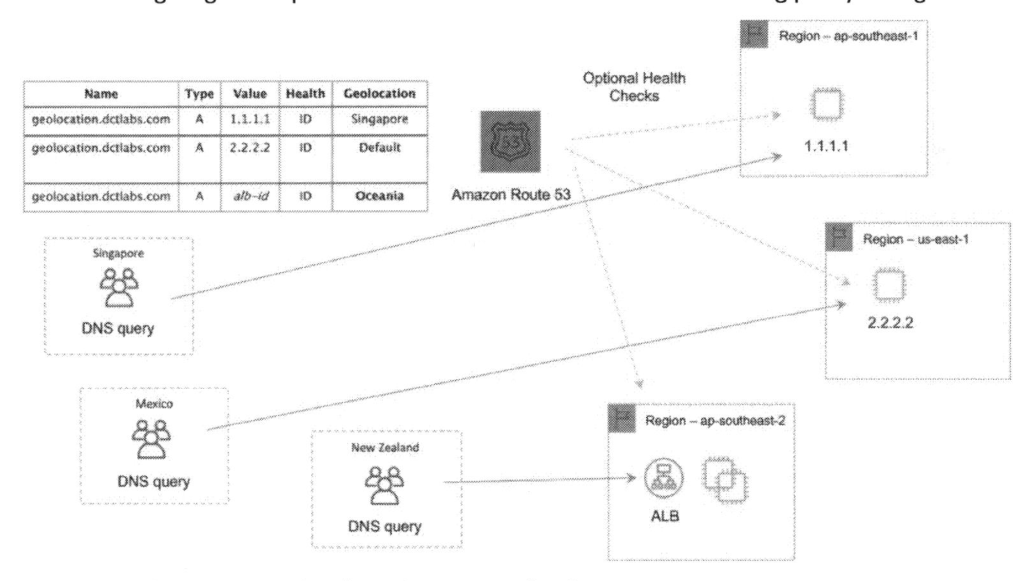

Geo-proximity routing policy (requires Route Flow):

- Use for routing traffic based on the location of resources and, optionally, shift traffic from resources in one location to resources in another.

Latency based routing:

- AWS maintains a database of latency from different parts of the world.
- Focused on improving performance by routing to the region with the lowest latency.
- You create latency records for your resources in multiple EC2 locations.

The following diagram depicts an Amazon Route 53 Latency based routing policy configuration:

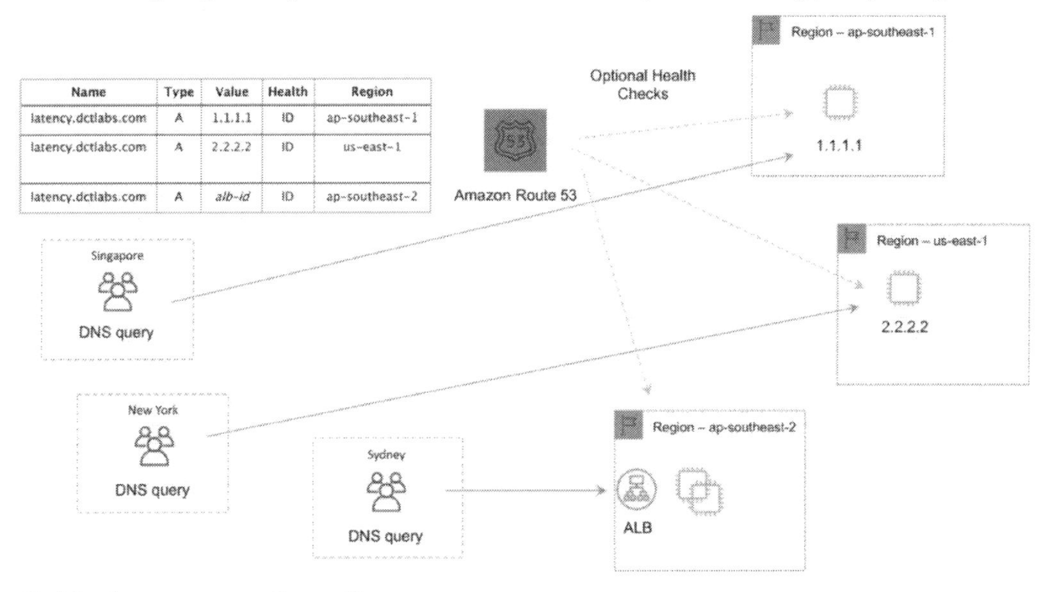

Name	Type	Value	Health	Region
latency.dctlabs.com	A	1.1.1.1	ID	ap-southeast-1
latency.dctlabs.com	A	2.2.2.2	ID	us-east-1
latency.dctlabs.com	A	*alb-id*	ID	ap-southeast-2

Multi-value answer routing policy:

- Use for responding to DNS queries with up to eight healthy records selected at random.

The following diagram depicts an Amazon Route 53 Multivalue routing policy configuration:

Weighted:

- Similar to simple but you can specify a weight per IP address.
- You create records that have the same name and type and assign each record a relative weight.
- Numerical value that favors one IP over another.
- To stop sending traffic to a resource you can change the weight of the record to 0.

The following diagram depicts an Amazon Route 53 Weighted routing policy configuration:

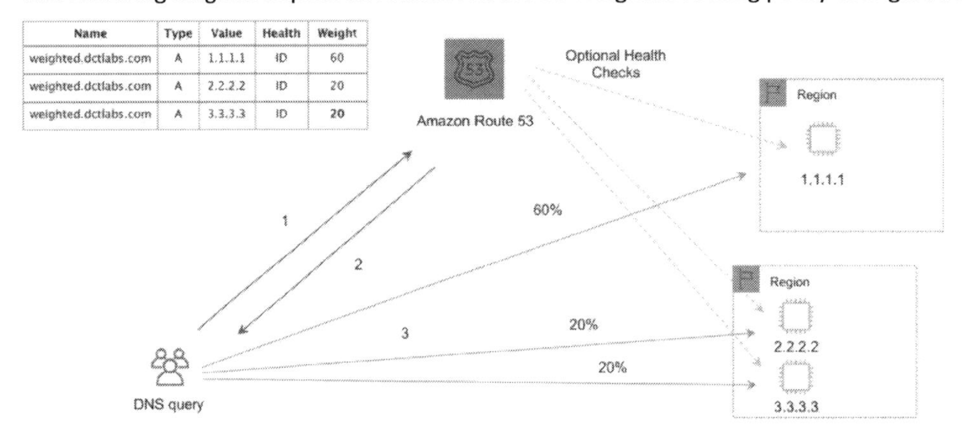

Name	Type	Value	Health	Weight
weighted.dctlabs.com	A	1.1.1.1	ID	60
weighted.dctlabs.com	A	2.2.2.2	ID	20
weighted.dctlabs.com	A	3.3.3.3	ID	**20**

TRAFFIC FLOW

Route 53 Traffic Flow provides Global Traffic Management (GTM) services.

Traffic flow policies allow you to create routing configurations for resources using routing types such as failover and geolocation.

Create policies that route traffic based on specific constraints, including latency, endpoint health, load, geo-proximity and geography.

Scenarios include:

- Adding a simple backup page in Amazon S3 for a website.
- Building sophisticated routing policies that consider an end user's geographic location, proximity to an AWS region, and the health of each of your endpoints.

Amazon Route 53 Traffic Flow also includes a versioning feature that allows you to maintain a history of changes to your routing policies, and easily roll back to a previous policy version using the console or API.

ROUTE 53 RESOLVER

Route 53 Resolver is a set of features that enable bi-directional querying between on-premises and AWS over private connections.

Used for enabling DNS resolution for hybrid clouds.

Route 53 Resolver Endpoints:

- Inbound query capability is provided by Route 53 Resolver Endpoints, allowing DNS queries that originate on-premises to resolve AWS hosted domains.
- Connectivity needs to be established between your on-premises DNS infrastructure and AWS through a Direct Connect (DX) or a Virtual Private Network (VPN).
- Endpoints are configured through IP address assignment in each subnet for which you would like to provide a resolver.

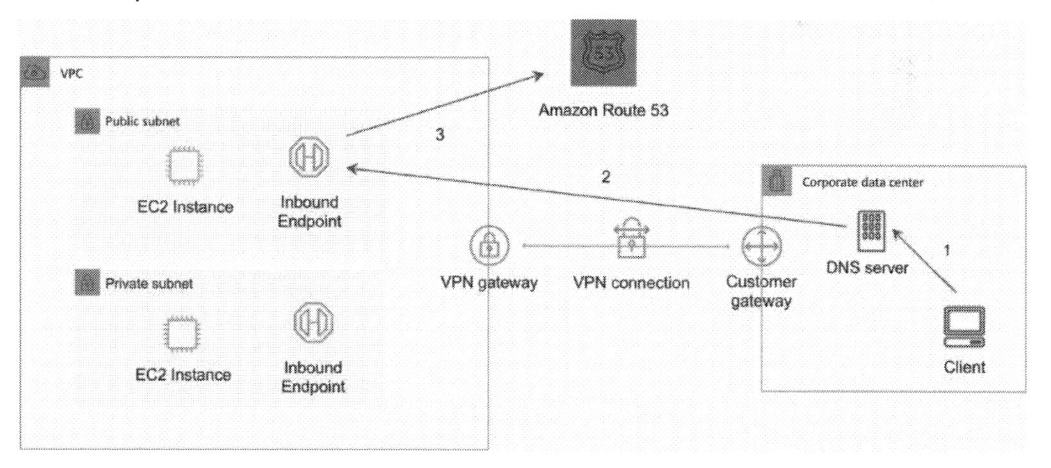

Conditional forwarding rules:

- Outbound DNS queries are enabled through the use of Conditional Forwarding Rules. .
- Domains hosted within your on-premises DNS infrastructure can be configured as forwarding rules in Route 53 Resolver.

- Rules will trigger when a query is made to one of those domains and will attempt to forward DNS requests to your DNS servers that were configured along with the rules.
- Like the inbound queries, this requires a private connection over DX or VPN.

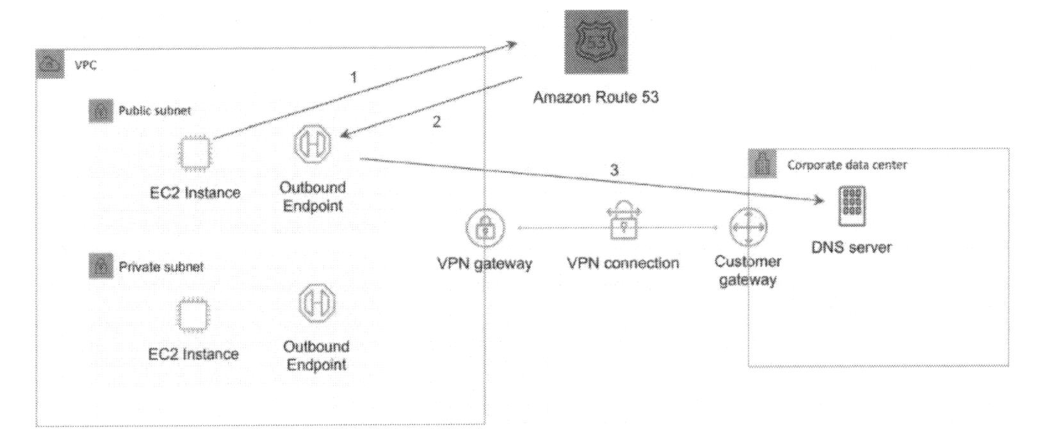

CHARGES

You pay per hosted zone per month (no partial months).

A hosted zone deleted within 12 hours of creation is not charged (queries are charges).

Additional charges for:

- Queries
- Traffic Flow
- Health Checks
- Route 53 Resolver ENIs + queries
- Domain names

Alias records are free of charge when the records are mapped to one of the following:

- Elastic Load Balancers
- Amazon CloudFront distributions
- AWS Elastic Beanstalk environments
- Amazon S3 buckets that are configured as website endpoints

Health checks are charged with different prices for AWS vs non-AWS endpoints.

You do not pay for the records that you add to your hosted zones.

Latency-based routing queries are more expensive.

Geo DNS and geo-proximity also have higher prices.

AWS GLOBAL ACCELERATOR

AWS Global Accelerator is a service that improves the availability and performance of applications with local or global users.

It provides static IP addresses that act as a fixed entry point to application endpoints in a single or multiple AWS Regions, such as Application Load Balancers, Network Load Balancers or EC2 instances.

Uses the AWS global network to optimize the path from users to applications, improving the performance of TCP and UDP traffic.

AWS Global Accelerator continually monitors the health of application endpoints and will detect an unhealthy endpoint and redirect traffic to healthy endpoints in less than 1 minute.

Details and Benefits

Uses redundant (two) static anycast IP addresses in different network zones (A and B).

The redundant pair are globally advertised.

Uses AWS Edge Locations – addresses are announced from multiple edge locations at the same time.

Addresses are associated to regional AWS resources or endpoints.

AWS Global Accelerator's IP addresses serve as the frontend interface of applications.

Intelligent traffic distribution: Routes connections to the closest point of presence for applications.

Targets can be Amazon EC2 instances or Elastic Load Balancers (ALB and NLB).

By using the static IP addresses, you don't need to make any client-facing changes or update DNS records as you modify or replace endpoints.

The addresses are assigned to your accelerator for as long as it exists, even if you disable the accelerator and it no longer accepts or routes traffic.

Does health checks for TCP only – not UDP.

Can assign target weight within a region to control routing and also "dial" up or down traffic to a region.

Fault tolerance:

- Has a fault-isolating design that increases the availability of your applications.
- AWS Global Accelerator allocates two IPv4 static addresses that are serviced by independent network zones.
- Similar to Availability Zones, these network zones are isolated units with their own set of physical infrastructure and service IP addresses from a unique IP subnet.
- If one IP address from a network zone becomes unavailable, due to network disruptions or IP address blocking by certain client networks, client applications can retry using the healthy static IP address from the other isolated network zone.

Global performance-based routing:

- AWS Global Accelerator uses the vast, congestion-free AWS global network to route TCP and UDP traffic to a healthy application endpoint in the closest AWS Region to the user.
- If there's an application failure, AWS Global Accelerator provides instant failover to the next best endpoint.

Fine-grained traffic control:

- AWS Global Accelerator gives you the option to dial up or dial down traffic to a specific AWS Region by using traffic dials.
- The traffic dial lets you easily do performance testing or blue/green deployment testing for new releases across different AWS Regions, for example.

- If an endpoint fails, AWS Global Accelerator assigns user traffic to the other endpoints, to maintain high availability.
- By default, traffic dials are set to 100% across all endpoint groups so that AWS Global Accelerator can select the best endpoint for applications.

Continuous availability monitoring:

- AWS Global Accelerator continuously monitors the health of application endpoints by using TCP, HTTP, and HTTPS health checks.
- It instantly reacts to changes in the health or configuration of application endpoints, and redirects user traffic to healthy endpoints that deliver the best performance and availability to end users.

Client affinity:

- AWS Global Accelerator enables you to build applications that require maintaining state.
- For stateful applications where you need to consistently route users to the same endpoint, you can choose to direct all requests from a user to the same endpoint, regardless of the port and protocol.

Distributed denial of service (DDoS) resiliency at the edge:

- By default, AWS Global Accelerator is protected by AWS Shield Standard, which minimizes application downtime and latency from denial of service attacks by using always-on network flow monitoring and automated in-line mitigation.
- You can also enable AWS Shield Advanced for automated resource-specific enhanced detection and mitigation, as well as 24x7 access to the AWS DDoS Response Team (DRT) for manual mitigations of sophisticated DDoS attacks.

AMAZON API GATEWAY

GENERAL API GATEWAY CONCEPTS

An Amazon API Gateway is a collection of resources and methods that are integrated with back-end HTTP endpoints, Lambda functions or other AWS services.

API Gateway is a fully managed service that makes it easy for developers to publish, maintain, monitor, and secure APIs at any scale.

API Gateway provides developers with a simple, flexible, fully managed, pay-as-you-go service that handles all aspects of creating and operating robust APIs for application back ends.

API Gateway handles all of the tasks involved in accepting and processing up to hundreds of thousands of concurrent API calls.

API calls include traffic management, authorization and access control, monitoring, and API version management.

Together with Lambda, API Gateway forms the app-facing part of the AWS serverless infrastructure.

Back-end services include Amazon EC2, AWS Lambda or any web application (public or private endpoints).

CloudFront is used as the public endpoint for API Gateway.

Supports API keys and Usage Plans for user identification, throttling or quota management.

Using CloudFront behind the scenes, custom domains, and SNI are supported.

Can be published as products and monetized on AWS Marketplace.

Collections can be deployed in stages.

Permissions to invoke a method are granted using IAM roles and policies or API Gateway custom authorizers.

An API can present a certificate to be authenticated by the back-end.

All of the APIs created with Amazon API Gateway expose HTTPS endpoints only (does not support unencrypted endpoints).

By default, API Gateway assigns an internal domain that automatically uses the API Gateway certificates.

When configuring your APIs to run under a custom domain name you can provide your own certificate.

Supported data formats include JSON, XML, query string parameters, and request headers.

Can enable Cross Origin Resource Sharing (CORS) for multiple domain use with Javascript/AJAX:

- Can be used to enable requests from domains other than the APIs domain.
- Allows the sharing of resources between different domains.
- The method (GET, PUT, POST etc) for which you will enable CORS must be available in the API Gateway API before you enable CORS.
- If CORS is not enabled and an API resource received requests from another domain the request will be blocked.
- Enable CORS on the APIs resources using the selected methods under the API Gateway.

Data types used with API Gateway:

- Any payload sent over HTTP (always encrypted over HTTPS).
- Data formats include JSON, XML, query string parameters and request headers.
- You can declare any content type for your APIs responses, and then use the transform templates to change the back-end response into your desired format.

You can add caching to API calls by provisioning an Amazon API Gateway cache and specifying its size in gigabytes.

ENDPOINTS

An *API endpoint* type refers to the hostname of the API.

The API endpoint type can be *edge-optimized*, *regional*, or *private*, depending on where the majority of your API traffic originates from.

Edge-Optimized Endpoint:

- An edge-optimized API endpoint is best for geographically distributed clients. API requests are routed to the nearest CloudFront Point of Presence (POP). This is the default endpoint type for API Gateway REST APIs.
- Edge-optimized APIs capitalize the names of HTTP headers (for example, Cookie).
- CloudFront sorts HTTP cookies in natural order by cookie name before forwarding the request to your origin. For more information about the way CloudFront processes cookies, see Caching Content Based on Cookies.

- Any custom domain name that you use for an edge-optimized API applies across all regions.

Regional Endpoint:

- A regional API endpoint is intended for clients in the same region.
- When a client running on an EC2 instance calls an API in the same region, or when an API is intended to serve a small number of clients with high demands, a regional API reduces connection overhead.
- For a regional API, any custom domain name that you use is specific to the region where the API is deployed.
- If you deploy a regional API in multiple regions, it can have the same custom domain name in all regions.
- You can use custom domains together with Amazon Route 53 to perform tasks such as latency-based routing.
- Regional API endpoints pass all header names through as-is.

Private Endpoint:

- A private API endpoint is an API endpoint that can only be accessed from your Amazon Virtual Private Cloud (VPC) using an interface VPC endpoint, which is an endpoint network interface (ENI) that you create in your VPC.
- Private API endpoints pass all header names through as-is.

The following diagram depicts the three different Amazon API Gateway endpoint types:

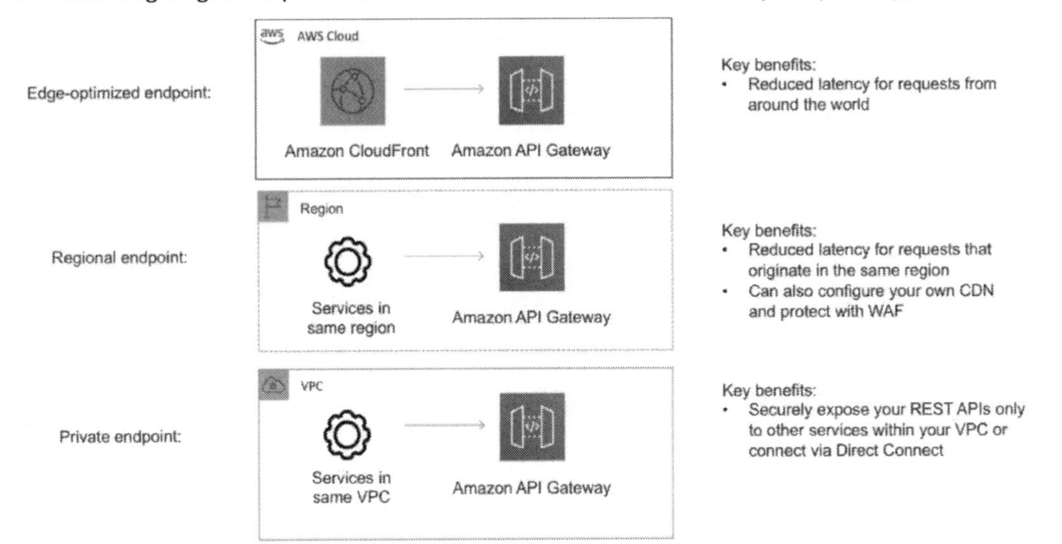

ADDITIONAL FEATURES AND BENEFITS

API Gateway provides several features that assist with creating and managing APIs:

- **Metering** – Define plans that meter and restrict third-party developer access to APIs.
- **Security** – API Gateway provides multiple tools to authorize access to APIs and control service operation access.
- **Resiliency** – Manage traffic with throttling so that backend operations can withstand traffic spikes.

- **Operations Monitoring** – API Gateway provides a metrics dashboard to monitor calls to services.
- **Lifecycle Management** – Operate multiple API versions and multiple stages for each version simultaneously so that existing applications can continue to call previous versions after new API versions are published.

API Gateway provides robust, secure, and scalable access to backend APIs and hosts multiple versions and release stages for your APIs.

You can create and distribute API Keys to developers.

Option to use AWS Sig-v4 to authorize access to APIs.

You can throttle and monitor requests to protect your backend.

API Gateway allows you to maintain a cache to store API responses.

SDK Generation for iOS, Android and JavaScript.

Reduced latency and distributed denial of service protection through the use of CloudFront.

Request/response data transformation and API mocking.

Provides Swagger support.

Resiliency through throttling rules based on the number of requests per second for each HTTP method (GET, PUT).

Throttling can be configured at multiple levels including Global and Service Call.

A cache can be created and specified in gigabytes (not enabled by default).

Caches are provisioned for a specific stage of your APIs.

Caching features include customizable keys and time-to-live (TTL) in seconds for your API data which enhances response times and reduces load on back-end services.

API Gateway can scale to any level of traffic received by an API.

LOGGING AND MONITORING

The Amazon API Gateway logs (near real time) back-end performance metrics such as API calls, latency, and error rates to CloudWatch.

You can monitor through the API Gateway dashboard (REST API) allowing you to visually monitor calls to the services.

API Gateway also meters utilization by third-party developers and the data is available in the API Gateway console and through APIs.

Amazon API Gateway is integrated with AWS CloudTrail to give a full auditable history of the changes to your REST APIs.

All API calls made to the Amazon API Gateway APIS to create, modify, delete, or deploy REST APIs are logged to CloudTrail.

CHARGES

With Amazon API Gateway, you only pay when your APIs are in use.

There are no minimum fees or upfront commitments.

You pay only for the API calls you receive, and the amount of data transferred out.

There are no data transfer out charges for Private APIs (however, AWS PrivateLink charges apply when using Private APIs in Amazon API Gateway).

Amazon API Gateway also provides optional data caching charged at an hourly rate that varies based on the cache size you select.

The API Gateway free tier includes one million API calls per month for up to 12 months.

AWS DIRECT CONNECT

AWS Direct Connect is a network service that provides an alternative to using the Internet to connect a customer's on-premise sites to AWS.

Data is transmitted through a private network connection between AWS and a customer's datacenter or corporate network.

Benefits:

- Reduce cost when using large volumes of traffic.
- Increase reliability (predictable performance).
- Increase bandwidth (predictable bandwidth).
- Decrease latency.

Each AWS Direct Connect connection can be configured with one or more virtual interfaces (VIFs).

Public VIFs allow access to public services such as S3, EC2, and DynamoDB.

Private VIFs allow access to your VPC.

Must use public IP addresses on public VIFs.

Must use private IP addresses on private VIFs.

Cannot do layer 2 over Direct Connect (L3 only).

From Direct Connect you can connect to all AZs **within the region.**

You can establish IPSec connections over public VIFs to remote regions.

Route propagation can be used to send customer side routes to the VPC.

You can only have one 0.0.0.0/0 (all IP addresses) entry per route table.

You can bind multiple ports for higher bandwidth.

Virtual interfaces are configured to connect to either AWS public services (e.g. EC2/S3) or private services (e.g. VPC based resources).

The diagram below shoes the components of AWS Direct Connect:

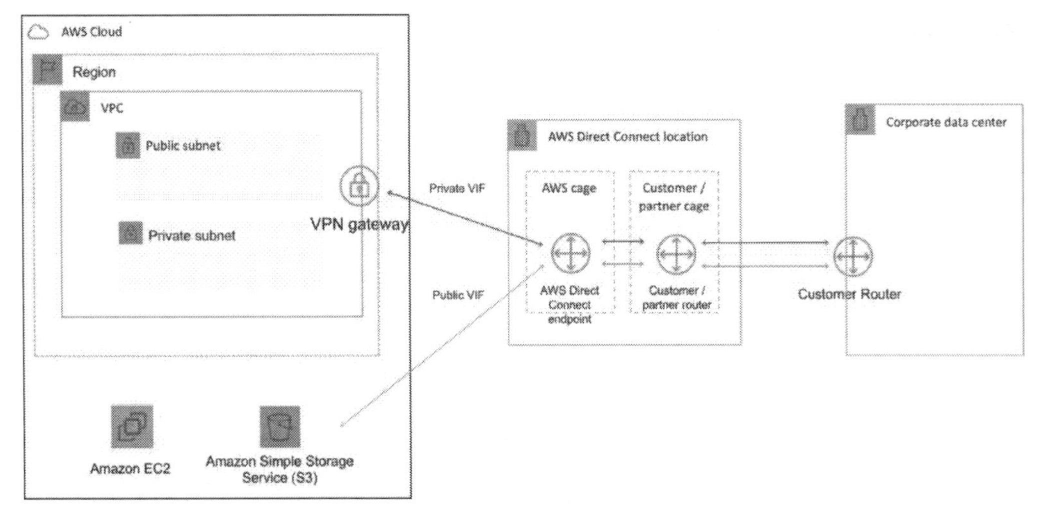

Direct Connect is charged by port hours and data transfer.

Available in 1Gbps and 10Gbps.

Speeds of 50Mbps, 100Mbps, 200Mbps, 300Mbps, 400Mbps, and 500Mbps can be purchased through AWS Direct Connect Partners.

Uses Ethernet trunking (802.1q).

Each connection consists of a single dedicated connection between ports on the customer router and an Amazon router.

for HA you must have 2 DX connections – can be active/active or active/standby.

Route tables need to be updated to point to a Direct Connect connection.

VPN can be maintained as a backup with a higher BGP priority.

Recommended to enable Bidirectional Forwarding Detection (BFD) for faster detection and failover.

You cannot extend your on-premise VLANs into the AWS cloud using Direct Connect.

Can aggregate up to 4 Direct Connect ports into a single connection using Link Aggregation Groups (LAG).

AWS Direct Connect supports both single (IPv4) and dual stack (IPv4/IPv6) configurations on public and private VIFs.

Technical requirements for connecting virtual interfaces:

- A public or private ASN. If you are using a public ASN you must own it. If you are using a private ASN, it must be in the 64512 to 65535 range.
- A new unused VLAN tag that you select.
- **Private Connection (VPC)** – The VPC Virtual Private Gateway (VGW) ID.
- **Public Connection** – Public IPs (/30) allocated by you for the BGP session.

AWS DIRECT CONNECT GATEWAY

Grouping of Virtual Private Gateways (VGWs) and Private Virtual Interfaces (VIFs) that belong to the same AWS account.

Direct Connect Gateway enables you to interface with VPCs in any AWS Region (except AWS China Region).

You associate an *AWS Direct Connect gateway* with either of the following gateways:

- A transit gateway when you have multiple VPCs in the same Region.
- A virtual private gateway.

Can share private virtual interface to interface with more than one Virtual Private Clouds (VPCs) reducing the number of BGP sessions.

A Direct Connect gateway is a globally available resource.

You can create the Direct Connect gateway in any public Region and access it from all other public Regions.

The diagram below depicts the components of an AWS Direct Connect Gateway configuration:

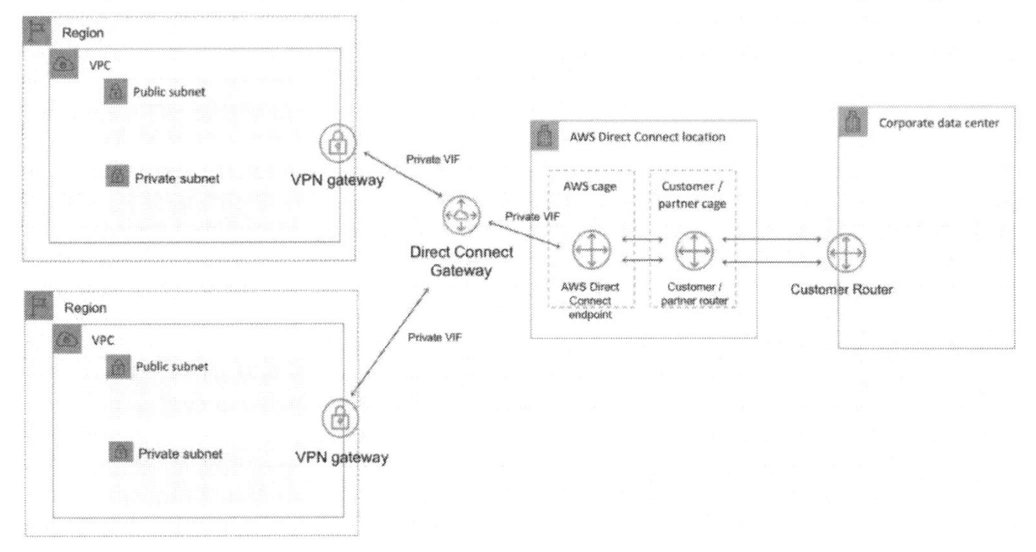

NETWORKING & CONTENT DELIVERY QUIZ QUESTIONS

Answers and explanations are provided below after the last question in this section.

Question 1: At which level do you attach an Internet gateway

1. Public Subnet
2. Private Subnet
3. Availability Zone
4. VPC

Question 2: What is the scope of a Virtual Private Cloud (VPC)?

1. Global
2. Regional
3. Availability Zone

Question 3: How should subnets be used for fault tolerance?

1. Create subnets that span multiple availability zones
2. Create subnets that have multiple Internet Gateways
3. Launch EC2 instances into subnets attached to a region
4. Launch EC2 instances into subnets created in different availability zones

Question 4: Your organization has a pre-production VPC and production VPC. You need to be able to setup routing between these VPCs using private IP addresses. How can this be done?

1. Configure a VPC endpoint
2. Add a route table entry for the opposite VPCs Internet gateway
3. Configure a peering connection
4. Use an Egress-only Internet gateway

Question 5: You created a new private subnet and created a route table with a path to a NAT gateway. However, EC2 instances launched into this subnet are not able to reach the Internet. Security Groups for the EC2 instances are setup correctly. What is the most likely explanation?

1. The security group for the NAT gateway is setup incorrectly.
2. You need to associate the new subnet with the new route table.
3. You need to add an entry for an Internet gateway.

Question 6: You need to apply a firewall to a group of EC2 instances launched in multiple subnets. Which option should be used?

1. Network Access Control List (ACL)
2. Operating system firewall
3. Security Group
4. IAM Policy

Question 7: An attack has been identified from a group of IP addresses. What's the quickest way to block these specific IP addresses from reaching the instances in your subnets?

1. Apply a Security Group to the instances in the subnets with a deny rule
2. Change the IP addresses used by the instances
3. Detach the Internet Gateway
4. Apply a Network ACL to the subnets involved with a deny rule

Question 8: An organization needs a private, high-bandwidth, low-latency connection to the AWS Cloud in order to establish hybrid cloud configuration with their on-premises cloud. What type of connection should they use?

1. AWS Managed VPN
2. AWS VPN CloudHub
3. AWS Direct Connect
4. Transit VPC

Question 9: An Architect needs to point the domain name dctlabs.com to the DNS name of an Elastic Load Balancer. Which type of record should be used?

1. MX record
2. A record
3. CNAME record
4. Alias record

Question 10: A company hosts copies of the same data in Amazon S3 buckets around the world and needs to ensure that customers connect to the nearest S3 bucket. Which Route 53 routing policy should be used?

1. Simple
2. Failover
3. Latency
4. Weighted

Question 11: A media organization offers news in local languages around the world. Which Route 53 routing policy should be used to direct readers to the website with the correct language?

1. Latency

2. Geolocation
3. Multivalue answer
4. Weighted

Question 12: An Architect is designing a web application that has points of presence in several regions around the world. The Architect would like to provide automatic routing to the nearest region, with failover possible to other regions. Customers should receive 2 IP addresses for whitelisting. How can this be achieved?

1. Use Route 53 latency-based routing
2. Use Amazon CloudFront
3. Use AWS Global Accelerator
4. Use Route 53 geolocation routing

Question 13: Which services does Amazon API Gateway use for its public endpoint?

1. AWS Lambda
2. Amazon CloudFront
3. Amazon S3
4. Amazon ECS

Question 14: A company provides videos for new employees around the world. They need to store the videos in one location and then provide low-latency access for the employees around the world. Which service would be best suited to providing fast access to the content?

1. Amazon S3
2. AWS Global Accelerator
3. Amazon CloudFront
4. AWS Lambda

Question 15: Which of the following are NOT valid origins for Amazon CloudFront?

1. Amazon S3 buckets
2. EC2 instance
3. AWS Lambda function
4. Elastic Load Balancer (ELB)

NETWORKING & CONTENT DELIVERY - ANSWERS

Question 1, Answer: 4

Explanation:

1 is incorrect. You do not attach Internet gateways to subnets.

2 is incorrect. You do not attach Internet gateways to subnets.

3 is incorrect. You do not attach Internet gateways to AZs.

4 is correct. Internet Gateways are attached to the VPC. You then need to add entries to the route tables for your public subnets to point to the IGW.

Question 2, Answer: 2

Explanation:

1 is incorrect. VPCs are not global.

2 is correct. VPCs are regional. You create VPCs in each region separately.

3 is incorrect. An availability zone exists within a region and a VPC can span subnets attached to all AZs in the region.

Question 3, Answer: 4

Explanation:

1 is incorrect. Subnets cannot span multiple AZs.

2 is incorrect. You cannot have multiple IGWs attached to a VPC.

3 is incorrect. You cannot attach a subnet to a region.

4 is correct. You should create multiple subnets each within a different AZ and launch EC2 instances running your application across these subnets.

Question 4, Answer: 3

Explanation:

1 is incorrect. A VPC endpoint can be used for sharing resources between VPCs but it is not used for direct routing between private IP addresses.

2 is incorrect. You cannot route between VPCs by using Internet gateways.

3 is correct. A peering connection enables you to route traffic via private IP addresses between two peered VPCs.

4 is incorrect. An egress-only Internet gateway is used for IPv6 traffic.

Question 5, Answer: 2

Explanation:

1 is incorrect. NAT gateways do not have security groups.

2 is correct. By default, new subnets are associated with the default route table. You need to assign the new route table in order for the instances to see the route to the NAT gateway.

3 is incorrect. You cannot use an Internet Gateway with a private subnet as the instances will not have public IP addresses.

Question 6, Answer: 3

Explanation:

1 is incorrect. Network ACLs are applied at the subnet level and will apply to all instances in the subnet, not just the group of EC2 instances.

2 is incorrect. Operating system-level firewalls require more administrative effort to maintain and are not the best option on AWS.

3 is correct. A Security Group can be applied to the group of EC2 instances. You can specify what ports and protocols are allowed to reach the instances and from what sources.

4 is incorrect. An IAM Policy is not a firewall.

Question 7, Answer: 4

Explanation:

1 is incorrect. You cannot apply deny rules with security groups.

2 is incorrect. This is not a good solution as it may break applications.

3 is incorrect. This would not block the specific IP addresses; it would stop all Internet connectivity.

4 is correct. You can apply deny rules with Network ACLs to block the specific IP addresses only.

Question 8, Answer: 3

Explanation:

1 is incorrect. AWS Managed VPN uses the public Internet, so it's not considered a private connection or low-latency.

2 is incorrect. AWS VPN CloudHub is used for creating a hub and spoke topology of VPN connections. Uses the public Internet not a private connection.

3 is correct. AWS Direct Connect uses private network connections into the AWS Cloud and is high-bandwidth and low-latency. This is good for establishing hybrid cloud configurations.

4 is incorrect. A Transit VPC is used for connecting VPCs across regions.

Question 9, Answer: 4

Explanation:

1 is incorrect. An MX record is a mail exchange record for email servers.

2 is incorrect. An A record simply points a name to an IP address.

3 is incorrect. A CNAME record cannot be pointed at a domain apex record like dctlabs.com.

4 is correct. An Alias record can be used with domain apex records and can point to an ELB.

Question 10, Answer: 3

Explanation:

1 is incorrect. The simple routing policy does not perform any routing based on location or latency.

2 is incorrect. The failover routing policy uses primary and secondary records for high availability.

3 is correct. The latency routing policy directs based on the lowest latency to the AWS resource. Latency increases over distance so this should ensure customers connect to the closest S3 bucket.

4 is incorrect. The weighted policy uses relative weights not location or latency.

Question 11, Answer: 2

Explanation:

1 is incorrect. The latency routing policy directs based on latency (distance) but does not allow you to specify geographic locations.

2 is correct. In this case you need to identify specific geographic locations and associate them with the correct language version.

3 is incorrect. This routing policy returns multiple answers for load balancing.

4 is incorrect. The weighted policy uses relative weights not geographic information.

Question 12, Answer: 3

Explanation:

1 is incorrect. Route 53 latency based routing does not provide automatic failover or 2 IP addresses.

2 is incorrect. Amazon CloudFront is a content delivery network. It does not perform automatic routing across regions and doesn't provide 2 IP addresses for whitelisting.

3 is correct. AWS Global Accelerator provides static IP addresses that act as a fixed entry point to application endpoints in a single or multiple AWS Regions. It uses 2 static anycast IP addresses.

4 is incorrect. Route 53 geolocation based routing does not provide automatic failover or 2 IP addresses.

Question 13, Answer: 2

Explanation:

1 is incorrect. AWS Lambda is not used as the public endpoint for API Gateway.

2 is correct. Amazon CloudFront is used as the public endpoint for API Gateway.

3 is incorrect. Amazon S3 is not used as the public endpoint for API Gateway.

4 is incorrect. Amazon ECS is not used as the public endpoint for API Gateway.

Question 14, Answer: 3

Explanation:

1 is incorrect. To provide low-latency access with Amazon S3 you would need to copy the videos to buckets in different regions around the world and then create a mechanism for directing employees to the local copy.

2 is incorrect. AWS Global Accelerator is used for directing users of applications to local points of presence around the world. It is not used for accessing content in S3, it's used with ELB and EC2.

3 is correct. CloudFront is a content delivery network and is ideal for this use case as it caches the content around the world, provides a single endpoint address, and uses a single source for the videos.

4 is incorrect. AWS Lambda is a compute service and not suited to this use case.

Question 15, Answer: 3

Explanation:

1 is incorrect. Amazon S3 buckets are a valid origin for CloudFront.

2 is incorrect. EC2 instances are a valid origin for CloudFront.

3 is correct. AWS Lambda is not a valid origin for Amazon CloudFront.

4 is incorrect. ELBs are a valid origin for CloudFront.

MANAGEMENT TOOLS

AMAZON CLOUDWATCH

Amazon CloudWatch is a monitoring service for AWS cloud resources and the applications you run on AWS.

CloudWatch vs CloudTrail:

CloudWatch	CloudTrail
Performance monitoring	Auditing
Log events across AWS services - think operations	Log API activity across AWS services - think activities
Higher-level comprehensive monitoring and eventing	More low-level granular
Log from multiple accounts	Log from multiple accounts
Logs stored indefinitely	Logs stored to S3 or CloudWatch indefinitely
Alarms history for 14 days	No native alarming; can use CloudWatch alarms

Used to collect and track metrics, collect and monitor log files, and set alarms.

Automatically react to changes in your AWS resources.

With CloudWatch you can monitor resources such as:

- EC2 instances.
- DynamoDB tables.
- RDS DB instances.
- Custom metrics generated by applications and services.
- Any log files generated by your applications.

Gain system-wide visibility into resource utilization.

Monitor application performance.

Monitor operational health.

CloudWatch is accessed via API, command-line interface, AWS SDKs, and the AWS Management Console.

CloudWatch integrates with IAM.

CloudWatch Logs:

- Amazon CloudWatch Logs lets you monitor and troubleshoot your systems and applications using your existing system, application and custom log files.

- You can use Amazon CloudWatch Logs to monitor, store, and access your log files from Amazon Elastic Compute Cloud (Amazon EC2) instances, AWS CloudTrail, Route 53, and other sources.
- CloudWatch Logs can be used for real time application and system monitoring as well as long term log retention.
- CloudWatch Logs keeps logs indefinitely by default.
- CloudTrail logs can be sent to CloudWatch Logs for real-time monitoring.
- CloudWatch Logs metric filters can evaluate CloudTrail logs for specific terms, phrases or values.

CloudWatch retains metric data as follows:

- Data points with a period of less than 60 seconds are available for 3 hours. These data points are high-resolution custom metrics.
- Data points with a period of 60 seconds (1 minute) are available for 15 days.
- Data points with a period of 300 seconds (5 minute) are available for 63 days.
- Data points with a period of 3600 seconds (1 hour) are available for 455 days (15 months).

AWS CLOUDTRAIL

AWS CloudTrail is a web service that records activity made on your account

A CloudTrail trail can be created which delivers log files to an Amazon S3 bucket.

CloudWatch vs CloudTrail:

CloudWatch	CloudTrail
Performance monitoring	Auditing
Log events across AWS services - think operations	Log API activity across AWS services - think activities
Higher-level comprehensive monitoring and eventing	More low-level granular
Log from multiple accounts	Log from multiple accounts
Logs stored indefinitely	Logs stored to S3 or CloudWatch indefinitely
Alarms history for 14 days	No native alarming; can use CloudWatch alarms

CloudTrail is about logging and saves a history of API calls for your AWS account.

Provides visibility into user activity by recording actions taken on your account.

API history enables security analysis, resource change tracking, and compliance auditing.

Logs API calls made via:

- AWS Management Console.
- AWS SDKs.

- Command line tools.
- Higher-level AWS services (such as CloudFormation).

CloudTrail records account activity and service events from most AWS services and logs the following records:

- The identity of the API caller.
- The time of the API call.
- The source IP address of the API caller.
- The request parameters.
- The response elements returned by the AWS service.

CloudTrail is per AWS account.

Trails can be enabled per region or a trail can be applied to all regions.

Trails can be configured to log data events and management events:

- **Data events:** These events provide insight into the resource operations performed on or within a resource. These are also known as data plane operations.
- **Management events:** Management events provide insight into management operations that are performed on resources in your AWS account. These are also known as control plane operations. Management events can also include non-API events that occur in your account.

CloudTrail log files are encrypted using S3 Server Side Encryption (SSE).

You can also enable encryption using SSE KMS for additional security.

A single KMS key can be used to encrypt log files for trails applied to all regions.

You can consolidate logs from multiple accounts using an S3 bucket:

1. Turn on CloudTrail in the paying account.
2. Create a bucket policy that allows cross-account access.
3. Turn on CloudTrail in the other accounts and use the bucket in the paying account.

You can integrate CloudTrail with CloudWatch Logs to deliver data events captured by CloudTrail to a CloudWatch Logs log stream.

CloudTrail log file integrity validation feature allows you to determine whether a CloudTrail log file was unchanged, deleted, or modified since CloudTrail delivered it to the specified Amazon S3 bucket.

AWS OPSWORKS

AWS OpsWorks is a configuration management service that provides managed instances of Chef and Puppet two very popular automation platforms.

Automates how applications are configured, deployed and managed.

Provide configuration management to deploy code, automate tasks, configure instances, perform upgrades etc.

OpsWorks lets you use Chef and Puppet to automate how servers are configured, deployed, and managed across your Amazon EC2 instances or on-premises compute environments.

OpsWorks is an automation platform that transforms infrastructure into code.

OpsWorks consists of Stacks and Layers:

- Stack are collections of resources needed to support a service or application.
- Stacks are containers of resources (EC2, RDS etc.) that you want to manage collectively.
- Every Stack contains one or more Layers and Layers automate the deployment of packages.
- Stacks can be cloned – but only within the same region.
- Layers represent different components of the application delivery hierarchy.
- EC2 instances, RDS instances, and ELBS are examples of Layers.

OpsWorks is a global service. But when you create a stack, you must specify a region and that stack can only control resources in that region.

There are three offerings: OpsWorks for Chef Automate, OpsWorks for Puppet Enterprise, and OpsWorks Stacks.

AWS OpsWorks for Chef Automate

- A fully-managed configuration management service that hosts Chef Automate, a suite of automation tools from Chef for configuration management, compliance and security, and continuous deployment.
- Completely compatible with tooling and cookbooks from the Chef community and automatically registers new nodes with your Chef server.
- Chef server stores recipes and configuration data.
- Chef client (node) is installed on each server.

AWS OpsWorks for Puppet Enterprise

- A fully-managed configuration management service that hosts Puppet Enterprise, a set of automation tools from Puppet for infrastructure and application management.

AWS OpsWorks Stacks

- An application and server management service that allows you to model your application as a stack containing different layers, such as load balancing, database, and application server.
- OpsWorks Stacks is an AWS creation and uses and embedded Chef Solo client installed on EC2 instances to run Chef recipes.

OpsWorks Stacks supports EC2 instances and on-premise servers as well as an agent.

AWS CLOUDFORMATION

AWS CloudFormation is a service that gives developers and businesses an easy way to create a collection of related AWS resources and provision them in an orderly and predictable fashion.

AWS CloudFormation provides a common language for you to describe and provision all the infrastructure resources in your cloud environment.

CloudFormation can be used to provision a broad range of AWS resources.

Think of CloudFormation as deploying infrastructure as code.

Elastic Beanstalk is more focused on deploying applications on EC2 (PaaS).

CloudFormation can deploy Elastic Beanstalk-hosted applications however the reverse is not possible.

Logical IDs are used to reference resources within the template.

Physical IDs identify resources outside of AWS CloudFormation templates, but only after the resources have been created.

Concept of templates, stacks and change sets:

Templates	The JSON or YAML text file that contains the instructions for building out the AWS environment
Stacks	The entire environment described by the template and created, updated, and deleted as a single unit
Change Sets	A summary of proposed changes to your stack that will allow you to see how those changes might impact your existing resources before implementing them

Templates:

- Architectural designs
- Create, update and delete templates
- Written in JSON or YAML
- CloudFormation determines the order of provisioning
- Don't need to worry about dependencies
- Modifies and updates templates in a controlled way (version control)
- Designer allows you to visualize using a drag and drop interface

Stacks:

- Deployed resources based on templates
- Create, update and delete stacks using templates
- Deployed through the Management Console, CLI or APIs

Template elements

Mandatory:

- File format and version
- List of resources and associated configuration values

Not mandatory:

- Template parameters (limited to 60)
- Output values (limited to 60)
- List of data tables

Puppet and Chef integration is supported.

Can use bootstrap scripts.

Can define deletion policies.

Provides WaitCondition function.

Can create roles in IAM.

VPCs can be created and customized.

VPC peering in the same AWS account can be performed.

Route 53 is supported.

Stack creation errors:

- Automatic rollback on error is enabled by default.
- You will be charged for resources provisioned even if there is an error.

Updating stacks:

- AWS CloudFormation provides two methods for updating stacks: direct update or creating and executing change sets.
- When you directly update a stack, you submit changes and AWS CloudFormation immediately deploys them.
- Use direct updates when you want to quickly deploy your updates.
- With change sets, you can preview the changes AWS CloudFormation will make to your stack, and then decide whether to apply those changes.

StackSets

- AWS CloudFormation StackSets extends the functionality of stacks by enabling you to create, update, or delete stacks across multiple accounts and regions with a single operation.
- Using an administrator account, you define and manage an AWS CloudFormation template, and use the template as the basis for provisioning stacks into selected target accounts across specified regions.
- An administrator account is the AWS account in which you create stack sets.
- A stack set is managed by signing in to the AWS administrator account in which it was created.
- A target account is the account into which you create, update, or delete one or more stacks in your stack set.

Before you can use a stack set to create stacks in a target account, you must set up a trust relationship between the administrator and target accounts.

Best Practices

- AWS provides Python "helper scripts" which can help you install software and start services on your EC2 instances.
- Use CloudFormation to make changes to your landscape rather than going directly into the resources.
- Make use of Change Sets to identify potential trouble spots in your updates.
- Use Stack Policies to explicitly protect sensitive portions of your stack.
- Use a version control system such as CodeCommit or GitHub to track changes to templates.

Charges

- There is no additional charge for AWS CloudFormation.
- You pay for AWS resources (such as Amazon EC2 instances, Elastic Load Balancing load balancers, etc.) created using AWS CloudFormation in the same manner as if you created them manually.

- You only pay for what you use, as you use it; there are no minimum fees and no required upfront commitments.

AWS CONFIG

GENERAL

AWS Config is a fully managed service that provides you with an AWS resource inventory, configuration history, and configuration change notifications to enable security and governance.

With AWS Config you can discover existing AWS resources, export a complete inventory of your AWS resources with all configuration details, and determine how a resource was configured at any point in time.

These capabilities enable compliance auditing, security analysis, resource change tracking, and troubleshooting.

Allow you to assess, audit and evaluate configurations of your AWS resources.

Very useful for Configuration Management as part of an ITIL program.

Creates a baseline of various configuration settings and files and can then track variations against that baseline.

AWS CONFIG VS CLOUDTRAIL

AWS CloudTrail records user API activity on your account and allows you to access information about this activity.

AWS Config records point-in-time configuration details for your AWS resources as Configuration Items (CIs).

You can use an AWS Config CI to answer "What did my AWS resource look like?" at a point in time.

You can use AWS CloudTrail to answer "Who made an API call to modify this resource?".

CONFIG RULES

A Config Rule represents desired configurations for a resource and is evaluated against configuration changes on the relevant resources, as recorded by AWS Config.

AWS Config Rules can check resources for certain desired conditions and if violations are found the resources are flagged as "noncompliant".

Examples of Config Rules:

- Is backup enabled on RDS?
- Is CloudTrail enabled on the AWS account?
- Are EBS volumes encrypted.

CONFIGURATION ITEMS

A Configuration Item (CI) is the configuration of a resource at a given point-in-time. A CI consists of 5 sections:

1. Basic information about the resource that is common across different resource types (e.g., Amazon Resource Names, tags).
2. Configuration data specific to the resource (e.g., EC2 instance type).
3. Map of relationships with other resources (e.g., EC2::Volume vol-3434df43 is "attached to instance" EC2 Instance i-3432ee3a).
4. AWS CloudTrail event IDs that are related to this state.
5. Metadata that helps you identify information about the CI, such as the version of this CI, and when this CI was captured.

CHARGES

With AWS Config, you are charged based on the number configuration items (CIs) recorded for supported resources in your AWS account.

AWS Config creates a configuration item whenever it detects a change to a resource type that it is recording.

AWS SYSTEMS MANAGER

AWS Systems Manager allows you to centralize operational data from multiple AWS services and automate tasks across your AWS resources.

You can create logical groups of resources such as applications, different layers of an application stack, or production versus development environments.

With Systems Manager, you can select a resource group and view its recent API activity, resource configuration changes, related notifications, operational alerts, software inventory, and patch compliance status.

You can also take action on each resource group depending on your operational needs.

Systems Manager provides a central place to view and manage your AWS resources, so you can have complete visibility and control over your operations.

Centralized console and toolset for a wide variety of system management tasks.

Designed for managing a large fleet of systems – tens or hundreds.

SSM Agent enables System Manager features and supports all OSs supported by OS as well as back to Windows Server 2003 and Raspbian.

SSM Agent installed by default on recent AWS-provided base AMIs for Linux and Windows.

Manages AWS-based and on-premises based systems via the agent.

The AWS Systems Manager console integrates with AWS Resource Groups, and it offers grouping capabilities in addition to other native integrations.

Systems Manager Inventory:

- AWS Systems Manager collects information about your instances and the software installed on them, helping you to understand your system configurations and installed applications.
- You can collect data about applications, files, network configurations, Windows services, registries, server roles, updates, and any other system properties.

- The gathered data enables you to manage application assets, track licenses, monitor file integrity, discover applications not installed by a traditional installer, and more.

Configuration Compliance:

- AWS Systems Manager lets you scan your managed instances for patch compliance and configuration inconsistencies.
- You can collect and aggregate data from multiple AWS accounts and Regions, and then drill down into specific resources that aren't compliant.
- By default, AWS Systems Manager displays data about patching and associations. You can also customize the service and create your own compliance types based on your requirements.

Automation:

- AWS Systems Manager allows you to safely automate common and repetitive IT operations and management tasks across AWS resources.
- With Systems Manager, you can create JSON documents that specify a specific list of tasks or use community published documents.
- These documents can be executed directly through the AWS Management Console, CLIs, and SDKs, scheduled in a maintenance window, or triggered based on changes to AWS resources through Amazon CloudWatch Events.
- You can track the execution of each step in the documents as well as require approvals for each step.
- You can also incrementally roll out changes and automatically halt when errors occur.

Run Command:

- Use Systems Manager Run Command to remotely and securely manage the configuration of your managed instances at scale. Use Run Command to perform on-demand changes like updating applications or running Linux shell scripts and Windows PowerShell commands on a target set of dozens or hundreds of instances.

Session Manager:

- AWS Systems Manager provides you safe, secure remote management of your instances at scale without logging into your servers, replacing the need for bastion hosts, SSH, or remote PowerShell.
- It provides a simple way of automating common administrative tasks across groups of instances such as registry edits, user management, and software and patch installations.
- Through integration with AWS Identity and Access Management (IAM), you can apply granular permissions to control the actions users can perform on instances.
- All actions taken with Systems Manager are recorded by AWS CloudTrail, allowing you to audit changes throughout your environment.

Patch Manager:

- AWS Systems Manager helps you select and deploy operating system and software patches automatically across large groups of Amazon EC2 or on-premises instances.
- Through patch baselines, you can set rules to auto-approve select categories of patches to be installed, such as operating system or high severity patches, and you can specify a list of patches that override these rules and are automatically approved or rejected.
- You can also schedule maintenance windows for your patches so that they are only applied during preset times.
- Systems Manager helps ensure that your software is up-to-date and meets your compliance policies.

Maintenance Windows:

- AWS Systems Manager lets you schedule windows of time to run administrative and maintenance tasks across your instances.
- This ensures that you can select a convenient and safe time to install patches and updates or make other configuration changes, improving the availability and reliability of your services and applications.

Distributor:

- Distributor is an AWS Systems Manager feature that enables you to securely store and distribute software packages in your organization.
- You can use Distributor with existing Systems Manager features like Run Command and State Manager to control the lifecycle of the packages running on your instances.

State Manager:

- AWS Systems Manager provides configuration management, which helps you maintain consistent configuration of your Amazon EC2 or on-premises instances.
- With Systems Manager, you can control configuration details such as server configurations, anti-virus definitions, firewall settings, and more.
- You can define configuration policies for your servers through the AWS Management Console or use existing scripts, PowerShell modules, or Ansible playbooks directly from GitHub or Amazon S3 buckets.
- Systems Manager automatically applies your configurations across your instances at a time and frequency that you define.
- You can query Systems Manager at any time to view the status of your instance configurations, giving you on-demand visibility into your compliance status.

Parameter Store:

- AWS Systems Manager provides a centralized store to manage your configuration data, whether plain-text data such as database strings or secrets such as passwords.
- This allows you to separate your secrets and configuration data from your code. Parameters can be tagged and organized into hierarchies, helping you manage parameters more easily.

- For example, you can use the same parameter name, “db-string”, with a different hierarchical path, “dev/db-string” or “prod/db-string”, to store different values.
- Systems Manager is integrated with AWS Key Management Service (KMS), allowing you to automatically encrypt the data you store.
- You can also control user and resource access to parameters using AWS Identity and Access Management (IAM). Parameters can be referenced through other AWS services, such as Amazon Elastic Container Service, AWS Lambda, and AWS CloudFormation.

MANAGEMENT TOOLS QUIZ QUESTIONS

Answers and explanations are provided below after the last question in this section.

Question 1:

You are a Solutions Architect at Digital Cloud Training. A client from a large multinational corporation is working on a deployment of a significant amount of resources into AWS. The client would like to be able to deploy resources across multiple AWS accounts and regions using a single toolset and template. You have been asked to suggest a toolset that can provide this functionality?

A. Use a CloudFormation template that creates a stack and specify the logical IDs of each account and region

B. Use a CloudFormation StackSet and specify the target accounts and regions in which the stacks will be created

C. Use a third-party product such as Terraform that has support for multiple AWS accounts and regions

D. This cannot be done, use separate CloudFormation templates per AWS account and region

Question 2:

A Solutions Architect needs to monitor application logs and receive a notification whenever a specific number of occurrences of certain HTTP status code errors occur. Which tool should the Architect use?

A. CloudWatch Events

B. CloudWatch Logs

C. CloudTrail Trails

D. CloudWatch Metrics

Question 3:

A Solutions Architect is designing the system monitoring and deployment layers of a serverless application. The system monitoring layer will manage system visibility through recording logs and metrics and the deployment layer will deploy the application stack and manage workload changes through a release management process.

The Architect needs to select the most appropriate AWS services for these functions. Which services and frameworks should be used for the system monitoring and deployment layers? (choose 2)

A. Use AWS X-Ray to package, test, and deploy the serverless application stack

B. Use Amazon CloudTrail for consolidating system and application logs and monitoring custom metrics

C. Use AWS Lambda to package, test, and deploy the serverless application stack

D. Use AWS SAM to package, test, and deploy the serverless application stack

E. Use Amazon CloudWatch for consolidating system and application logs and monitoring custom metrics

Question 4:

A systems integration consultancy regularly deploys and manages multi-tiered web services for customers on AWS. The SysOps team are facing challenges in tracking changes that are made to the web services and rolling back when problems occur.

Which of the approaches below would BEST assist the SysOps team?

A. Use AWS Systems Manager to manage all updates to the web services

B. Use CodeDeploy to manage version control for the web services

C. Use Trusted Advisor to record updates made to the web services

D. Use CloudFormation templates to deploy and manage the web services

Question 5:

An event in CloudTrail is the record of an activity in an AWS account. What are the two types of events that can be logged in CloudTrail? (choose 2)

A. System Events which are also known as instance level operations

B. Management Events which are also known as control plane operations

C. Platform Events which are also known as hardware level operations

D. Data Events which are also known as data plane operations

E. API events which are also known as CloudWatch events

Question 6:

Your company currently uses Puppet Enterprise for infrastructure and application management. You are looking to move some of your infrastructure onto AWS and would like to continue to use the same tools in the cloud. What AWS service provides a fully managed configuration management service that is compatible with Puppet Enterprise?

A. Elastic Beanstalk

B. CloudFormation

C. OpsWorks

D. CloudTrail

Question 7:

The operations team in your company are looking for a method to automatically respond to failed system status check alarms that are being received from an EC2 instance. The system in question is experiencing intermittent problems with its operating system software.

Which two steps will help you to automate the resolution of the operating system software issues? (choose 2)

A. Create a CloudWatch alarm that monitors the “StatusCheckFailed_System” metric

B. Create a CloudWatch alarm that monitors the “StatusCheckFailed_Instance” metric

C. Configure an EC2 action that recovers the instance

D. Configure an EC2 action that terminates the instance

E. Configure an EC2 action that reboots the instance

MANAGEMENT TOOLS - ANSWERS

Question 1 answer: B

Explanation:

AWS CloudFormation StackSets extends the functionality of stacks by enabling you to create, update, or delete stacks across multiple accounts and regions with a single operation.

Using an administrator account, you define and manage an AWS CloudFormation template, and use the template as the basis for provisioning stacks into selected target accounts across specified regions. An administrator account is the AWS account in which you create stack sets.

A stack set is managed by signing in to the AWS administrator account in which it was created. A target account is the account into which you create, update, or delete one or more stacks in your stack set.

Before you can use a stack set to create stacks in a target account, you must set up a trust relationship between the administrator and target accounts.

A regular CloudFormation template cannot be used across regions and accounts. You would need to create copies of the template and then manage updates.

You do not need to use a third-party product such as Terraform as this functionality can be delivered through native AWS technology.

Question 2 answer: B

Explanation:

You can use **CloudWatch Logs** to monitor applications and systems using log data. For example, CloudWatch Logs can track the number of errors that occur in your application logs and send you a notification whenever the rate of errors exceeds a threshold you specify. This is the best tool for this requirement.

Amazon CloudWatch Events delivers a near real-time stream of system events that describe changes in Amazon Web Services (AWS) resources. Though you can generate custom application-level events and publish them to CloudWatch Events this is not the best tool for monitoring application logs.

CloudTrail is used for monitoring API activity on your account, not for monitoring application logs.

CloudWatch Metrics are the fundamental concept in CloudWatch. A metric represents a time-ordered set of data points that are published to CloudWatch. You cannot use a metric alone; it is used when setting up monitoring for any service in CloudWatch.

Question 3 answer: D,E

Explanation:

AWS Serverless Application Model (AWS SAM) is an extension of AWS CloudFormation that is used to package, test, and deploy serverless applications.

With Amazon CloudWatch, you can access system metrics on all the AWS services you use, consolidate system and application level logs, and create business key performance indicators (KPIs) as custom metrics for your specific needs.

AWS Lambda is used for executing your code as functions, it is not used for packaging, testing and deployment. AWS Lambda is used with AWS SAM.

AWS X-Ray lets you analyze and debug serverless applications by providing distributed tracing and service maps to easily identify performance bottlenecks by visualizing a request end-to-end.

Question 4 answer: D

Explanation:

When you provision your infrastructure with AWS CloudFormation, the AWS CloudFormation template describes exactly what resources are provisioned and their settings. Because these templates are text files, you simply track differences in your templates to track changes to your infrastructure, similar to the way developers control revisions to source code. For example, you can use a version control system with your templates so that you know exactly what changes were made, who made them, and when. If at any point you need to reverse changes to your infrastructure, you can use a previous version of your template.

AWS Systems Manager gives you visibility and control of your infrastructure on AWS. Systems Manager provides a unified user interface so you can view operational data from multiple AWS services and allows you to automate operational tasks across your AWS resources. However, CloudFormation would be the preferred method of maintaining the state of the overall architecture.

AWS CodeDeploy is a deployment service that automates application deployments to Amazon EC2 instances, on-premises instances, or serverless Lambda function.

AWS Trusted Advisor is an online resource to help you reduce cost, increase performance, and improve security by optimizing your AWS environment, Trusted Advisor provides real time guidance to help you provision your resources following AWS best practices.

Question 5 answer: B,D

Explanation:

Trails can be configured to log Data events and Management events:

- **Data events:** These events provide insight into the resource operations performed on or within a resource. These are also known as data plane operations
- **Management events:** Management events provide insight into management operations that are performed on resources in your AWS account. These are also known as control plane operations. Management events can also include non-API events that occur in your account

Question 6 answer: C

Explanation:

The only service that would allow you to continue to use the same tools is OpsWorks. AWS OpsWorks is a configuration management service that provides managed instances of Chef and Puppet. OpsWorks lets you use Chef and Puppet to automate how servers are configured, deployed, and managed across your Amazon EC2 instances or on-premises compute environments.

Question 7 answer: B,E

Explanation:

EC2 status checks are performed every minute and each returns a pass or a fail status. If all checks pass, the overall status of the instance is OK. If one or more checks fail, the overall status is impaired.

System status checks detect (StatusCheckFailed_System) problems with your instance that require AWS involvement to repair whereas **Instance status checks** (StatusCheckFailed_Instance) detect problems that require your involvement to repair.

The action to *recover* the instance is only supported on specific instance types and can be used only with StatusCheckFailed_System.

Configuring an action to terminate the instance would not help resolve system software issues as the instance would be terminated.

MEDIA SERVICES

AMAZON ELASTIC TRANSCODER

Amazon Elastic Transcoder is a highly scalable, easy to use and cost-effective way for developers and businesses to convert (or "transcode") video and audio files from their source format into versions that will playback on devices like smartphones, tablets and PCs.

Supports a wide range of input and output formats, resolutions, bitrates, and frame rates.

Also offers features for automatic video bit rate optimization, generation of thumbnails, overlay of visual watermarks, caption support, DRM packaging, progressive downloads, encryption and more.

Picks up files from an input S3 bucket and saves the output to an output S3 bucket.

Uses a JSON API, and SDKs are provided for Python, Node.js, Java, .NET, PHP, and Ruby.

Provides transcoding pre-sets for popular formats.

You are charged based on the duration of the content and the resolution or format of the media.

MEDIA SERVICES QUIZ QUESTIONS

Answers and explanations are provided below after the last question in this section.

Question 1:

You are undertaking a project to make some audio and video files that your company uses for onboarding new staff members available via a mobile application. You are looking for a cost-effective way to convert the files from their current formats into formats that are compatible with smartphones and tablets. The files are currently stored in an S3 bucket.

What AWS service can help with converting the files?

A. MediaConvert

B. Data Pipeline

C. Elastic Transcoder

D. Rekognition

Question 2:

Which service provides a way to convert video and audio files from their source format into versions that will playback on devices like smartphones, tablets and PCs?

A. Amazon Elastic Transcoder

B. AWS Glue

C. Amazon Rekognition

D. Amazon Comprehend

MEDIA SERVICES - ANSWERS

Question 1 answer: C

Explanation:

Amazon Elastic Transcoder is a highly scalable, easy to use and cost-effective way for developers and businesses to convert (or "transcode") video and audio files from their source format into versions that will playback on devices like smartphones, tablets and PCs.

MediaConvert converts file-based content for broadcast and multi-screen delivery.

Data Pipeline helps you move, integrate, and process data across AWS compute and storage resources, as well as your on-premises resources.

Rekognition is a deep learning-based visual analysis service.

Question 2 answer: A

Explanation:

Amazon Elastic Transcoder is a highly scalable, easy to use and cost-effective way for developers and businesses to convert (or "transcode") video and audio files from their source format into versions that will playback on devices like smartphones, tablets and PCs.

AWS Glue is a fully managed extract, transform, and load (ETL) service that makes it easy for customers to prepare and load their data for analytics.

Amazon Rekognition makes it easy to add image and video analysis to your applications.

Amazon Comprehend is a natural language processing (NLP) service that uses machine learning to find insights and relationships in text.

ANALYTICS

AMAZON EMR

Amazon EMR is a web service that enables businesses, researchers, data analysts, and developers to easily and cost-effectively process vast amounts of data.

EMR utilizes a hosted Hadoop framework running on Amazon EC2 and Amazon S3.

Managed Hadoop framework for processing huge amounts of data.

Also support Apache Spark, HBase, Presto and Flink.

Most commonly used for log analysis, financial analysis, or extract, translate and loading (ETL) activities.

A Step is a programmatic task for performing some process on the data (e.g. count words).

A cluster is a collection of EC2 instances provisioned by EMR to run your Steps.

EMR uses Apache Hadoop as its distributed data processing engine, which is an open source, Java software framework that supports data-intensive distributed applications running on large clusters of commodity hardware.

EMR is a good place to deploy Apache Spark, an open-source distributed processing used for big data workloads which utilizes in-memory caching and optimized query execution.

You can also launch Presto clusters. Presto is an open-source distributed SQL query engine designed for fast analytic queries against large datasets.

EMR launches all nodes for a given cluster in the same Amazon EC2 Availability Zone.

You can access Amazon EMR by using the AWS Management Console, Command Line Tools, SDKS, or the EMR API.

With EMR you have access to the underlying operating system (you can SSH in).

AMAZON KINESIS

GENERAL

Amazon Kinesis makes it easy to collect, process, and analyze real-time, streaming data so you can get timely insights and react quickly to new information.

Collection of services for processing streams of various data.

Data is processed in "shards" – with each shard able to ingest 1000 records per second.

There is a default limit of 500 shards, but you can request an increase to unlimited shards.

A record consists of a partition key, sequence number, and data blob (up to 1 MB).

Transient data store – default retention of 24 hours but can be configured for up to 7 days.

There are four types of Kinesis service and these are detailed below.

KINESIS VIDEO STREAMS

Kinesis Video Streams makes it easy to securely stream video from connected devices to AWS for analytics, machine learning (ML), and other processing.

Durably stores, encrypts, and indexes video data streams, and allows access to data through easy-to-use APIs.

Producers provide data streams.

Stores data for 24 hours by default, up to 7 days.

Stores data in shards – 5 transaction per second for reads, up to a max read rate of 2MB per second and 1000 records per second for writes up to a max of 1MB per second.

Consumers receive and process data.

Can have multiple shards in a stream.

Supports encryption at rest with server-side encryption (KMS) with a customer master key.

KINESIS DATA STREAMS

Kinesis Data Streams enables you to build custom applications that process or analyze streaming data for specialized needs.

Kinesis Data Streams enables real-time processing of streaming big data.

Kinesis Data Streams is useful for rapidly moving data off data producers and then continuously processing the data.

Kinesis Data Streams **stores data** for later processing by applications (key difference with Firehose which delivers data directly to AWS services).

Common use cases include:

- Accelerated log and data feed intake.
- Real-time metrics and reporting.
- Real-time data analytics.
- Complex stream processing.

The following diagram illustrates the high-level architecture of Kinesis Data Streams.

- Producers continually push data to Kinesis Data Streams.
- Consumers process the data in real time.
- Consumers can store their results using an AWS service such as Amazon DynamoDB, Amazon Redshift, or Amazon S3.
- Kinesis Streams applications are consumers that run on EC2 instances.
- Shards are uniquely identified groups or data records in a stream.
- Records are the data units stored in a Kinesis Stream.

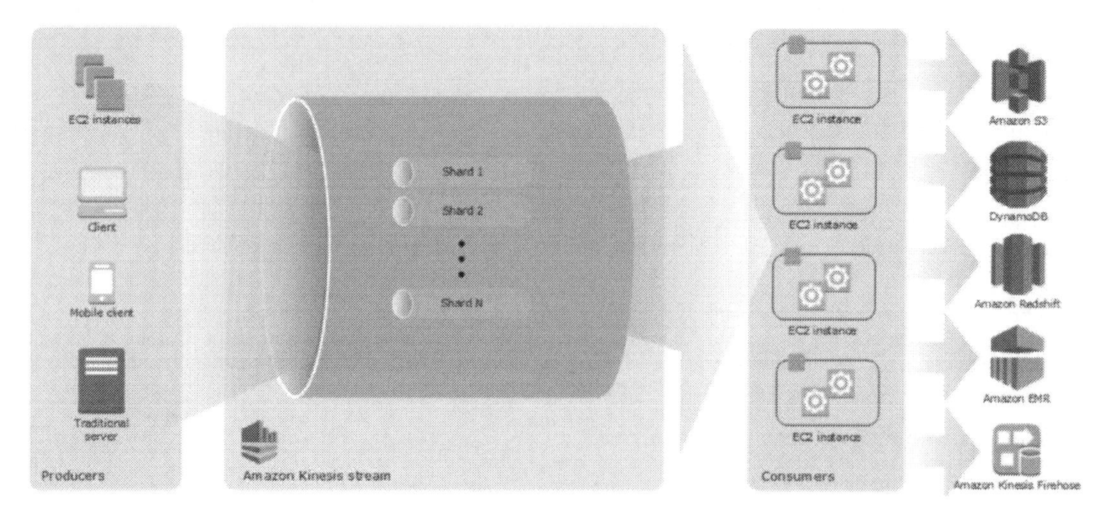

A producer creates the data that makes up the stream.

Producers can be used through the following:

- Kinesis Streams API.
- Kinesis Producer Library (KPL).
- Kinesis Agent.

A record is the unit of data stored in a Amazon Kinesis data stream.

A record is composed of a sequence number, partition key, and data blob.

By default, records of a stream are accessible for up to 24 hours from the time they are added to the stream (can be raised to 7 days by enabling extended data retention).

A data blob is the data of interest your data producer adds to a data stream.

The maximum size of a data blob (the data payload before Base64-encoding) within one record is 1 megabyte (MB).

A shard is the base throughput unit of an Amazon Kinesis data stream.

One shard provides a capacity of 1MB/sec data input and 2MB/sec data output.

Each shard can support up to 1000 PUT records per second.

A stream is composed of one or more shards.

Consumers are the EC2 instances that analyze the data received from a stream.

Consumers are known as Amazon Kinesis Streams Applications.

When the data rate increases, add more shards to increase the size of the stream.

Remove shards when the data rate decreases.

Partition keys are used to group data by shard within a stream.

Kinesis Streams uses KMS master keys for encryption.

To read from or write to an encrypted stream the producer and consumer applications must have permission to access the master key.

Kinesis Data Streams replicates synchronously across three AZs.

KINESIS DATA FIREHOSE

Kinesis Data Firehose is the easiest way to load streaming data into data stores and analytics tools.

Captures, transforms, and loads streaming data.

Enables near real-time analytics with existing business intelligence tools and dashboards.

Kinesis Data Streams can be used as the source(s) to Kinesis Data Firehose.

You can configure Kinesis Data Firehose to transform your data before delivering it.

With Kinesis Data Firehose you don't need to write an application or manage resources.

Firehose can batch, compress, and encrypt data before loading it.

Firehose synchronously replicates data across three AZs as it is transported to destinations.

Each delivery stream stores data records for up to 24 hours.

A source is where your streaming data is continuously generated and captured.

A delivery stream is the underlying entity of Amazon Kinesis Data Firehose.

A record is the data of interest your data producer sends to a delivery stream.

The maximum size of a record (before Base64-encoding) is 1000 KB.

A destination is the data store where your data will be delivered.

Firehose Destinations include:

- Amazon S3
- Amazon Redshift
- Amazon Elasticsearch Service
- Splunk

Producers provide data streams.

No shards, totally automated.

Can encrypt data with an existing AWS Key Management Service (KMS) key.

Server-side-encryption can be used if Kinesis Streams is used as the data source.

Firehose can invoke an AWS Lambda function to transform incoming data before delivering it to a destination.

For Amazon S3 destinations, streaming data is delivered to your S3 bucket. If data transformation is enabled, you can optionally back up source data to another Amazon S3 bucket:

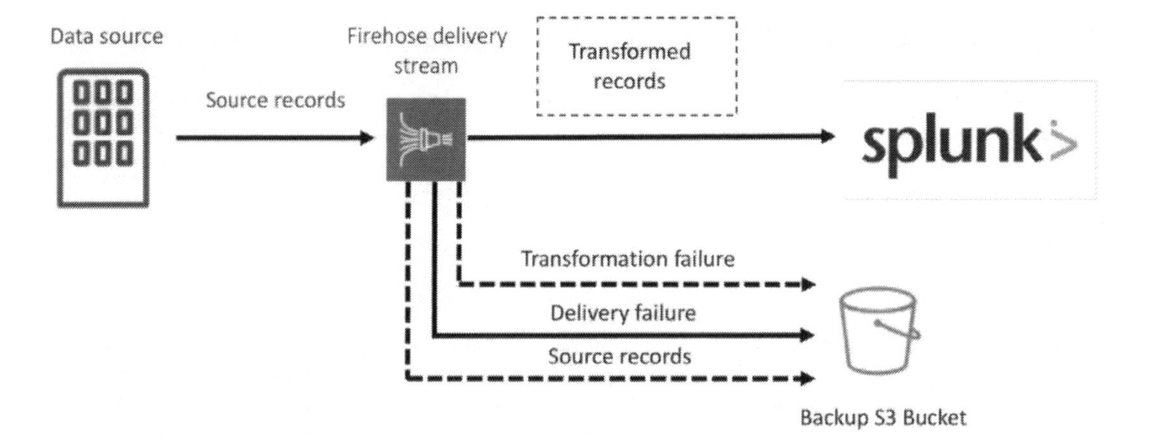

For Amazon Redshift destinations, streaming data is delivered to your S3 bucket first. Kinesis Data Firehose then issues an Amazon Redshift **COPY** command to load data from your S3 bucket to your Amazon Redshift cluster. If data transformation is enabled, you can optionally back up source data to another Amazon S3 bucket:

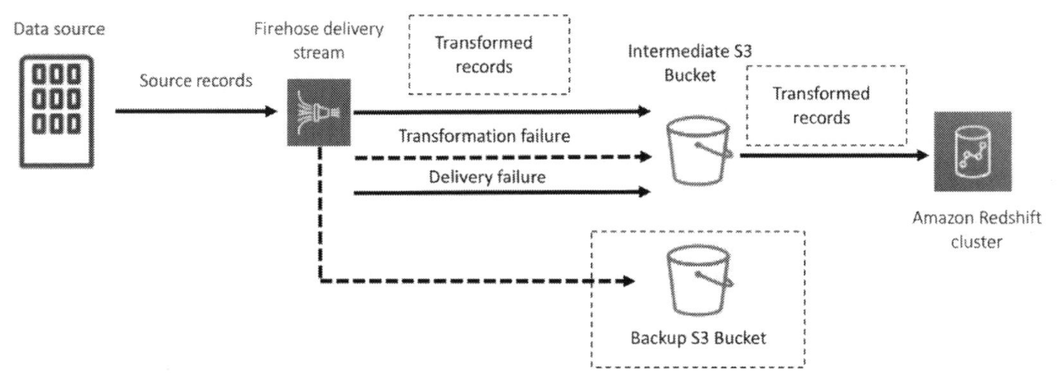

For Amazon Elaticsearch destinations, streaming data is delivered to your Amazon ES cluster, and it can optionally be backed up to your S3 bucket concurrently:

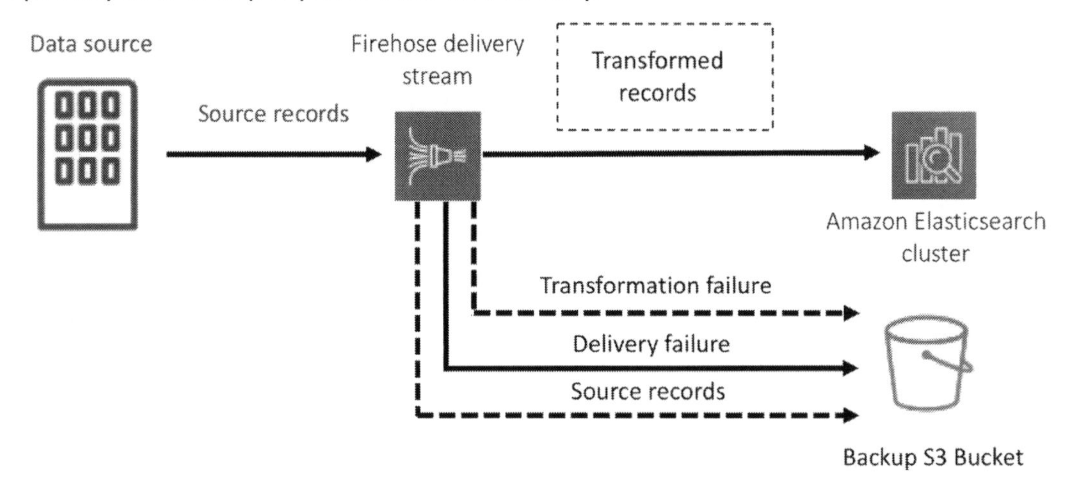

For Splunk destinations, streaming data is delivered to Splunk, and it can optionally be backed up to your S3 bucket concurrently:

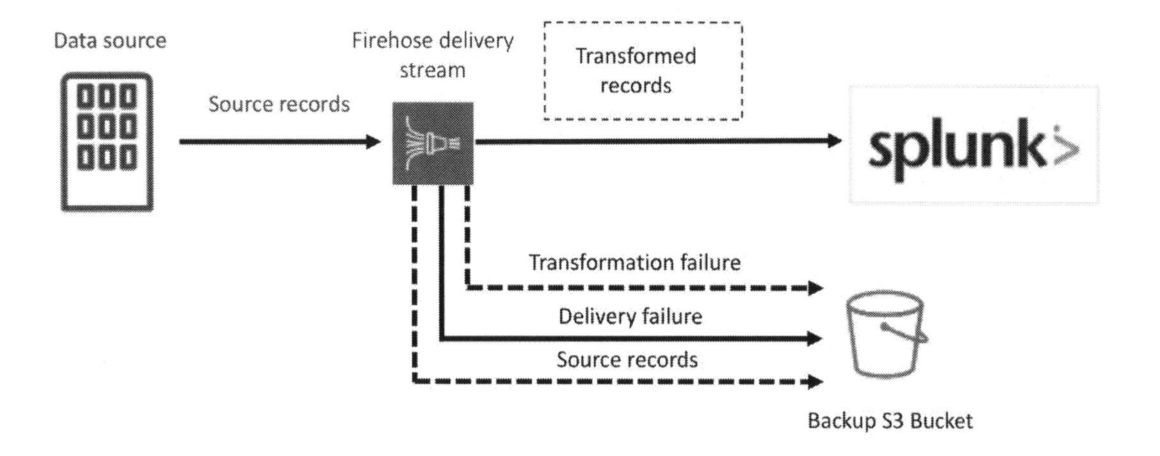

KINESIS DATA ANALYTICS

Amazon Kinesis Data Analytics is the easiest way to process and analyze real-time, streaming data.

Can use standard SQL queries to process Kinesis data streams.

Provides real-time analysis.

Use cases:

- Generate time-series analytics.
- Feed real-time dashboards.
- Create real-time alerts and notifications.

Quickly author and run powerful SQL code against streaming sources.

Can ingest data from Kinesis Streams and Kinesis Firehose.

Output to S3, RedShift, Elasticsearch and Kinesis Data Streams.

Sits over Kinesis Data Streams and Kinesis Data Firehose.

A Kinesis Data Analytics application consists of three components:

- Input – the streaming source for your application.
- Application code – a series of SQL statements that process input and produce output.
- Output – one or more in-application streams to hold intermediate results.

Kinesis Data Analytics supports two types of inputs: streaming data sources and reference data sources:

- A streaming data source is continuously generated data that is read into your application for processing.
- A reference data source is static data that your application uses to enrich data coming in from streaming sources.

Can configure destinations to persist the results.

Supports Kinesis Streams and Kinesis Firehose (S3, RedShift, ElasticSearch) as destinations.

IAM can be used to provide Kinesis Analytics with permissions to read records from sources and write to destinations.

AMAZON ATHENA

AMAZON ATHENA GENERAL

Amazon Athena is an interactive query service that makes it easy to analyze data in Amazon S3 using standard SQL.

Athena is serverless, so there is no infrastructure to manage, and you pay only for the queries that you run.

Athena is easy to use – simply point to your data in Amazon S3, define the schema, and start querying using standard SQL.

Amazon Athena uses Presto with full standard SQL support and works with a variety of standard data formats, including CSV, JSON, ORC, Apache Parquet and Avro.

While Amazon Athena is ideal for quick, ad-hoc querying and integrates with Amazon QuickSight for easy visualization, it can also handle complex analysis, including large joins, window functions, and arrays.

Amazon Athena uses a managed Data Catalog to store information and schemas about the databases and tables that you create for your data stored in Amazon S3.

With Amazon Athena, you don't have to worry about managing or tuning clusters to get fast performance.

Athena is optimized for fast performance with Amazon S3.

Athena automatically executes queries in parallel, so that you get query results in seconds, even on large datasets.

Most results are delivered within seconds.

With Athena, there's no need for complex ETL jobs to prepare data for analysis.

This makes it easy for anyone with SQL skills to quickly analyze large-scale datasets.

Athena is out-of-the-box integrated with AWS Glue Data Catalog, allowing you to create a unified metadata repository across various services, crawl data sources to discover schemas and populate your Catalog with new and modified table and partition definitions, and maintain schema versioning.

You can also use Glue's fully-managed ETL capabilities to transform data or convert it into columnar formats to optimize cost and improve performance.

USE CASES

Query services like Amazon Athena, data warehouses like Amazon Redshift, and sophisticated data processing frameworks like Amazon EMR, all address different needs and use cases.

Amazon Redshift provides the fastest query performance for enterprise reporting and business intelligence workloads, particularly those involving extremely complex SQL with multiple joins and sub-queries.

Amazon EMR makes it simple and cost-effective to run highly distributed processing frameworks such as Hadoop, Spark, and Presto when compared to on-premises deployments. Amazon EMR is flexible – you can run custom applications and code, and define specific compute, memory, storage, and application parameters to optimize your analytic requirements.

Amazon Athena provides the easiest way to run ad-hoc queries for data in S3 without the need to setup or manage any servers.

The table below shows the primary use case and situations for using a few AWS query and analytics services:

AWS Service	Primary Use Case	When to use
Amazon Athena	Query	Run interactive queries against data directly in Amazon S3 without worrying about formatting data or managing infrastructure. Can use with other services such as Amazon RedShift
Amazon RedShift	Data Warehouse	Pull data from many sources, format and organize it, store it, and suppor complex, high speed queries that produce business reports.
Amazon EMR	Data Processing	Highly distributed processing frameworks such as Hadoop, Spark, and Presto. Run a wide variety of scale-out data processing tasks for applications such as machine learning, graph analytics, data transformation, streaming data.
AWS Glue	ETL Service	Transform and move data to various destinations. Used to prepare and load data for analytics. Data source can be S3, RedShift or other database Glue Data Catalog can be queried by Athena, EMR and RedShift Spectrum

PRICING

With Amazon Athena, you pay only for the queries that you run.

You are charged based on the amount of data scanned by each query.

You can get significant cost savings and performance gains by compressing, partitioning, or converting your data to a columnar format, because each of those operations reduces the amount of data that Athena needs to scan to execute a query.

AWS GLUE

AWS GLUE GENERAL

AWS Glue is a fully-managed, pay-as-you-go, extract, transform, and load (ETL) service that automates the time-consuming steps of data preparation for analytics.

AWS Glue automatically discovers and profiles data via the Glue Data Catalog, recommends and generates ETL code to transform your source data into target schemas.

AWS Glue runs the ETL jobs on a fully managed, scale-out Apache Spark environment to load your data into its destination.

AWS Glue also allows you to setup, orchestrate, and monitor complex data flows.

You can create and run an ETL job with a few clicks in the AWS Management Console.

Simply point AWS Glue to your data stored on AWS, and AWS Glue discovers data and stores the associated metadata (e.g. table definition and schema) in the AWS Glue Data Catalog.

Once cataloged, data is immediately searchable, queryable, and available for ETL.

AWS Glue consists of a Data Catalog which is a central metadata repository, an ETL engine that can automatically generate Scala or Python code, and a flexible scheduler that handles dependency resolution, job monitoring, and retries.

Together, these automate much of the undifferentiated heavy lifting involved with discovering, categorizing, cleaning, enriching, and moving data, so you can spend more time analyzing your data.

AWS Glue crawlers connect to a source or target data store, progress through a prioritized list of classifiers to determine the schema for the data, and then creates metadata in the AWS Glue Data Catalog.

The metadata is stored in tables in a data catalog and used in the authoring process of ETL jobs.

You can run crawlers on a schedule, on-demand, or trigger them based on an event to ensure that your metadata is up-to-date.

AWS Glue automatically generates the code to extract, transform, and load data.

Simply point AWS Glue to a source and target, and AWS Glue creates ETL scripts to transform, flatten, and enrich the data.

The code is generated in Scala or Python and written for Apache Spark.

AWS Glue helps clean and prepare data for analysis by providing a Machine Learning Transform called FindMatches for deduplication and finding matching records.

USE CASES

Use AWS Glue to discover properties of data, transform it, and prepare it for analytics.

Glue can automatically discover both structured and semi-structured data stored in data lakes on Amazon S3, data warehouses in Amazon Redshift, and various databases running on AWS.

It provides a unified view of data via the Glue Data Catalog that is available for ETL, querying and reporting using services like Amazon Athena, Amazon EMR, and Amazon Redshift Spectrum.

Glue automatically generates Scala or Python code for ETL jobs that you can further customize using tools you are already familiar with.

AWS Glue is serverless, so there are no compute resources to configure and manage.

ANALYTICS QUIZ QUESTIONS

Answers and explanations are provided below after the last question in this section.

Question 1:

A user is testing a new service that receives location updates from 5,000 rental cars every hour. Which service will collect data and automatically scale to accommodate production workload?

A. Amazon EC2

B. Amazon Kinesis Firehose

C. Amazon EBS

D. Amazon API Gateway

Question 2:

Which AWS service can be used to prepare and load data for analytics using an extract, transform and load (ETL) process?

A. AWS Lambda

B. Amazon Athena

C. AWS Glue

D. Amazon EMR

Question 3:

A Solutions Architect is designing a solution for a financial application that will receive trading data in large volumes. What is the best solution for ingesting and processing a very large number of data streams in near real time?

A. Amazon EMR

B. Amazon Kinesis Firehose

C. Amazon Redshift

D. Amazon Kinesis Data Streams

Question 4:

You have recently enabled Access Logs on your Application Load Balancer (ALB). One of your colleagues would like to process the log files using a hosted Hadoop service. What configuration changes and services can be leveraged to deliver this requirement?

A. Configure Access Logs to be delivered to DynamoDB and use EMR for processing the log files

B. Configure Access Logs to be delivered to S3 and use Kinesis for processing the log files

C. Configure Access Logs to be delivered to S3 and use EMR for processing the log files

D. Configure Access Logs to be delivered to EC2 and install Hadoop for processing the log files

Question 5:

A Solutions Architect is designing the messaging and streaming layers of a serverless application. The messaging layer will manage communications between components and the streaming layer will manage real-time analysis and processing of streaming data.

The Architect needs to select the most appropriate AWS services for these functions. Which services should be used for the messaging and streaming layers? (choose 2)

A. Use Amazon Kinesis for collecting, processing and analyzing real-time streaming data

B. Use Amazon EMR for collecting, processing and analyzing real-time streaming data

C. Use Amazon SNS for providing a fully managed messaging service

D. Use Amazon SWF for providing a fully managed messaging service

E. Use Amazon CloudTrail for collecting, processing and analyzing real-time streaming data

ANALYTICS - ANSWERS

Question 1 answer: B

Explanation:

What we need here is a service that can streaming collect streaming data. The only option available is Kinesis Firehose which captures, transforms, and loads streaming data into "destinations" such as S3, RedShift, Elasticsearch and Splunk.

Amazon EC2 is not suitable for collecting streaming data.

EBS is a block-storage service in which you attach volumes to EC2 instances, this does not assist with collecting streaming data (see previous point).

Amazon API Gateway is used for hosting and managing APIs not for receiving streaming data.

Question 2 answer: C

Explanation:

AWS Glue is a fully managed extract, transform, and load (ETL) service that makes it easy for customers to prepare and load their data for analytics.

Amazon Elastic Map Reduce (EMR) provides a managed Hadoop framework that makes it easy, fast, and cost-effective to process vast amounts of data across dynamically scalable Amazon EC2 instances.

Amazon Athena is an interactive query service that makes it easy to analyze data in Amazon S3 using standard SQL.

AWS Lambda is a serverless application that runs code as functions in response to events.

Question 3 answer: D

Explanation:

Kinesis Data Streams enables you to build custom applications that process or analyze streaming data for specialized needs. It enables real-time processing of streaming big data and can be used for rapidly moving data off data producers and then continuously processing the data. Kinesis Data Streams stores data for later processing by applications (key difference with Firehose which delivers data directly to AWS services).

Kinesis Firehose can allow transformation of data and it then delivers data to supported services.

RedShift is a data warehouse solution used for analyzing data.

EMR is a hosted Hadoop framework that is used for analytics.

Question 4 answer: C

Explanation:

Access Logs can be enabled on ALB and configured to store data in an S3 bucket. Amazon EMR is a web service that enables businesses, researchers, data analysts, and developers to easily and cost-effectively process vast amounts of data. EMR utilizes a hosted Hadoop framework running on Amazon EC2 and Amazon S3.

Neither Kinesis nor EC2 provide a hosted Hadoop service.

You cannot configure access logs to be delivered to DynamoDB.

Question 5 answer: A,C

Explanation:

Amazon Kinesis makes it easy to collect, process, and analyze real-time streaming data. With Amazon Kinesis Analytics, you can run standard SQL or build entire streaming applications using SQL.

Amazon Simple Notification Service (Amazon SNS) provides a fully managed messaging service for pub/sub patterns using asynchronous event notifications and mobile push notifications for microservices, distributed systems, and serverless applications.

Amazon Elastic Map Reduce runs on EC2 instances so is not serverless.

Amazon Simple Workflow Service is used for executing tasks not sending messages.

Amazon CloudTrail is used for recording API activity on your account.

AWS SECURITY, IDENTITY & COMPLIANCE

AWS IAM

GENERAL IAM CONCEPTS

IAM is used to securely control individual and group access to AWS resources.

IAM makes it easy to provide multiple users secure access to AWS resources.

IAM can be used to manage:

- Users
- Groups
- Access policies
- Roles
- User credentials
- User password policies
- Multi-factor authentication (MFA)
- API keys for programmatic access (CLI)

Provides centralized control of your AWS account.

Enables shared access to your AWS account.

By default, new users are created with NO access to any AWS services – they can only login to the AWS console.

Permission must be explicitly granted to allow a user to access an AWS service.

IAM users are individuals who have been granted access to an AWS account.

Each IAM user has three main components:

- A user-name
- A password
- Permissions to access various resources

You can apply granular permissions with IAM.

You can assign users individual security credentials such as access keys, passwords, and multi-factor authentication devices.

IAM is not used for application-level authentication.

Identity Federation (including AD, Facebook etc.) can be configured allowing secure access to resources in an AWS account without creating an IAM user account.

Multi-factor authentication (MFA) can be enabled/enforced for the AWS account and for individual users under the account.

MFA uses an authentication device that continually generates random, six-digit, single-use authentication codes.

You can authenticate using an MFA device in the following three ways:

- Through the **AWS Management Console** – the user is prompted for a user name, password and authentication code.
- Using the **AWS API** – restrictions are added to IAM policies and developers can request temporary security credentials and pass MFA parameters in their AWS STS API requests.
- Using the **AWS CLI** by obtaining temporary security credentials from STS (aws sts get-session-token).

It is a best practice to use MFA for all users and to use U2F or hardware MFA devices for all privileged users.

IAM is universal (global) and does not apply to regions.

IAM is eventually consistent.

IAM replicates data across multiple data centers around the world.

The "root account" is the account created when you setup the AWS account. It has complete Admin access and is the only account that has this access by default.

It is a best practice to not use the root account for anything other than billing.

Power user access allows all permissions except the management of groups and users in IAM.

Temporary security credentials consist of the AWS access key ID, secret access key, and security token.

IAM can assign temporary security credentials to provide users with temporary access to services/resources.

To sign-in you must provide your account ID or account alias in addition to a user name and password.

The sign-in URL includes the account ID or account alias, e.g.:

https://***My_AWS_Account_ID***.signin.aws.amazon.com/console/.

Alternatively, you can sign-in at the following URL and enter your account ID or alias manually:

https://console.aws.amazon.com/.

IAM integrates with many different AWS services.

IAM supports PCI DSS compliance.

AWS recommend that you use the AWS SDKs to make programmatic API calls to IAM.

However, you can also use the IAM Query API to make direct calls to the IAM web service.

IAM INFRASTRUCTURE ELEMENTS

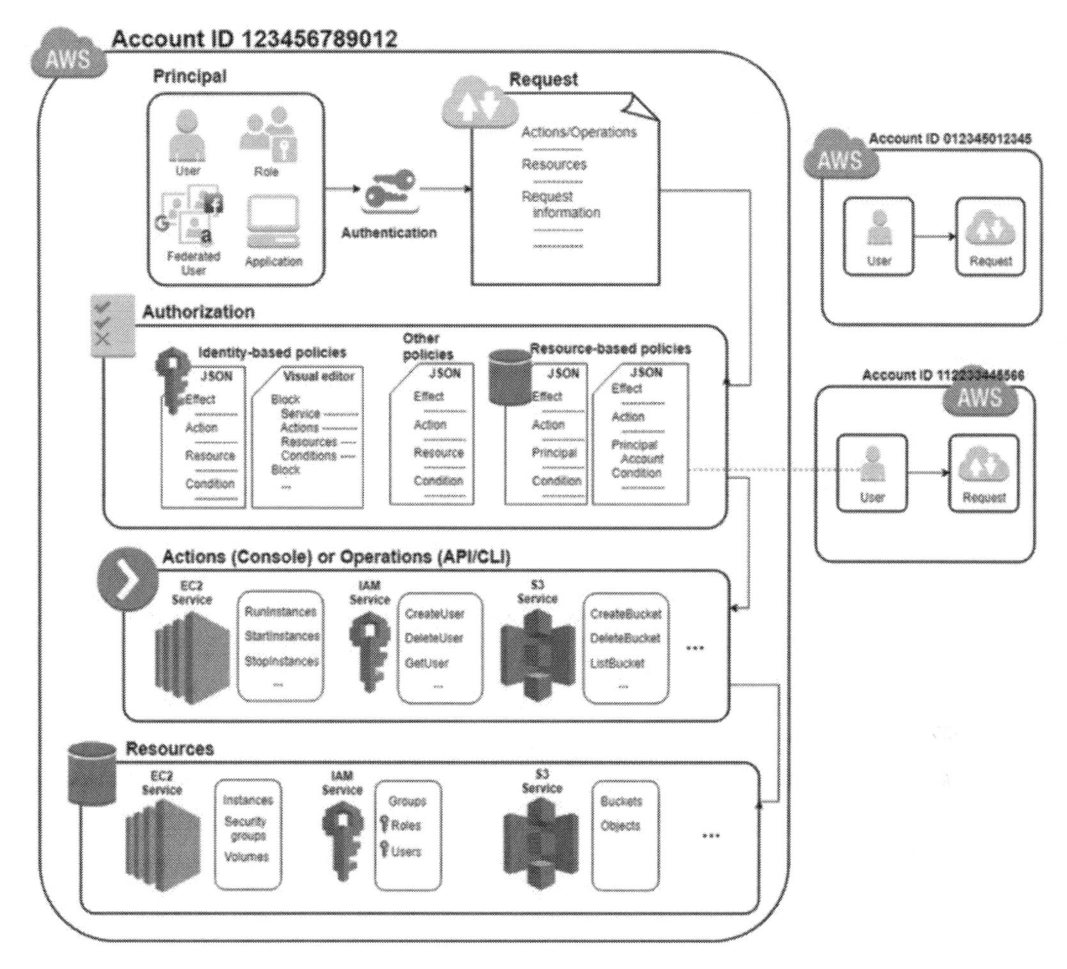

Principals:

- An entity that can take an action on an AWS resource.
- Your administrative IAM user is your first principal.
- You can allow users and services to assume a role.
- IAM supports federated users.
- IAM supports programmatic access to allow an application to access your AWS account.
- IAM users, roles, federated users, and applications are all AWS principals

Requests:

- Principals send requests via the Console, CLI, SDKs, or APIs.

Requests are:

- Actions (or operations) that the principal wants to perform.
- Resources upon which the actions are performed.
- Principal information including the environment from which the request was made.

Request context - AWS gathers the request information:

- Principal (requester).
- Aggregate permissions associated with the principal.
- Environment data, such as IP address, user agent, SSL status etc.
- Resource data, or data that is related to the resource being requested.

Authentication:

- A principal sending a request must be authenticated to send a request to AWS.
- To authenticate from the console, you must sign in with your user name and password.
- To authenticate from the API or CLI, you must provide your access key and secret key.

Authorization:

- IAM uses values from the request context to check for matching policies and determines whether to allow or deny the request.
- IAM policies are stored in IAM as JSON documents and specify the permissions that are allowed or denied.
- IAM policies can be:
    - User (identity) based policies
    - Resource-based policies
- IAM checks each policy that matches the context of your request.
- If a single policy has a deny action IAM denies the request and stops evaluating (explicit deny).
- **Evaluation logic:**
    - By default, all requests are denied (implicit deny).
    - An explicit allow overrides the implicit deny.
    - An explicit deny overrides any explicit allows.
- Only the root user has access to all resources in the account by default.

Actions:

- Actions are defined by a service.
- Actions are the things you can do to a resource such as viewing, creating, editing, deleting.
- Any actions on resources that are not explicitly allowed are denied.
- To allow a principal to perform an action you must include the necessary actions in a policy that applies to the principal or the affected resource.

Resources:

- A resource is an entity that exists within a service.
- E.g. EC2 instances, S3 buckets, IAM users, and DynamoDB tables.
- Each AWS service defines a set of actions that can be performed on the resource.
- After AWS approves the actions in your request, those actions can be performed on the related resources within your account.

AUTHENTICATION METHODS

Console password:

- A password that the user can enter to sign into interactive sessions such as the AWS Management Console.
- You can allow users to change their own passwords.
- You can allow selected IAM users to change their passwords by disabling the option for all users and using an IAM policy to grant permissions for the selected users.

Access Keys:

- A combination of an **access key ID** and a **secret access key.**
- You can assign two active access keys to a user at a time.
- These can be used to make programmatic calls to AWS when using the **API** in program code or at a command prompt when using the **AWS CLI** or the **AWS PowerShell** tools.
- You can create, modify, view or rotate access keys.
- When created IAM returns the access key ID and secret access key.
- The secret access is returned only at creation time and if lost a new key must be created.
- Ensure access keys and secret access keys are stored securely.
- Users can be given access to change their own keys through IAM policy (not from the console).
- You can disable a user's access key which prevents it from being used for API calls.

Server certificates:

- SSL/TLS certificates that you can use to authenticate with some AWS services.
- AWS recommends that you use the AWS Certificate Manager (ACM) to provision, manage and deploy your server certificates.
- Use IAM only when you must support HTTPS connections in a region that is not supported by ACM.

The following diagram shows the different methods of authentication available with IAM:

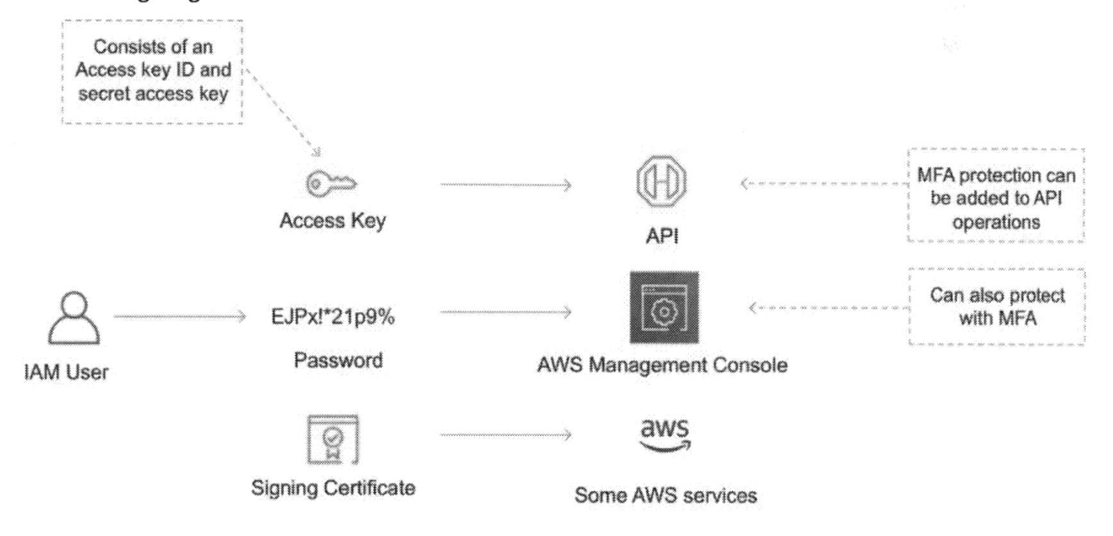

IAM USERS

An IAM user is an entity that represents a person or service.

Can be assigned:

- An access key ID and secret access key for programmatic access to the AWS API, CLI, SDK, and other development tools.
- A password for access to the management console.

By default, users cannot access anything in your account.

The account root user credentials are the email address used to create the account and a password.

The root account has full administrative permissions, and these cannot be restricted.

Best practice for root accounts:

- Don't use the root user credentials.
- Don't share the root user credentials.
- Create an IAM user and assign administrative permissions as required.
- Enable MFA.

IAM users can be created to represent applications and these are known as "service accounts".

You can have up to 5000 users per AWS account.

Each user account has a friendly name and an ARN which uniquely identifies the user across AWS.

A unique ID is also created which is returned only when you create the user using the API, Tools for Windows PowerShell or the AWS CLI.

You should create individual IAM accounts for users (best practice not to share accounts).

The Access Key ID and Secret Access Key are not the same as a password and cannot be used to login to the AWS console.

The Access Key ID and Secret Access Key can only be generated once and must be regenerated if lost.

A password policy can be defined for enforcing password length, complexity etc. (applies to all users).

You can allow or disallow the ability to change passwords using an IAM policy.

Access keys and passwords should be changed regularly.

GROUPS

Groups are collections of users and have policies attached to them.

A group is not an identity and cannot be identified as a principal in an IAM policy.

Use groups to assign permissions to users.

Use the principal of least privilege when assigning permissions.

You cannot nest groups (groups within groups).

ROLES

Roles are created and then "assumed" by trusted entities and define a set of permissions for making AWS service requests.

With IAM Roles you can delegate permissions to resources for users and services without using permanent credentials (e.g. user name and password).

IAM users or AWS services can assume a role to obtain temporary security credentials that can be used to make AWS API calls.

You can delegate using roles.

There are no credentials associated with a role (password or access keys).

IAM users can temporarily assume a role to take on permissions for a specific task.

A role can be assigned to a federated user who signs in using an external identity provider.

Temporary credentials are primarily used with IAM roles and automatically expire.

Roles can be assumed temporarily through the console or programmatically with the **AWS CLI**, **Tools for Windows PowerShell** or **API.**

IAM roles with EC2 instances:

- IAM roles can be used for granting applications running on EC2 instances permissions to AWS API requests using instance profiles.
- Only one role can be assigned to an EC2 instance at a time.
- A role can be assigned at the **EC2 instance creation time or at any time afterwards.**
- When using the AWS CLI or API instance profiles must be created manually (it's automatic and transparent through the console).
- Applications retrieve temporary security credentials from the instance metadata.

Role Delegation:

- Create an IAM role with two policies:
  - Permissions policy – grants the user of the role the required permissions on a resource.
  - Trust policy – specifies the trusted accounts that are allowed to assume the role.
- Wildcards (*) cannot be specified as a principal.
- A permissions policy must also be attached to the user in the trusted account.

POLICIES

Policies are documents that define permissions and can be applied to users, groups and roles.

Policy documents are written in JSON (key value pair that consists of an attribute and a value).

All permissions are implicitly denied by default.

The most restrictive policy is applied.

The IAM policy simulator is a tool to help you understand, test, and validate the effects of access control policies.

The Condition element can be used to apply further conditional logic.

The diagram below provides some more information on the relationship between IAM roles, users, groups and policies.

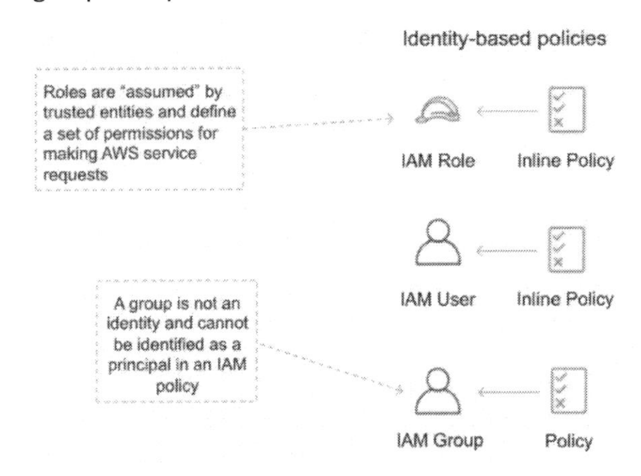

IAM Policies:

- Policies are documents that define permissions and can be applied to users, groups and roles
- Written in JSON
- All permissions are implicitly denied by default
- With multiple policies the most restrictive policy is applied
- The Condition element can be used to apply further conditional logic

SECURITY TOKEN SERVICE (STS)

The AWS Security Token Service (STS) is a web service that enables you to request temporary, limited-privilege credentials for IAM users or for users that you authenticate (federated users).

By default, AWS STS is available as a global service, and all AWS STS requests go to a single endpoint at https://sts.amazonaws.com

You can optionally send your AWS STS requests to endpoints in any region (can reduce latency).

All regions are enabled for STS by default but can be disabled.

The region in which temporary credentials are requested must be enabled.

Credentials will always work globally.

STS supports AWS CloudTrail, which records AWS calls for your AWS account and delivers log files to an S3 bucket.

Temporary security credentials work almost identically to long-term access key credentials that IAM users can use, with the following differences:

- Temporary security credentials are short-term.
- They can be configured to last anywhere from a few minutes to several hours.
- After the credentials expire, AWS no longer recognizes them or allows any kind of access to API requests made with them.
- Temporary security credentials are not stored with the user but are generated dynamically and provided to the user when requested.
- When (or even before) the temporary security credentials expire, the user can request new credentials, as long as the user requesting them still has permission to do so.

Advantages of STS are:

- You do not have to distribute or embed long-term AWS security credentials with an application.
- You can provide access to your AWS resources to users without having to define an AWS identity for them (temporary security credentials are the basis for IAM Roles and ID Federation).
- The temporary security credentials have a limited lifetime, so you do not have to rotate them or explicitly revoke them when they're no longer needed.

- After temporary security credentials expire, they cannot be reused (you can specify how long the credentials are valid for, up to a maximum limit).

The AWS STS API action returns temporary security credentials that consist of:

- An access key which consists of an access key ID and a secret ID.
- A session token.
- Expiration or duration of validity.
- Users (or an application that the user runs) can use these credentials to access your resources.

With STS you can request a session token using one of the following APIs:

- AssumeRole – can only be used by IAM users (can be used for MFA).
- AssumeRoleWithSAML – can be used by any user who passes a SAML authentication response that indicates authentication from a known (trusted) identity provider.
- AssumeRoleWithWebIdentity – can be used by a user who passes a web identity token that indicates authentication from a known (trusted) identity provider.
- GetSessionToken – can be used by an IAM user or AWS account root user (can be used for MFA).
- GetFederationToken – can be used by an IAM user or AWS account root user.

AWS recommends using Cognito for identity federation with Internet identity providers.

Users can come from three sources:

Federation (typically AD):

- Uses SAML 2.0.
- Grants temporary access based on the users AD credentials.
- Does not need to be a user in IAM.
- Single sign-on allows users to login to the AWS console without assigning IAM credentials.

Federation with Mobile Apps:

- Use Facebook/Amazon/Google or other OpenID providers to login.

Cross Account Access:

- Lets users from one AWS account access resources in another.
- To make a request in a different account the resource in that account must have an attached resource-based policy with the permissions you need.
- Or you must assume a role (identity-based policy) within that account with the permissions you need.

There are a couple of ways STS can be used:

Scenario 1:

1. Develop an Identity Broker to communicate with LDAP and AWS STS.
2. Identity Broker always authenticates with LDAP first, then with AWS STS.
3. Application then gets temporary access to AWS resources.

Scenario 2:

1. Develop an Identity Broker to communicate with LDAP and AWS STS.

2. Identity Broker authenticates with LDAP first, then gets an IAM role associated with the user.
3. Application then authenticates with STS and assumes that IAM role.
4. Application uses that IAM role to interact with the service.

IAM BEST PRACTICES

- Lock Away Your AWS Account Root User Access Keys.
- Create Individual IAM Users.
- Use Groups to Assign Permissions to IAM Users.
- Grant Least Privilege.
- Get Started Using Permissions with AWS Managed Policies.
- Use Customer Managed Policies Instead of Inline Policies.
- Use Access Levels to Review IAM Permissions.
- Configure a Strong Password Policy for Your Users.
- Enable MFA.
- Use Roles for Applications That Run on Amazon EC2 Instances.
- Use Roles to Delegate Permissions.
- Do Not Share Access Keys.
- Rotate Credentials Regularly.
- Remove Unnecessary Credentials.
- Use Policy Conditions for Extra Security.
- Monitor Activity in Your AWS Account.

AWS ACCOUNTS

AWS ORGANIZATIONS

AWS Organizations helps you centrally govern your environment as you grow and scale your workloads on AWS.

Organizations helps you to centrally manage billing; control access, compliance, and security; and share resources across your AWS accounts.

Using AWS Organizations, you can automate account creation, create groups of accounts to reflect your business needs, and apply policies for these groups for governance.

You can also simplify billing by setting up a single payment method for all of your AWS accounts.

Through integrations with other AWS services, you can use Organizations to define central configurations and resource sharing across accounts in your organization.

AWS Organizations is available to all AWS customers at no additional charge.

The AWS Organizations API enables automation for account creation and management.

Available in two feature sets:

- Consolidated billing
- All features

By default, organizations support consolidated billing features.

Consolidated billing separates paying accounts and linked accounts.

You can use AWS Organizations to set up a single payment method for all the AWS accounts in your organization through consolidated billing.

With consolidated billing, you can see a combined view of charges incurred by all your accounts.

Can also take advantage of pricing benefits from aggregated usage, such as volume discounts for Amazon EC2 and Amazon S3.

Limit of 20 linked accounts for consolidated billing (default).

Policies can be assigned at different points in the hierarchy.

Can help with cost control through volume discounts.

Unused reserved EC2 instances are applied across the group.

Paying accounts should be used for billing purposes only.

Billing alerts can be setup at the paying account which shows billing for all linked accounts.

Core concepts:

- **AWS Organization** - An organization is a collection of AWS accounts that you can organize into a hierarchy and manage centrally.
- **AWS Account** - An AWS account is a container for your AWS resources.
- **Master Account** - A master account is the AWS account you use to create your organization.
- **Member Account** - A member account is an AWS account, other than the master account, that is part of an organization.
- **Administrative Root** - An administrative root is the starting point for organizing your AWS accounts. The administrative root is the top-most container in your organization's hierarchy.
- **Organizational Unit (OU)** - An organizational unit (OU) is a group of AWS accounts within an organization. An OU can also contain other OUs enabling you to create a hierarchy.
- **Policy** - A policy is a "document" with one or more statements that define the controls that you want to apply to a group of AWS accounts. AWS Organizations supports a specific type of policy called a Service Control Policy (SCP). An SCP defines the AWS service actions, such as Amazon EC2 RunInstances, that are available for use in different accounts within an organization.

Migrating accounts between organizations:

- Accounts can be migrated between organizations.
- You must have root or IAM access to both the member and master accounts.
- Use the AWS Organizations console for just a few accounts.
- Use the AWS Organizations API or AWS Command Line Interface (AWS CLI) if there are many accounts to migrate.
- Billing history and billing reports for all accounts stay with the master account in an organization.

- Before migration download any billing or report history for any member accounts that you want to keep.
- When a member account leaves an organization, all charges incurred by the account are charged directly to the standalone account.
- Even if the account move only takes a minute to process, it is likely that some charges will be incurred by the member account.

AWS RESOURCE ACCESS MANAGER

AWS Resource Access Manager (RAM) is a service that enables you to easily and securely share AWS resources with any AWS account or within your AWS Organization.

You can share AWS Transit Gateways, Subnets, AWS License Manager configurations, and Amazon Route 53 Resolver rules resources with RAM.

RAM eliminates the need to create duplicate resources in multiple accounts, reducing the operational overhead of managing those resources in every single account you own.

You can create resources centrally in a multi-account environment, and use RAM to share those resources across accounts in **three simple steps**:

1. Create a Resource Share
2. Specify resources
3. Specify accounts

RAM is available at no additional charge.

Key benefits:

- **Reduce Operational Overhead** - Procure AWS resources centrally, and use RAM to share resources such as subnets or License Manager configurations with other accounts. This eliminates the need to provision duplicate resources in every account in a multi-account environment.
- **Improve Security and Visibility** - RAM leverages existing policies and permissions set in AWS Identity and Access Management (IAM) to govern the consumption of shared resources. RAM also provides comprehensive visibility into shared resources to set alarms and visualize logs through integration with Amazon CloudWatch and AWS CloudTrail.
- **Optimize Costs** - Sharing resources such as AWS License Manager configurations across accounts allows you to leverage licenses in multiple parts of your company to increase utilization and optimize costs.

RESOURCE GROUPS

You can use resource groups to organize your AWS resources.

In AWS, a resource is an entity that you can work with.

Resource groups make it easier to manage and automate tasks on large numbers of resources at one time.

Resource groups allow you to group resources and then tag them.

The Tag Editor assists with finding resources and adding tags.

You can access Resource Groups through any of the following entry points:

- On the navigation bar of the AWS Management Console.
- In the AWS Systems Manager console, from the left navigation pane entry for Resource Groups.
- By using the Resource Groups API, in AWS CLI commands or AWS SDK programming languages.

A resource group is a collection of AWS resources that are all in the same AWS region, and that match criteria provided in a query.

In Resource Groups, there are two types of queries on which you can build a group.

Both query types include resources that are specified in the format AWS::service::resource.

- **Tag-based** - Tag-based queries include lists of resources and tags. Tags are keys that help identify and sort your resources within your organization. Optionally, tags include values for keys.
- **AWS CloudFormation stack-based** - In an AWS CloudFormation stack-based query, you choose an AWS CloudFormation stack in your account in the current region, and then choose resource types within the stack that you want to be in the group. You can base your query on only one AWS CloudFormation stack.

Resource groups can be nested; a resource group can contain existing resource groups in the same region.

AWS DIRECTORY SERVICE

GENERAL

AWS provide a number of directory types.

The following three types currently feature on the exam and will be covered on this page:

- Active Directory Service for Microsoft Active Directory
- Simple AD
- AD Connector

As an alternative to the AWS Directory service you can build your own Microsoft AD DCs in the AWS cloud (on EC2):

- When you build your own you can join an existing on-premise Active Directory domain (replication mode).
- You must establish a VPN (on top of Direct Connect if you have it).
- Replication mode is less secure than establishing trust relationships.

The table below summarizes the directory services covered on this page as well as a couple of others, and provides some typical use cases:

Directory Service Option	Description	Use Case
AWS Cloud Directory	Cloud-native directory to share and control access to hierarchical data between applications	Cloud applications that need hierarchical data with complex relationships
Amazon Cognito	Sign-up and sign-in functionality that scales to millions of users and federated to public social media services	Develop consumer apps or SaaS
AWS Directory Service for Microsoft Active Directory	AWS-managed full Microsoft AD running on Windows Server 2012 R2	Enterprises that want hosted Microsoft AD or you need LDAP for Linux apps
AD Connector	Allows on-premises users to log into AWS services with their existing AD credentials. Also allows EC2 instances to join AD domain	Single sign-on for on-premises employees and for adding EC2 instances to the domain
Simple AD	Low scale, low cost, AD implementation based on Samba	Simple user directory, or you need LDAP compatibility

ACTIVE DIRECTORY SERVICE FOR MICROSOFT ACTIVE DIRECTORY

Fully managed AWS services on AWS infrastructure.

Best choice if you have more than 5000 users and/or need a trust relationship set up.

Includes software patching, replication, automated backups, replacing failed DCs and monitoring.

Runs on a Windows Server.

Can perform schema extensions.

Works with SharePoint, Microsoft SQL Server and .Net apps.

You can setup trust relationships to extend authentication from on-premises Active Directories into the AWS cloud.

On-premise users and groups can access resources in either domain using SSO.

Requires a VPN or Direct Connect connection.

Can be used as a standalone AD in the AWS cloud.

When used standalone users can access 3rd party applications such as Microsoft O365 through federation.

You can also use Active Directory credentials to authenticate to the AWS management console without having to set up SAML authentication.

AWS Microsoft AD supports AWS applications including Workspaces, WorkDocs, QuickSight, Chime, Amazon Connect, and RDS for Microsoft SQL Server.

The following diagram shows some of the use cases for your AWS Microsoft AD directory, including the ability to grant your users access to external cloud applications and allow your on-premises AD users to manage and have access to resources in the AWS Cloud.

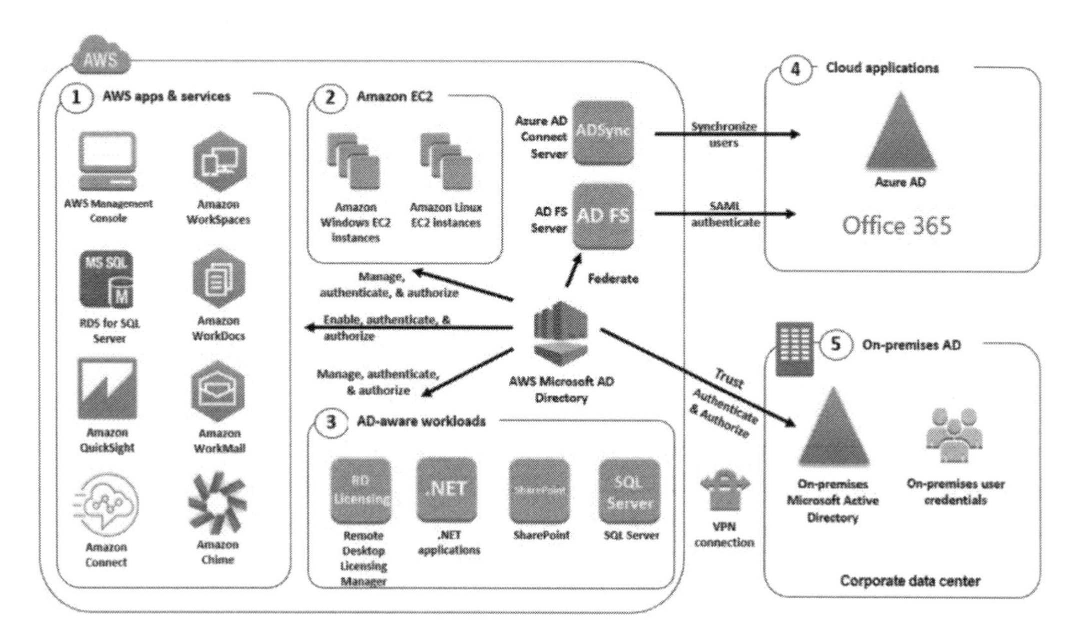

Includes security features such as:

- Fine-grained password policy management
- LDAP encryption through SSL/TLS
- HIPAA and PCI DSS approved
- Multi-factor authentication through integration with existing RADIUS-based MFA infrastructure

Monitoring provided through CloudTrail, notifications through SNS, daily automated snapshots.

Scalable service that scales by adding Domain Controllers.

Deployed in a HA configuration across two AZs in the same region.

AWS Microsoft AD does not support replication mode where replication to an on-premise AD takes place.

Two editions:

- Standard Edition is optimized to be a primary directory for small and midsize businesses with up to 5,000 employees. It provides you enough storage capacity to support up to 30,000 directory objects, such as users, groups, and computers.

- Enterprise Edition is designed to support enterprise organizations with up to 500,000 directory objects.

Directory Sharing:

- AWS Directory Service for Microsoft Active Directory allows you to use a directory in one account and share it with multiple accounts and VPCs.
- There is an hourly sharing charge for each additional account to which you share a directory.
- There is no sharing charge for additional VPCs to which you share a directory, or for the account in which you install the directory.

SIMPLE AD

An inexpensive Active Directory-compatible service with common directory features.

Standalone, fully managed, directory on the AWS cloud.

Simple AD is generally the least expensive option.

Best choice for less than 5000 users and doesn't need advanced AD features.

Powered by SAMBA 4 Active Directory compatible server.

Can create users and control access to applications on AWS.

Provides a subset of the features provided by AWS MS AD.

Features include:

- Manage user accounts.
- Manage groups.
- Apply group policies.
- Securely connect to EC2 instances.
- Kerberos-based SSO.
- Supports joining Linux or Windows based EC2 instances.

AWS provides monitoring, daily snapshots, and recovery services.

Manual snapshots possible.

Simple AD is compatible with WorkSpaces, WorkDocs, Workmail and QuickSight.

You can also sign on to the AWS management console with Simple AD user accounts to manage AWS resources.

Available in two editions:

- Small – supports up to 500 users (approximately 2000 objects).
- Large – supports up to 5000 users (approximately 20,000 objects).

AWS creates two directory servers and DNS servers on two different subnets within an AZ.

Simple AD does not support:

- DNS dynamic updates.
- Schema extensions.
- Multi-factor authentication.

- Communication over LDAPS.
- PowerShell AD cmdlets.
- FSMO role transfer.

Not compatible with RDS SQL server.

Does not support trust relationships with other domains (use AWS MS AD).

AD CONNECTOR

AD Connector is a directory gateway for redirecting directory requests to your on-premise Active Directory.

AD Connector eliminates the need for directory synchronization and the cost and complexity of hosting a federation infrastructure.

Connects your existing on-premise AD to AWS.

Best choice when you want to use an existing Active Directory with AWS services.

AD Connector comes in two sizes:

- Small – designed for organizations up to 500 users.
- Large – designed for organizations up to 5000 users.

The VPC must be connected to your on-premise network via VPN or Direct Connect.

When users log in to AWS applications AD connector forwards sign-in requests to your on-premise AD DCs.

You can also join EC2 instances to your on-premise AD through AD Connector.

You can also login to the AWS Management Console using your on-premise AD DCs for authentication.

Not compatible with RDS SQL.

You can use AD Connector for multi-factor authentication using RADIUS-based MFA infrastructure.

AD CONNECTOR VS SIMPLE AD

The table below describes some of the key differences to consider when choosing AD Connector or Simple AD:

AD Connector	Simple AD
Must have an existing AD	Standalone AD based on Samba
Existing AD users can access AWS assets via IAM roles	Supports user accounts, groups, group policies, and domains
Supports MFA via existing RADIUS-based MFA infrastructure	Kerberos-based SSO
	MFA not supported
	Trust relationships not supported

AWS KEY MANAGEMENT STORE (KMS)

AWS Key Management Store (KMS) is a managed service that enables you to easily encrypt your data.

AWS KMS provides a highly available key storage, management, and auditing solution for you to encrypt data within your own applications and control the encryption of stored data across AWS services.

AWS KMS allows you to centrally manage and securely store your keys. These are known as customer master keys or CMKs.

You can generate CMKs in KMS, in an AWS CloudHSM cluster, or import them from your own key management infrastructure.

These master keys are protected by hardware security modules (HSMs) and are only ever used within those modules.

You can submit data directly to KMS to be encrypted or decrypted using these master keys.

You set usage policies on these keys that determine which users can use them to encrypt and decrypt data and under which conditions.

KMS is tightly integrated into many AWS services like Lambda, S3, EBS, EFS, DynamoDB, SQS etc.

AWS KMS is integrated with AWS services and client-side toolkits that use a method known as envelope encryption to encrypt your data.

Under this method, KMS generates data keys which are used to encrypt data and are themselves encrypted using your master keys in KMS.

Data keys are not retained or managed by KMS.

AWS services encrypt your data and store an encrypted copy of the data key along with the data it protects.

When a service needs to decrypt your data they request KMS to decrypt the data key using your master key.

If the user requesting data from the AWS service is authorized to decrypt under your master key policy, the service will receive the decrypted data key from KMS with which it can decrypt the data and return it in plaintext.

All requests to use your master keys are logged in AWS CloudTrail so you can understand who used which key under which context and when they used it.

You can control who manages and accesses keys via IAM users and roles.

You can audit the use of keys via CloudTrail.

KMS differs from Secrets Manager as its purpose-built for encryption key management.

KMS is validated by many compliance schemes (e.g. PCI DSS Level 1, FIPS 140-2 Level 2).

You can perform the following key management functions in AWS KMS:

- Create keys with a unique alias and description.
- Import your own key material.
- Define which IAM users and roles can manage keys.
- Define which IAM users and roles can use keys to encrypt and decrypt data.
- Choose to have AWS KMS automatically rotate your keys on an annual basis.
- Temporarily disable keys so they cannot be used by anyone.

- Re-enable disabled keys.
- Delete keys that you no longer use.
- Audit use of keys by inspecting logs in AWS CloudTrail.
- Create custom key stores*.
- Connect and disconnect custom key stores*.
- Delete custom key stores*.

* The use of custom key stores requires CloudHSM resources to be available in your account.

Typically, data is encrypted in one of the following three scenarios:

1. You can use KMS APIs directly to encrypt and decrypt data using your master keys stored in KMS.
2. You can choose to have AWS services encrypt your data using your master keys stored in KMS. In this case data is encrypted using data keys that are protected by your master keys in KMS.
3. You can use the AWS Encryption SDK that is integrated with AWS KMS to perform encryption within your own applications, whether they operate in AWS or not.

Custom Key Store:

- The AWS KMS custom key store feature combines the controls provided by AWS CloudHSM with the integration and ease of use of AWS KMS.
- You can configure your own CloudHSM cluster and authorize KMS to use it as a dedicated key store for your keys rather than the default KMS key store.
- When you create keys in KMS you can chose to generate the key material in your CloudHSM cluster. Master keys that are generated in your custom key store never leave the HSMs in the CloudHSM cluster in plaintext and all KMS operations that use those keys are only performed in your HSMs.
- In all other respects master keys stored in your custom key store are consistent with other KMS CMKs.

Key deletion:

- You can schedule a customer master key and associated metadata that you created in AWS KMS for deletion, with a configurable waiting period from 7 to 30 days.
- This waiting period allows you to verify the impact of deleting a key on your applications and users that depend on it.
- The default waiting period is 30 days.
- You can cancel key deletion during the waiting period.

Limits:

- You can create up to 1000 customer master keys per account per region.
- As both enabled and disabled customer master keys count towards the limit, AWS recommend deleting disabled keys that you no longer use.
- AWS managed master keys created on your behalf for use within supported AWS services do not count against this limit.
- There is no limit to the number of data keys that can be derived using a master key and used in your application or by AWS services to encrypt data on your behalf.

AWS CLOUDHSM

The AWS CloudHSM service helps you meet corporate, contractual and regulatory compliance requirements for data security by using dedicated Hardware Security Module (HSM) instances within the AWS cloud.

AWS and AWS Marketplace partners offer a variety of solutions for protecting sensitive data within the AWS platform, but for some applications and data subject to contractual or regulatory mandates for managing cryptographic keys, additional protection may be necessary.

CloudHSM complements existing data protection solutions and allows you to protect your encryption keys within HSMs that are designed and validated to government standards for secure key management.

CloudHSM allows you to securely generate, store and manage cryptographic keys used for data encryption in a way that keys are accessible only by you.

A Hardware Security Module (HSM) provides secure key storage and cryptographic operations within a tamper-resistant hardware device.

HSMs are designed to securely store cryptographic key material and use the key material without exposing it outside the cryptographic boundary of the hardware.

You can use the CloudHSM service to support a variety of use cases and applications, such as database encryption, Digital Rights Management (DRM), Public Key Infrastructure (PKI), authentication and authorization, document signing, and transaction processing.

Runs on a dedicated hardware device, single tenanted.

The table below describes the latest version of CloudHSM and how it differs from its predecessor:

	"Classic" CloudHSM	**Current CloudHSM**
Device	safeNET Luna SA	Proprietary
Pricing	Upfront cost required ($5000)	No upfront cost, pay per hour
High Availability	Have to buy a second device	Clustered
FIPS 140-2	Level 2	Level 3

When you use the AWS CloudHSM service you create a CloudHSM Cluster.

Clusters can contain multiple HSM instances, spread across multiple Availability Zones in a region. HSM instances in a cluster are automatically synchronized and load-balanced.

You receive dedicated, single-tenant access to each HSM instance in your cluster. Each HSM instance appears as a network resource in your Amazon Virtual Private Cloud (VPC).

Adding and removing HSMs from your Cluster is a single call to the AWS CloudHSM API (or on the command line using the AWS CLI).

After creating and initializing a CloudHSM Cluster, you can configure a client on your EC2 instance that allows your applications to use the cluster over a secure, authenticated network connection.

Must be within a VPC and can be accessed via VPC Peering.

Applications don't need to be in the same VPC but but the server or instance on which your application and the HSM client are running must have network (IP) reachability to all HSMs in the cluster.

Does not natively integrate with many AWS services like KMS, but instead requires custom application scripting.

Offload SSL from web server, act as an issuing CA, enable TDE for Oracle databases. The table below compares CloudHSM against KMS:

	CloudHSM	AWS KMS
Tenancy	Single-tenant HSM	Multi-tenant AWS service
Availability	Customer-managed durability and available	Highly available and durable key storage and management
Root of Trust	Customer managed root of trust	AWS managed root of trust
FIPS 140-2	Level 3	Level 2 / Level 3 in some areas
3rd Party Support	Broad 3rd Party Support	Broad AWS service support

AMAZON COGNITO

AMAZON COGNITO GENERAL

Amazon Cognito lets you add user sign-up, sign-in, and access control to your web and mobile apps quickly and easily.

Amazon Cognito provides authentication, authorization, and user management for your web and mobile apps.

Your users can sign in directly with a user name and password, or through a third party such as Facebook, Amazon, or Google.

The two main components of AWS Cognito are user pools and identity pools:

- User pools are user directories that provide sign-up and sign-in options for your app users.
- Identity pools enable you to grant your users access to other AWS services.

You can use identity pools and user pools separately or together.

AWS Cognito works with external identity providers that support SAML or OpenID Connect, social identity providers (such as Facebook, Twitter, Amazon).

Cognito Identity provides temporary security credentials to access your app's backend resources in AWS or any service behind Amazon API Gateway.

You can use Amazon, Facebook, Twitter, Digits, Google and any other OpenID Connect compatible identity provider.

You can also integrate your own identity provider.

Cognito exposes server-side APIs.

Users can sign-up and sign-in using email, phone number, or user name.

End users of an application can also sign in with SMS-based MFA.

There is an import tool for migrating users into an Amazon Cognito User Pool.

USER POOLS

A user pool is a user directory in Amazon Cognito.

With a user pool, users can sign in to your web or mobile app through Amazon Cognito.

Users can also sign in through social identity providers like Facebook or Amazon, and through SAML identity providers.

Whether users sign in directly or through a third party, all members of the user pool have a directory profile that you can access through an SDK.

User pools provide:

- Sign-up and sign-in services.
- A built-in, customizable web UI to sign in users.
- Social sign-in with Facebook, Google, and Login with Amazon, as well as sign-in with SAML identity providers from your user pool.
- User directory management and user profiles.
- Security features such as multi-factor authentication (MFA), checks for compromised credentials, account takeover protection, and phone and email verification.
- Customized workflows and user migration through AWS Lambda triggers.

After successfully authenticating a user, Amazon Cognito issues JSON web tokens (JWT) that you can use to secure and authorize access to your own APIs, or exchange for AWS credentials.

IDENTITY POOLS

Amazon Cognito identity pools (federated identities) enable you to create unique identities for your users and federate them with identity providers.

With an identity pool, you can obtain temporary, limited-privilege AWS credentials to access other AWS services. Amazon Cognito identity pools support the following identity providers:

- Public providers: Login with Amazon (Identity Pools), Facebook (Identity Pools), Google (Identity Pools).
- Amazon Cognito User Pools
- Open ID Connect Providers (Identity Pools)
- SAML Identity Providers (Identity Pools)
- Developer Authenticated Identities (Identity Pools)

AMAZON COGNITO SYNC

Amazon Cognito Sync is an AWS service and client library that enables cross-device syncing of application-related user data.

You can use it to synchronize user profile data across mobile devices and the web without requiring your own backend.

The client libraries cache data locally so your app can read and write data regardless of device connectivity status.

When the device is online, you can synchronize data, and if you set up push sync, notify other devices immediately that an update is available.

AWS WAF AND SHIELD

AWS WAF AND AWS SHIELD GENERAL

AWS WAF and AWS Shield help protect your AWS resources from web exploits and DDoS attacks.

AWS WAF is a web application firewall service that helps protect your web apps from common exploits that could affect app availability, compromise security, or consume excessive resources.

AWS Shield provides expanded DDoS attack protection for your AWS resources. Get 24/7 support from the DDoS response team and detailed visibility into DDoS events.

We'll now go into more detail on each service.

AWS WEB APPLICATION FIREWALL (WAF)

AWS WAF is a web application firewall that helps protect your web applications from common web exploits that could affect application availability, compromise security, or consume excessive resources.

AWS WAF helps protect web applications from attacks by allowing you to configure rules that allow, block, or monitor (count) web requests based on conditions that you define.

These conditions include IP addresses, HTTP headers, HTTP body, URI strings, SQL injection and cross-site scripting.

AWS WAF gives you control over which traffic to allow or block to your web applications by defining customizable web security rules.

New rules can be deployed within minutes, letting you respond quickly to changing traffic patterns.

When AWS services receive requests for web sites, the requests are forwarded to AWS WAF for inspection against defined rules.

Once a request meets a condition defined in the rules, AWS WAF instructs the underlying service to either block or allow the request based on the action you define.

With AWS WAF you pay only for what you use.

AWS WAF pricing is based on how many rules you deploy and how many web requests your web application receives.

There are no upfront commitments.

AWS WAF is tightly integrated with Amazon CloudFront and the Application Load Balancer (ALB), services.

When you use AWS WAF on Amazon CloudFront, rules run in all AWS Edge Locations, located around the world close to end users.

This means security doesn't come at the expense of performance.

Blocked requests are stopped before they reach your web servers.

When you use AWS WAF on an Application Load Balancer, your rules run in region and can be used to protect internet-facing as well as internal load balancers.

WEB TRAFFIC FILTERING

AWS WAF lets you create rules to filter web traffic based on conditions that include IP addresses, HTTP headers and body, or custom URIs.

This gives you an additional layer of protection from web attacks that attempt to exploit vulnerabilities in custom or third-party web applications.

In addition, AWS WAF makes it easy to create rules that block common web exploits like SQL injection and cross site scripting.

AWS WAF allows you to create a centralized set of rules that you can deploy across multiple websites.

This means that in an environment with many websites and web applications you can create a single set of rules that you can reuse across applications rather than recreating that rule on every application you want to protect.

FULL FEATURE API

AWS WAF can be completely administered via APIs.

This provides organizations with the ability to create and maintain rules automatically and incorporate them into the development and design process.

For example, a developer who has detailed knowledge of the web application could create a security rule as part of the deployment process.

This capability to incorporate security into your development process avoids the need for complex handoffs between application and security teams to make sure rules are kept up to date.

AWS WAF can also be deployed and provisioned automatically with AWS CloudFormation sample templates that allow you to describe all security rules you would like to deploy for your web applications delivered by Amazon CloudFront.

AWS WAF is integrated with Amazon CloudFront, which supports custom origins outside of AWS – this means you can protect web sites not hosted in AWS.

Support for IPv6 allows the AWS WAF to inspect HTTP/S requests coming from both IPv6 and IPv4 addresses.

REAL-TIME VISIBILITY

AWS WAF provides real-time metrics and captures raw requests that include details about IP addresses, geo locations, URIs, User-Agent and Referers.

AWS WAF is fully integrated with Amazon CloudWatch, making it easy to setup custom alarms when thresholds are exceeded, or particular attacks occur.

This information provides valuable intelligence that can be used to create new rules to better protect applications.

AWS SHIELD

AWS Shield is a managed Distributed Denial of Service (DDoS) protection service that safeguards applications running on AWS.

AWS Shield provides always-on detection and automatic inline mitigations that minimize application downtime and latency, so there is no need to engage AWS Support to benefit from DDoS protection.

There are two tiers of AWS Shield – Standard and Advanced.

AWS SHIELD STANDARD

All AWS customers benefit from the automatic protections of AWS Shield Standard, at no additional charge.

AWS Shield Standard defends against most common, frequently occurring network and transport layer DDoS attacks that target web sites or applications.

When using AWS Shield Standard with Amazon CloudFront and Amazon Route 53, you receive comprehensive availability protection against all known infrastructure (Layer 3 and 4) attacks.

AWS SHIELD ADVANCED

Provides higher levels of protection against attacks targeting applications running on Amazon Elastic Compute Cloud (EC2), Elastic Load Balancing (ELB), Amazon CloudFront, AWS Global Accelerator and Amazon Route 53 resources.

In addition to the network and transport layer protections that come with Standard, AWS Shield Advanced provides additional detection and mitigation against large and sophisticated DDoS attacks, near real-time visibility into attacks, and integration with AWS WAF, a web application firewall.

AWS Shield Advanced also gives you 24×7 access to the AWS DDoS Response Team (DRT) and protection against DDoS related spikes in your Amazon Elastic Compute Cloud (EC2), Elastic Load Balancing (ELB), Amazon CloudFront, AWS Global Accelerator and Amazon Route 53 charges.

AWS Shield Advanced is available globally on all Amazon CloudFront, AWS Global Accelerator, and Amazon Route 53 edge locations.

Origin servers can be Amazon S3, Amazon Elastic Compute Cloud (EC2), Elastic Load Balancing (ELB), or a custom server outside of AWS.

AWS Shield Advanced includes DDoS cost protection, a safeguard from scaling charges as a result of a DDoS attack that causes usage spikes on protected Amazon EC2, Elastic Load Balancing (ELB), Amazon CloudFront, AWS Global Accelerator, or Amazon Route 53.

If any of the AWS Shield Advanced protected resources scale up in response to a DDoS attack, you can request credits via the regular AWS Support channel.

SECURITY, IDENTITY & COMPLIANCE QUIZ QUESTIONS

Answers and explanations are provided below after the last question in this section.

Question 1:

A company needs to deploy virtual desktops for its customers in an AWS VPC, and would like to leverage their existing on-premise security principles. AWS Workspaces will be used as the virtual desktop solution.

Which set of AWS services and features will meet the company's requirements?

A. A VPN connection. AWS Directory Services

B. A VPN connection, VPC NACLs and Security Groups

C. A VPN connection, VPC NACLs and Security Groups

D. Amazon EC2, and AWS IAM

Question 2:

To improve security in your AWS account you have decided to enable multi-factor authentication (MFA). You can authenticate using an MFA device in which two ways? (choose 2)

A. Locally to EC2 instances

B. Through the AWS Management Console

C. Using biometrics

D. Using a key pair

E. Using the AWS API

Question 3:

Your company would like to restrict the ability of most users to change their own passwords whilst continuing to allow a select group of users within specific user groups.

What is the best way to achieve this? (choose 2)

A. Under the IAM Password Policy deselect the option to allow users to change their own passwords

B. Create an IAM Policy that grants users the ability to change their own password and attach it to the groups that contain the users

C. Create an IAM Role that grants users the ability to change their own password and attach it to the groups that contain the users

D. Create an IAM Policy that grants users the ability to change their own password and attach it to the individual user accounts

E. Disable the ability for all users to change their own passwords using the AWS Security Token Service

Question 4:

Your company has started using the AWS CloudHSM for secure key storage. A recent administrative error resulted in the loss of credentials to access the CloudHSM. You need access to data that was encrypted using keys stored on the hardware security module.

How can you recover the keys that are no longer accessible?

A. There is no way to recover your keys if you lose your credentials

B. Log a case with AWS support and they will use MFA to recover the credentials

C. Restore a snapshot of the CloudHSM

D. Reset the CloudHSM device and create a new set of credentials

Question 5:

The AWS Acceptable Use Policy describes permitted and prohibited behavior on AWS and includes descriptions of prohibited security violations and network abuse. According to the policy, what is AWS's position on penetration testing?

A. AWS do not allow any form of penetration testing

B. AWS allow penetration testing by customers on their own VPC resources

C. AWS allow penetration for some resources with prior authorization

D. AWS allow penetration testing for all resources

Question 6:

You have been asked to come up with a solution for providing single sign-on to existing staff in your company who manage on-premise web applications and now need access to the AWS management console to manage resources in the AWS cloud.

Which product combinations provide the best solution to achieve this requirement?

A. Use your on-premise LDAP directory with IAM

B. Use IAM and MFA

C. Use the AWS Secure Token Service (STS) and SAML

D. Use IAM and Amazon Cognito

Question 7:

You are a Developer working for Digital Cloud Training. You are planning to write some code that creates a URL that lets users who sign in to your organization's network securely access the AWS Management Console. The URL will include a sign-in token that you get from AWS that authenticates the user to AWS. You are using Microsoft Active Directory Federation Services as your identity provider (IdP) which is compatible with SAML 2.0.

Which of the steps below will you need to include when developing your custom identity broker? (choose 2)

A. Generate a pre-signed URL programmatically using the AWS SDK for Java or the AWS SDK for .NET

B. Call the AWS Security Token Service (AWS STS) AssumeRole or GetFederationToken API operations to obtain temporary security credentials for the user

C. Delegate access to the IdP through the "Configure Provider" wizard in the IAM console

D. Call the AWS federation endpoint and supply the temporary security credentials to request a sign-in token

E. Assume an IAM Role through the console or programmatically with the AWS CLI, Tools for Windows PowerShell or API

Question 8:

A health club is developing a mobile fitness app that allows customers to upload statistics and view their progress. Amazon Cognito is being used for authentication, authorization and user management and users will sign-in with Facebook IDs.

In order to securely store data in DynamoDB, the design should use temporary AWS credentials. What feature of Amazon Cognito is used to obtain temporary credentials to access AWS services?

A. User Pools

B. Identity Pools

C. SAML Identity Providers

D. Key Pairs

SECURITY, IDENTITY & COMPLIANCE - ANSWERS

Question 1 answer: A

Explanation:

A security principle is an individual identity such as a user account within a directory. The AWS Directory service includes: Active Directory Service for Microsoft Active Directory, Simple AD, AD Connector. One of these services may be ideal depending on detailed requirements. The Active Directory Service for Microsoft AD and AD Connector both require a VPN or Direct Connect connection.

A VPN with NACLs and security groups will not deliver the required solution. AWS Directory Service with IAM or EC2 with IAM are also not sufficient for leveraging on-premise security principles. You must have a VPN.

Question 2 answer: A,E

Explanation:

You can authenticate using an MFA device in the following ways:

- Through the AWS Management Console – the user is prompted for a user name, password and authentication code
- Using the AWS API – restrictions are added to IAM policies and developers can request temporary security credentials and pass MFA parameters in their AWS STS API requests
- Using the AWS CLI by obtaining temporary security credentials from STS (aws sts get-session-token)

Question 3 answer: A,B

Explanation:

A password policy can be defined for enforcing password length, complexity etc. (applies to all users).

You can allow or disallow the ability to change passwords using an IAM policy and you should attach this to the group that contains the users, not to the individual users themselves.

You cannot use an IAM role to perform this function.

The AWS STS is not used for controlling password policies.

Question 4 answer: A

Explanation:

Amazon does not have access to your keys or credentials and therefore has no way to recover your keys if you lose your credentials.

Question 5 answer: C

Explanation:

Permission is required for all penetration tests.

You must complete and submit the AWS Vulnerability / Penetration Testing Request Form to request authorization for penetration testing to or originating from any AWS resources.

There is a limited set of resources on which penetration testing can be performed.

Question 6 answer: C

Explanation:

Single sign-on using federation allows users to login to the AWS console without assigning IAM credentials.

The AWS Security Token Service (STS) is a web service that enables you to request temporary, limited-privilege credentials for IAM users or for users that you authenticate (such as federated users from an on-premise directory).

Federation (typically Active Directory) uses SAML 2.0 for authentication and grants temporary access based on the users AD credentials. The user does not need to be a user in IAM.

You cannot use your on-premise LDAP directory with IAM, you must use federation.

Enabling multi-factor authentication (MFA) for IAM is not a federation solution.

Amazon Cognito is used for authenticating users to web and mobile apps not for providing single sign-on between on-premises directories and the AWS management console.

Question 7 answer: B,D

Explanation:

The aim of this solution is to create a single sign-on solution that enables users signed in to the organization's Active Directory service to be able to connect to AWS resources. When developing a custom identity broker you use the AWS STS service.

The AWS Security Token Service (STS) is a web service that enables you to request temporary, limited-privilege credentials for IAM users or for users that you authenticate (federated users). The steps performed by the custom identity broker to sign users into the AWS management console are:

1. Verify that the user is authenticated by your local identity system
2. Call the AWS Security Token Service (AWS STS) AssumeRole or GetFederationToken API operations to obtain temporary security credentials for the user
3. Call the AWS federation endpoint and supply the temporary security credentials to request a sign-in token
4. Construct a URL for the console that includes the token
5. Give the URL to the user or invoke the URL on the user's behalf

You cannot generate a pre-signed URL for this purpose using SDKs, delegate access through the IAM console or directly assume IAM roles.

Question 8 answer: B

Explanation:

With an identity pool, users can obtain temporary AWS credentials to access AWS services, such as Amazon S3 and DynamoDB.

A user pool is a user directory in Amazon Cognito. With a user pool, users can sign in to web or mobile apps through Amazon Cognito, or federate through a third-party identity provider (IdP).

SAML Identity Providers are supported IDPs for identity pools but cannot be used for gaining temporary credentials for AWS services.

Key pairs are used in Amazon EC2 for access to instances.

APPLICATION INTEGRATION

AMAZON SNS

Amazon Simple Notification Service (Amazon SNS) is a web service that makes it easy to set up, operate, and send notifications from the cloud.

Amazon SNS is used for building and integrating loosely-coupled, distributed applications.

Provides instantaneous, push-based delivery (no polling).

Uses simple APIs and easy integration with applications.

Flexible message delivery is provided over multiple transport protocols.

Offered under an inexpensive, pay-as-you-go model with no up-front costs.

The web-based AWS Management Console offers the simplicity of a point-and-click interface.

Data type is JSON.

SNS supports a wide variety of needs including event notification, monitoring applications, workflow systems, time-sensitive information updates, mobile applications, and any other application that generates or consumes notifications.

SNS Subscribers:

- HTTP
- HTTPS
- Email
- Email-JSON
- SQS
- Application
- Lambda

SNS supports notifications over multiple transport protocols:

- HTTP/HTTPS – subscribers specify a URL as part of the subscription registration.
- Email/Email-JSON – messages are sent to registered addresses as email (text-based or JSON-object).
- SQS – users can specify an SQS standard queue as the endpoint.
- SMS – messages are sent to registered phone numbers as SMS text messages.

Topic names are limited to 256 characters.

SNS supports CloudTrail auditing for authenticated calls.

SNS provides durable storage of all messages that it receives (across multiple AZs).

Users pay $0.50 per 1 million Amazon SNS Requests, $0.06 per 100,000 notification deliveries over HTTP, and $2.00 per 100,000 notification deliveries over email.

AMAZON SQS

GENERAL SQS CONCEPTS

Amazon Simple Queue Service (Amazon SQS) is a web service that gives you access to message queues that store messages waiting to be processed.

SQS offers a reliable, highly-scalable, hosted queue for storing messages in transit between computers.

SQS is used for distributed/decoupled applications.

SQS can be used with RedShift, DynamoDB, EC2, ECS, RDS, S3 and Lambda.

SQS uses a message-oriented API.

SQS uses pull based (polling) not push based.

Messages are 256KB in size.

Messages can be kept in the queue from 1 minute to 14 days (default is 4 days).

The visibility timeout is the amount of time a message is invisible in the queue after a reader picks up the message.

If a job is processed within the visibility timeout the message will be deleted.

If a job is not processed within the visibility timeout the message will become visible again (could be delivered twice).

The maximum visibility timeout for an Amazon SQS message is 12 hours.

An Amazon SQS message can contain up to 10 metadata attributes.

The table below compares solution requirements that are more suitable for Amazon Kinesis Data Streams and Amazon SQS:

Kinesis Data Streams	Amazon SQS
Routing related records to the same record processor	Messaging semantics such as message-level ack/fail and visibility timeout
Maintaining the order of records	Individual message delay of up to 15 minutes
Connecting multiple consumers to a stream concurrently	Seamless and automatic scalability (Kinesis requires planning and provisioning shards)
Store records for up to 7 days and then consume whilst maintaining order	

POLLING

SQS uses short polling and long polling.

Short polling:

- Does not wait for messages to appear in the queue.
- It queries only a subset of the available servers for messages (based on weighted random execution).

- Short polling is the default.
- ReceiveMessageWaitTime is set to 0.
- More requests are used, which implies higher cost.

Long polling:

- Uses fewer requests and reduces cost.
- Eliminates false empty responses by querying all servers.
- SQS waits until a message is available in the queue before sending a response.
- Requests contain at least one of the available messages up to the maximum number of messages specified in the ReceiveMessage action.
- Shouldn't be used if your application expects an immediate response to receive message calls.
- ReceiveMessageWaitTime is set to a non-zero value (up to 20 seconds).
- Same charge per million requests as short polling.

QUEUES

Queue names must be unique within a region.

Queues can be either standard or first-in-first-out (FIFO).

Standard queues provide a loose-FIFO capability that attempts to preserve the order of messages.

Because standard queues are designed to be massively scalable using a highly distributed architecture, receiving messages in the exact order they are sent is not guaranteed.

Standard queues provide at-least-once delivery, which means that each message is delivered at least once.

FIFO (first-in-first-out) queues preserve the exact order in which messages are sent and received.

If you use a FIFO queue, you don't have to place sequencing information in your message.

FIFO queues provide exactly-once processing, which means that each message is delivered once and remains available until a consumer processes it and deletes it.

Standard Queues	FIFO Queues
Unlimited Throughput: Standard queues support a nearly unlimited number of transactions per second (TPS) per API action. **At-Least-Once Delivery:** A message is delivered at least once, but occasionally more than one copy of a message is delivered. **Best-Effort Ordering:** Occasionally, messages might be delivered in an order different from which they were sent.	**High Throughput:** By default, FIFO queues support up to 300 messages per second (300 send, receive, or delete operations per second). When you batch 10 messages per operation (maximum), FIFO queues can support up to 3,000 messages per second. To request a limit increase, file a support request. **Exactly-Once Processing:** A message is delivered once and remains available until a consumer processes and deletes it. Duplicates aren't introduced into the queue. **First-In-First-Out Delivery:** The order in which messages are sent and received is strictly preserved (i.e. First-In-First-Out).

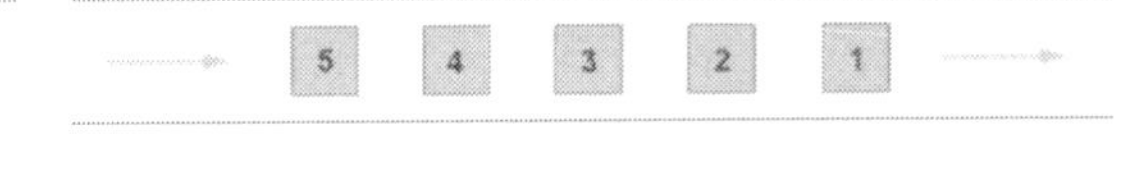

LIMITS

In-flight messages are messages that have been picked up by a consumer but not yet deleted from the queue.

Standard queues have a limit of 120,000 in-flight messages per queue.

FIFO queues have a limit of 20,000 in-flight messages per queue.

Queue names can be up to 80 characters.

Messages are retained for 4 days by default up to 14 days.

FIFO queues support up to 3000 messages per second when batching or 300 per second otherwise.

The maximum messages size is 256KB.

SCALABILITY AND DURABILITY

You can have multiple queues with different priorities.

Scaling is performed by creating more queues.

SQS stores all message queues and messages within a single, highly-available AWS region with multiple redundant AZs.

SECURITY

You can use IAM policies to control who can read/write messages.

Authentication can be used to secure messages within queues (who can send and receive).

SQS supports HTTPS and supports TLS versions 1.0, 1.1, 1.2.

SQS is PCI DSS level 1 compliant and HIPAA eligible.

Server-side encryption (SSE) lets you transmit sensitive data in encrypted queues (AWS KMS):

- SSE encrypts messages as soon as SQS receives them.

- The messages are stored in encrypted form and SQS decrypts messages only when they are sent to an authorized consumer.
- Uses AES 256 bit encryption.
- Not available in all regions.
- Standard and FIFO queues.
- Body of message is encrypted.
- **The following is not encrypted:**
    - Queue metadata.
    - Message metadata.
    - Per-queue metrics.

MONITORING

CloudWatch is integrated with SQS and you can view and monitor queue metrics.

CloudWatch metrics are automatically collected every 5 minutes.

CloudWatch considers a queue to be active for up to 6 hours if it contains any messages or if any API action accesses it.

No charge for CloudWatch (no detailed monitoring).

CloudTrail captures API calls from SQS and logs to a specified S3 bucket.

AMAZON SIMPLE WORKFLOW SERVICE (SWF)

Amazon Simple Workflow Service (SWF) is a web service that makes it easy to coordinate work across distributed application components.

Create distributed asynchronous systems as workflows.

Supports both sequential and parallel processing.

Tracks the state of your workflow which you interact and update via API.

Best suited for human-enabled workflows like an order fulfilment system or for procedural requests.

AWS recommends that for new applications customers consider Step Functions instead of SWF.

SWF enables applications for a range of use cases, including media processing, web application back-ends, business process workflows, and analytics pipelines, to be designed as a coordination of tasks.

Registration is a one-time step that you perform for each different type of workflow and activity.

SWF has a completion time of up to 1 year for workflow executions.

SWF uses a task-oriented API.

SWF ensures a task is assigned once and never duplicated.

SWF keeps track of all the tasks and events in an application.

A domain is a logical container for application resources such as workflows, activities, and executions.

Workers are programs that interact with Amazon SWF to get tasks, process received tasks, and return the results.

The decider is a program that controls the coordination of tasks, i.e. their ordering, concurrency, and scheduling according to the application logic.

SWF applications include the following logical components:

- Domains.
- Workflows.
- Activities.
- Task Lists.
- Workers.
- Workflow Execution.

AMAZON MQ

Amazon MQ is a managed message broker service for ActiveMQ that makes it easy to set up and operate message brokers in the cloud, so you can migrate your messaging and applications without rewriting code.

Amazon MQ supports industry-standard APIs and protocols so you can migrate messaging and applications without rewriting code.

Amazon MQ provides cost-efficient and flexible messaging capacity – you pay for broker instance and storage usage as you go.

Amazon MQ manages the administration and maintenance of ActiveMQ brokers and automatically provisions infrastructure for high availability.

With Amazon MQ, you can use the AWS Management Console, AWS CloudFormation, the Command Line Interface (CLI), or simple API calls to launch a production-ready message broker in minutes.

It's a managed implementation of Apache ActiveMQ.

Fully managed and highly available within a region.

Amazon MQ stores your messages redundantly across multiple Availability Zones (AZs).

Active/standby brokers are designed for high availability. In the event of a failure of the broker, or even a full AZ outage, Amazon MQ automatically fails over to the standby broker so you can continue sending and receiving messages.

ActiveMQ API and support for JMS, NMS, MQTT, and WebSockets.

Designed as a drop-in replacement for on-premise message brokers.

Use SQS if you're creating a new application from scratch.

Use MQ if you want an easy low-hassle path to migrate from existing message brokers to AWS.

Amazon MQ provides encryption of your messages at rest and in transit.

It's easy to ensure that your messages are securely stored in an encrypted format. Connections to the broker use SSL, and access can be restricted to a private endpoint within your Amazon VPC, which allows you to isolate your broker in your own virtual network.

You can configure security groups to control network access to your broker.

Amazon MQ is integrated with Amazon CloudWatch and AWS CloudTrail. With CloudWatch you can monitor metrics on your brokers, queues, and topics.

The following table describes related services and typical use cases for them:

Service	What it does	Example Use Cases
Simple Notification Service (SNS)	Set up, operate, and send notifications from the cloud	Send email notification when CloudWatch alarm is triggered
Step Functions	Out-of-the-box coordination of AWS service components with visual workflow	Order processing workflow
Simple Workflow Service (SWF)	Need to support external processes or specialized execution logic	Human-enabled workflows like an order fulfilment system or for procedural requests AWS recommends that for new applications customers consider Step Functions instead of SWF
Simple Queue Service (SQS)	Messaging queue; store and forward patterns	Building distributed / decoupled applications
Amazon MQ	Managed message broker based on Apache MQ	Easy low-hassle path to migrate from existing message brokers to AWS

AWS STEP FUNCTIONS

AWS Step Functions makes it easy to coordinate the components of distributed applications as a series of steps in a visual workflow.

You can quickly build and run state machines to execute the steps of your application in a reliable and scalable fashion.

How it works:

1. Define the steps of your workflow in the JSON-based Amazon States Language. The visual console automatically graphs each step in the order of execution.
2. Start an execution to visualize and verify the steps of your application are operating as intended. The console highlights the real-time status of each step and provides a detailed history of every execution.
3. AWS Step Functions operates and scales the steps of your application and underlying compute for you to help ensure your application executes reliably under increasing demand.

Managed workflow and orchestration platform.

Scalable and highly available.

Define your app as a state machine.

Create tasks, sequential steps, parallel steps, branching paths or timers.

Amazon State Language declarative JSON.

Apps can interact and update the stream via Step Function API.

Visual interface describes flow and real-time status.

Detailed logs of each step execution.

Benefits and Features:

- **Built-in error handling** – AWS Step Functions tracks the state of each step, so you can automatically retry failed or timed-out tasks, catch specific errors, and recover gracefully, whether the task takes seconds or months to complete.
- **Automatic Scaling** – AWS Step Functions automatically scales the operations and underlying compute to run the steps of your application for you in response to changing workloads. Step Functions scales automatically to help ensure the performance of your application workflow remains consistently high as the frequency of requests increases.
- **Pay per use** – With AWS Step Functions, you pay only for the transition from one step of your application workflow to the next, called a state transition. Billing is metered by state transition, regardless of how long each state persists (up to one year).
- **Execution event history** – AWS Step Functions creates a detailed event log for every execution, so when things do go wrong, you can quickly identify not only where, but why. All of the execution history is available visually and programmatically to quickly troubleshoot and remediate failures.
- **High availability** – AWS Step Functions has built-in fault tolerance. Step Functions maintains service capacity across multiple Availability Zones in each region to help protect application workflows against individual machine or data center facility failures. There are no maintenance windows or scheduled downtimes.

- **Administrative security** – AWS Step Functions is integrated with AWS Identity and Access Management (IAM). IAM policies can be used to control access to the Step Functions APIs.

The following table describes **related services and typical use cases** for them:

Service	What it does	Example Use Cases
Simple Notification Service (SNS)	Set up, operate, and send notifications from the cloud	Send email notification when CloudWatch alarm is triggered
Step Functions	Out-of-the-box coordination of AWS service components with visual workflow	Order processing workflow
Simple Workflow Service (SWF)	Need to support external processes or specialized execution logic	Human-enabled workflows like an order fulfilment system or for procedural requests AWS recommends that for new applications customers consider Step Functions instead of SWF
Simple Queue Service (SQS)	Messaging queue; store and forward patterns	Building distributed / decoupled applications
Amazon MQ	Managed message broker based on Apache MQ	Easy low-hassle path to migrate from existing message brokers to AWS

APPLICATION INTEGRATION QUIZ QUESTIONS

Answers and explanations are provided below after the last question in this section.

Question 1:

There is expected to be a large increase in write intensive traffic to a website you manage that registers users onto an online learning program. You are concerned about writes to the database being dropped and need to come up with a solution to ensure this does not happen. Which of the solution options below would be the best approach to take?

A. Update the application to write data to an SQS queue and provision additional EC2 instances to process the data and write it to the database

B. Use RDS in a multi-AZ configuration to distribute writes across AZs

C. Update the application to write data to an S3 bucket and provision additional EC2 instances to process the data and write it to the database

D. Use CloudFront to cache the writes and configure the database as a custom origin

Question 2:

You are using a series of Spot instances that process messages from an SQS queue and store results in a DynamoDB table. Shortly after picking up a message from the queue AWS terminated the Spot instance. The Spot instance had not finished processing the message. What will happen to the message?

A. The message will be lost as it would have been deleted from the queue when processed

B. The message will remain in the queue and be immediately picked up by another instance

C. The message will become available for processing again after the visibility timeout expires

D. The results may be duplicated in DynamoDB as the message will likely be processed multiple times

Question 3:

You are developing a multi-tier application that includes loosely-coupled, distributed application components and need to determine a method of sending notifications instantaneously. Using SNS which transport protocols are supported? (choose 2)

A. FTP

B. Email-JSON

C. HTTPS

D. Amazon SWF

E. AWS Lambda

Question 4:

A Solutions Architect is creating the business process workflows associated with an order fulfilment system. What AWS service can assist with coordinating tasks across distributed application components?

A. Amazon STS
B. Amazon SQS
C. Amazon SWF
D. Amazon SNS

Question 5:

You are a developer at Digital Cloud Training. An application stack you are building needs a message bus to decouple the application components from each other. The application will generate up to 300 messages per second without using batching. You need to ensure that a message is only delivered once, and duplicates are not introduced into the queue. It is not necessary to maintain the order of the messages.

Which SQS queue type will you use?

A. Standard queues
B. Long polling queues
C. Auto Scaling queues
D. FIFO queues

Question 6:

A client is in the design phase of developing an application that will process orders for their online ticketing system. The application will use a number of front-end EC2 instances that pick-up orders and place them in a queue for processing by another set of back-end EC2 instances. The client will have multiple options for customers to choose the level of service they want to pay for.

The client has asked how he can design the application to process the orders in a prioritized way based on the level of service the customer has chosen?

A. Create multiple SQS queues, configure the front-end application to place orders onto a specific queue based on the level of service requested and configure the back-end instances to sequentially poll the queues in order of priority
B. Create a combination of FIFO queues and Standard queues and configure the applications to place messages into the relevant queue based on priority
C. Create a single SQS queue, configure the front-end application to place orders on the queue in order of priority and configure the back-end instances to poll the queue and pick up messages in the order they are presented
D. Create multiple SQS queues, configure exactly-once processing and set the maximum visibility timeout to 12 hours

APPLICATION INTEGRATION - ANSWERS

Question 1 answer: A

Explanation:

This is a great use case for Amazon Simple Queue Service (Amazon SQS). SQS is a web service that gives you access to message queues that store messages waiting to be processed and offers a reliable, highly-scalable, hosted queue for storing messages in transit between computers. SQS is used for distributed/decoupled applications. In this circumstance SQS will reduce the risk of writes being dropped and it the best option presented.

RDS in a multi-AZ configuration will not help as writes are only made to the primary database.

Though writing data to an S3 bucket could potentially work, it is not the best option as SQS is recommended for decoupling application components.

The CloudFront option is bogus as you cannot configure a database as a custom origin in CloudFront.

Question 2 answer: C

Explanation:

The visibility timeout is the amount of time a message is invisible in the queue after a reader picks up the message. If a job is processed within the visibility timeout the message will be deleted. If a job is not processed within the visibility timeout the message will become visible again (could be delivered twice). The maximum visibility timeout for an Amazon SQS message is 12 hours.

The message will not be lost and will not be immediately picked up by another instance. As mentioned above it will be available for processing in the queue again after the timeout expires.

As the instance had not finished processing the message it should only be fully processed once. Depending on your application process however it is possible some data was written to DynamoDB.

Question 3 answer: B,C

Explanation:

Note that the questions asks you which transport protocols are supported, NOT which subscribers - therefore Lambda is not supported

SNS supports notifications over multiple transport protocols:

- HTTP/HTTPS – subscribers specify a URL as part of the subscription registration
- Email/Email-JSON – messages are sent to registered addresses as email (text-based or JSON-object)
- SQS – users can specify an SQS standard queue as the endpoint
- SMS – messages are sent to registered phone numbers as SMS text messages

Question 4 answer: C

Explanation:

Amazon Simple Workflow Service (SWF) is a web service that makes it easy to coordinate work across distributed application components. SWF enables applications for a range of use cases, including media processing, web application back-ends, business process workflows, and analytics pipelines, to be designed as a coordination of tasks.

Amazon Security Token Service (STS) is used for requesting temporary credentials.

Amazon Simple Queue Service (SQS) is a message queue used for decoupling application components.

Amazon Simple Notification Service (SNS) is a web service that makes it easy to set up, operate, and send notifications from the cloud.

SNS supports notifications over multiple transports including HTTP/HTTPS, Email/Email-JSON, SQS and SMS.

Question 5 answer: D

Explanation:

The key fact you need to consider here is that duplicate messages cannot be introduced into the queue. For this reason alone you must use a FIFO queue. The statement about it not being necessary to maintain the order of the messages is meant to confuse you, as that might lead you to think you can use a standard queue, but standard queues don't guarantee that duplicates are not introduced into the queue.

FIFO (first-in-first-out) queues preserve the exact order in which messages are sent and received – note that this is not required in the question but exactly once processing is. FIFO queues provide exactly-once processing, which means that each message is delivered once and remains available until a consumer processes it and deletes it.

Standard queues provide a loose-FIFO capability that attempts to preserve the order of messages. Standard queues provide at-least-once delivery, which means that each message is delivered at least once.

Long polling is configuration you can apply to a queue, it is not a queue type.

There is no such thing as an Auto Scaling queue.

Question 6 answer: A

Explanation:

The best option is to create multiple queues and configure the application to place orders onto a specific queue based on the level of service. You then configure the back-end instances to poll these queues in order or priority, so they pick up the higher priority jobs first.

Creating a combination of FIFO and standard queues is incorrect as creating a mixture of queue types is not the best way to separate the messages, and there is nothing in this option that explains how the messages would be picked up in the right order.

Creating a single queue and configuring the applications to place orders on the queue in order of priority would not work as standard queues offer best-effort ordering so there's no guarantee that the messages would be picked up in the correct order.

Creating multiple SQS queues and configuring exactly-once processing (only possible with FIFO) would not ensure that the order of the messages is prioritized.

AWS DESKTOP & APP STREAMING

AMAZON WORKSPACES

Amazon WorkSpaces is a managed desktop computing service running on the AWS cloud.

WorkSpaces allows customers to easily provision cloud-based desktops that allow end-users to access documents and applications.

Supported client-side devices include Windows and Mac computers, Chromebooks, iPads, Fire tablets, Android tablets, and Chrome and Firefox web browsers.

WorkSpaces offers bundles that come with a Windows 7 or Windows 10 desktop experience, powered by Windows Server 2008 R2 and Windows Server 2016 respectively.

By default, users can personalize their workspaces, but this can be locked down.

By default, you will be given local administrator access.

Workspaces are persistent.

The user volume (D:) on the WorkSpace is backed up every 12 hours.

You do not need an AWS account to login to workspaces.

CONCLUSION

We trust that these training notes have helped you to gain a complete understanding of the facts you need to know to pass the AWS Certified Solutions Architect Associate exam first time.

The exam covers a broad set of technologies. It's vital to ensure you are armed with the knowledge to answer whatever questions come up in your certification exam. We recommend reviewing these training notes until you're confident in all areas.

BEFORE TAKING THE AWS EXAM

Get Hands-On experience with AWS

AWS certification exams such as the Solutions Architect Associate test your hands-on knowledge and experience with the AWS platform. It's therefore super important to have some real experience before you sit the exam.

Our AWS Certified Solutions Architect Associate Hands-On Labs course provides a practical approach to learning. Through over 20 hours of videos you will learn how to architect and build solutions on Amazon Web Services. By the end of the course you will have a strong experience-based skillset. This is the best way to develop strong hands-on skills and will really help you when it comes time to answer exam questions.

Assess your exam readiness with the online Exam Simulator - over 500 unique practice questions

The Digital Cloud Training practice questions are the closest to the actual exam question format and the only exam-difficulty questions on the market. If you can pass these mock exams, you're well set to ace the real thing! To learn more, visit:

AWS Certified Solutions Architect Associate Practice Exams

Reach out with any questions you may have

If anything is not 100% to your liking, please email us at feedback@digitalcloud.training. We promise to address all questions and concerns. For technical support, contact us at:

support@digitalcloud.training.

Also, remember to join our private Facebook group to ask questions and share knowledge and exam tips with the AWS community:

https://www.facebook.com/groups/awscertificationqa

BONUS OFFER

To gain access to your **free practice exam with 65 exam-difficulty questions** on the interactive online exam simulator, visit https://digitalcloud.training/free-aws-practice-questions-solutions-architect/ or simply scan this QR code.

For those who have already purchased the full set of practice questions, please note that the 65 questions are included in the pool of 500 questions.

SMALL FAVOR

If you like reading course reviews, please consider paying it forward. It's the best way you can help us improve our courses and help your fellow students make the right choices. We celebrate every honest review and truly appreciate it. You can leave a review at any time by visiting amazon.com/ryp.

Best wishes for your AWS certification journey!

OTHER BOOKS & COURSES BY NEAL DAVIS

AWS CERTIFIED SOLUTIONS ARCHITECT ASSOCIATE HANDS-ON LABS VIDEO COURSE

AVAILABLE ON DIGITALCLOUD.TRAINING

This popular AWS Certified Solutions Architect Associate (SAA-C02) video course is delivered through practical AWS Hands-On Labs.

You will be looking over my shoulder and building applications on Amazon Web Services. By the end of the course , you will have a strong experience-based skillset thanks to the guided AWS Practice Labs.

We will use a process of repetition and incremental learning to ensure that you retain the knowledge as repeated practice is the best way to learn and build your cloud skills. We take you from opening your first AWS Free Tier account through to creating complex multi-tier architectures, always sticking to the **SAA-C02 exam blueprint** to ensure you're learning practical skills and also preparing for your exam.

We back the +20 hours of AWS Hands-On Labs with high-quality logical diagrams so you can visualize what you're building and check your progress.

Our AWS Hands-On Labs teach you how to design and build multi-tier web architectures with services such as EC2 Auto Scaling, Elastic Load Balancing, Route 53, ECS, Lambda, API Gateway and Elastic File System.

To learn more, visit:

https://digitalcloud.training/aws-training-courses/

AWS CERTIFIED SOLUTIONS ARCHITECT ASSOCIATE (ONLINE) PRACTICE TESTS

AVAILABLE ON DIGITALCLOUD.TRAINING

Get access to the **online Exam Simulator** from Digital Cloud Training with over 500 Questions plus 6 sets of practice exams with 65 Questions each. All questions are unique, 100% scenario-based and conform to the latest AWS SAA-C02 exam blueprint.

Our AWS Practice Tests are delivered in 3 different modes:

Simulation mode: the number of questions, time limit, and pass mark are the same as the real AWS exam. You must complete the exam before you are able to check your score and review answers and explanations.

Training mode: You are shown the answer and explanation for every question after clicking "check". Upon completion of the exam the score report shows your overall score and performance in each knowledge area.

Knowledge reviews: Collections of practice questions for a specific knowledge area. When you complete a practice exam you can use the score report to identify your strengths and weaknesses and then use the knowledge reviews to focus your efforts where they're needed most.

Each exam includes questions from the four domains of the AWS exam blueprint. All questions are also available in the knowledge reviews where they are split into more than 15 categories for focused training.

To learn more on how to fast-track your AWS Certified Solutions Architect Associate Exam Success, visit:

https://digitalcloud.training/aws-certified-solutions-architect-associate-practice-tests-2019/

AWS CERTIFIED SOLUTIONS ARCHITECT ASSOCIATE (OFFLINE) PRACTICE TESTS

AVAILABLE ON AMAZON ONLY

The AWS Solutions Architect Associate certification is extremely valuable in the Cloud Computing industry today and preparing to answer the difficult scenario-based questions requires a significant commitment in time and effort.

The latest **SAA-C02 exam** is composed entirely of scenario-based questions that test your knowledge and experience working with Amazon Web Services. Our practice tests are patterned to reflect the difficulty of the AWS exam and are the closest to the real AWS exam experience available anywhere.

There are **6 practice exams with 65 questions** each covering the five domains of the AWS exam blueprint. Each set of questions is repeated once without answers and explanations, and once with answers and explanations, so you get to choose from two methods of preparation:

- **To simulate the exam experience and assess your exam readiness**, use the "PRACTICE QUESTIONS ONLY" sets.
- **To use the practice questions as a learning tool**, use the "PRACTICE QUESTIONS, ANSWERS & EXPLANATIONS" sets to view the answers and read the in-depth explanations as you move through the questions.

These Practice Questions will prepare you for your AWS exam in the following ways:

- **Master the new 2020 exam pattern**: All 390 practice questions are based on the SAA-C02 exam blueprint and use the question format of the real AWS exam
- **6 sets of exam-difficulty practice questions**: Presented with and without answers so you can study or simulate an exam
- **Ideal exam prep tool that will shortcut your study time**: Assess your exam readiness to maximize your chance of passing the AWS exam first time

The exam covers a broad set of technologies and it's vital to ensure you are armed with the knowledge to answer whatever questions come up in your certification exam. We recommend reviewing these practice questions until you're confident in all areas and ready to ace your AWS exam.

To learn more, visit: https://www.amazon.com/gp/product/1079185720.

AWS CERTIFIED CLOUD PRACTITIONER VIDEO COURSE

AVAILABLE ON DIGITALCLOUD.TRAINING

We have fully aligned this instructor-led video training with the AWS Certified Cloud Practitioner exam blueprint and structured the course so that you can study at a pace that suits you best. We start with some basic background to get everyone up to speed on what cloud computing is, before progressing through each knowledge domain.

Here's why this ultimate exam prep is your best chance to ace your AWS certification exam:

HIGHLY FLEXIBLE COURSE STRUCTURE: We understand that not everyone has the time to go through lengthy lectures. That's why we give you options to maximize your time efficiency and accommodate different learning styles.

6 HOURS OF THEORY LECTURES: You can move quickly through the course, focusing on the theory lectures that are 100% conform with the CLF-C01 exam blueprint - everything you need to know to pass your exam first attempt.

4 HOURS OF GUIDED HANDS-ON EXERCISES: To gain more practical experience with AWS services, you have the option to explore the guided hands-on exercises.

1 HOUR OF EXAM-CRAM LECTURES: Get through the key exam facts in the shortest time possible with the exam-cram lectures that you'll find at the end of each section.

HIGH-QUALITY VISUALS: We've spared no effort to create a highly visual training course with lots of table and graphs to illustrate the concepts. All practical exercises are backed by logical diagrams so you can visualize what we're building.

To learn more, visit: https://digitalcloud.training/aws-certified-cloud-practitioner-training-course/

AWS CERTIFIED CLOUD PRACTITIONER (ONLINE) PRACTICE TESTS

AVAILABLE ON DIGITALCLOUD.TRAINING

Get access to the online Exam Simulator from Digital Cloud Training with over 500 Practice questions plus 6 sets of practice exams with 65 Questions each. All questions are unique and conform to the latest AWS CLF-C01 exam blueprint.

Our AWS Practice Tests are delivered in 3 different modes:

Simulation mode: the number of questions, time limit and pass mark are the same as the real AWS exam. You need to complete the exam before you get to check your score and review answers and explanations.

Training mode: You are shown the answer and explanation for every question after clicking "check". Upon completion of the exam, the score report shows your overall score and performance in each knowledge area.

Knowledge reviews: Collections of practice questions for a specific knowledge area. When you complete a practice exam you can use the score report to identify your strengths and weaknesses and then use the knowledge reviews to focus your efforts where they are needed most.

To learn more on how to fast-track your AWS Certified Cloud Practitioner Exam Success, visit:

https://digitalcloud.training/aws-certified-cloud-practitioner-practice-tests-2019/

AWS CERTIFIED CLOUD PRACTITIONER (OFFLINE) PRACTICE TESTS

AVAILABLE ON AMAZON ONLY

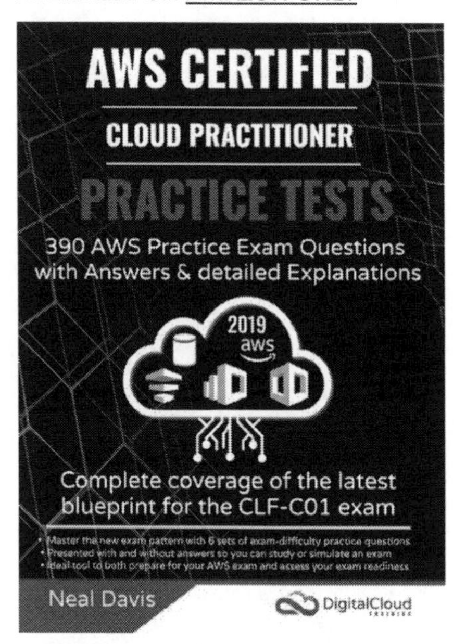

The **AWS Cloud Practitioner** exam is a foundational level exam that nonetheless includes tricky questions that test your knowledge and experience of the AWS Cloud. Our practice tests are patterned to reflect the difficulty of the AWS exam and are the closest to the real AWS exam experience available.

There are **6 practice exams with 65 questions each** covering the five domains of the AWS CLF-C01 exam blueprint. Each set of questions is repeated once without answers and explanations, and once with answers and explanations, so you get to choose from two methods of preparation:

1. To simulate the exam experience and assess your exam readiness, use the "**PRACTICE QUESTIONS ONLY**" sets.
2. To use the practice questions as a learning tool, use the "**PRACTICE QUESTIONS, ANSWERS & EXPLANATIONS**" sets to view the answers and read the in-depth explanations as you move through the questions.

These Practice Questions will prepare you for your AWS exam in the following ways:

Master the latest exam pattern: All 390 practice questions are based on the latest version of the CLF-C01 exam blueprint and use the question format of the real AWS exam

6 sets of exam-difficulty practice questions: Presented with and without answers so you can study or simulate an exam

Ideal exam prep tool that will shortcut your study time: Assess your exam readiness to maximize your chance of passing the AWS exam first time.

To learn more, visit:

https://www.amazon.com/gp/product/1081271949

AWS CERTIFIED CLOUD PRACTITIONER TRAINING NOTES

AVAILABLE ON AMAZON AND DIGITALCLOUD.TRAINING

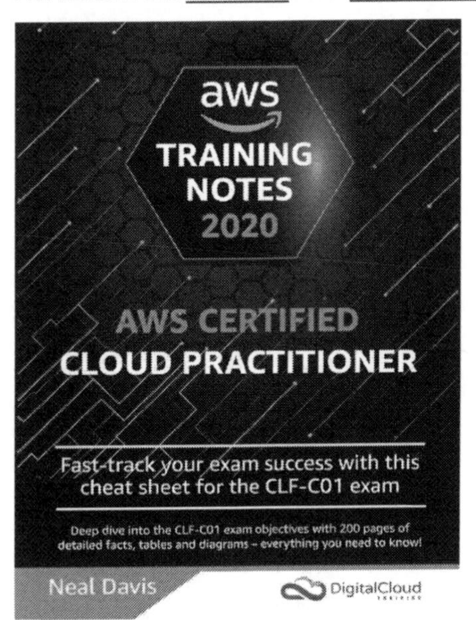

Save valuable time by getting straight to the facts you need to know to be successful and ensure you pass your AWS Certified Cloud Practitioner exam first time!

This book is based on the CLF-C01 exam blueprint and provides a deep dive into the subject matter in a concise and easy-to-read format so you can fast-track your time to success.

The Cloud Practitioner certification is a great first step into the world of Cloud Computing and requires a foundational knowledge of the AWS Cloud, its architectural principles, value proposition, billing and pricing, key services and more.

AWS Solutions Architect and successful instructor, Neal Davis, has consolidated the information you need to be successful from numerous training sources and AWS FAQ pages to save you time.

In addition to the book, you are provided with access to a 65-question practice exam on an interactive exam simulator to evaluate your progress and ensure you're prepared for the style and difficulty of the real AWS exam.

This book can help you prepare for your AWS exam in the following ways:

• Deep dive into the CLF-C01 exam objectives with over 200 pages of detailed facts, tables, and diagrams – everything you need to know!

• Familiarize yourself with the exam question format with the practice questions included in each section.

• Use our online exam simulator to evaluate progress and ensure you're ready for the real thing.

To learn more, visit:

https://digitalcloud.training/product/aws-certified-cloud-practitioner-offline-training-notes/

ABOUT THE AUTHOR

Neal Davis is the founder of Digital Cloud Training, AWS Cloud Solutions Architect and successful IT instructor. With more than 20 years of experience in the tech industry, Neal is a true expert in virtualization and cloud computing. His passion is to help others achieve career success by offering in-depth AWS certification training resources.

Neal started **Digital Cloud Training** to provide a variety of training resources for Amazon Web Services (AWS) certifications that represent a higher standard of quality than is otherwise available in the market.

Digital Cloud Training provides **AWS Certification exam preparation resources** including instructor-led Video Courses, guided Hands-on Labs, in-depth Training Notes, Exam-Cram lessons for quick revision, Quizzes to test your knowledge and exam-difficulty Practice Exams to assess your exam readiness.

With Digital Cloud Training, you get access to highly experienced staff who support you on your AWS Certification journey and help you elevate your career through achieving highly valuable certifications. Join the AWS Community of over 40,000 happy students that are currently enrolled in Digital Cloud Training courses

Connect with Neal / Digital Cloud Training on social media:

digitalcloud.training

facebook.com/digitalcloudtraining/

linkedin.com/company/digitalcloudtraining

Twitter @DigitalCloudT

Instagram @digitalcloudtraining

Made in the USA
San Bernardino, CA
19 March 2020